COLLECTED POEMS
1943-1995

COLLECTED POEMS
1943-1995

ROY McFADDEN

introduced by Philip Hobsbaum

LAGAN PRESS
BELFAST
1996

Published by
Lagan Press
PO Box 110 BT12 4AB, Belfast

The publishers wish to acknowledge the financial assistance
of the Arts Council of Northern Ireland in the production of this book.

ISBN: 1 873687 16 8
1 873687 21 4
Author: McFadden, Roy
Title: Collected Poems 1943-1995
1996

Cover: Roy McFadden by Rowel Friers
Cover Design by December Publications
Set in New Baskerville
Printed by Noel Murphy Printing, Belfast

Not
To or For
But
From

The word's compassion; for
Everything that has lived.
— 'First Funeral'

CONTENTS

Preface xv
Introduction xix

THE HUNGER MARCHERS:
Poems 1990-1995
New Year's Eve *3*
Magee's Nursery *3*
The Low Glen *4*
Another Place *4*
Miss Purdy in Old Age *5*
Tiveragh *5*
The White Rabbit *6*
A Dog, An Afternoon *7*
An Exhibition of Themselves *7*
Herbertson at Forty *8*
The Hunger-Marchers *8*
Proxy *9*
5 Anglesea Road, Dublin *10*
Confirmation Class *10*
Remembering Orpheus *11*
Miss Walters *11*
Irish Street,
    Downpatrick 1886 *12*
The Garden Seat *13*
Burns Night *14*
Class of 1926 *15*
McKelvey Revisits Scenes
    of Childhood *16*
Autograph Album *16*
Prior Title *17*
Belgravia in Winter *18*
Jump *19*
Miniature *19*

**AFTER SEYMOUR'S
FUNERAL** (1990)
Bed and Breakfast *23*
The Innocent Eye *23*
Hyde Park *24*

The Dancers, Sloane Street *24*
The Hill *25*
The Stuffed Fox *26*
A Dead Chief *26*
Jack Yeats
    at Fitzwilliam Square *27*
Carrie Coates *28*
The Upanishads *29*
Detail for a Painting *30*
June Blossom *31*
Sunday-School Excursion *32*
Night Out *32*
Idyll *33*
Pim *33*
The Foster Twins *34*
The Invisible Menders *35*
Gallagher's Donkey *35*
The Little Black Rose *36*
End of Season *37*
There and Back *37*
After Seymour's Funeral *38*
Hans Crescent *42*
Parvenus *43*
Old Style *43*
Old Knock Graveyard *44*
My Mother's Young Sister *45*
A Small Incident in Town *45*
A Man Observed
    Standing Beside a Grave *46*
The Statute of Limitations *46*
Old Tennis Courts *47*
For the Record *48*
Grand Old Man *48*
William Cowper *49*
Three Cousins *50*
House Under Construction *51*
The Rockery *52*
The Bar Library *53*
The Silverman Plea *53*
Mr McAlonen *54*
Emigrants *55*

Three Cats 55
Evictions 58
The Little B.A. 58
Captain Thompson 59
Gone Away 61

**LETTERS TO
THE HINTERLAND** (1986)
2 September 1939 65
34 Tite Street 65
Style 66
Victories 66
The Disappeared Ones 67
Old Mr Kershaw 67
The Colonel 68
The House 69
The Den 70
First Blood 70
Side Ward 71
Shop Soil 72
Interpolation 72
Doctor Serafico 73
Telling 76
Poetry Reading 76
Oil Painting:
    The Manse at Raloo 78
An Attic in Holborn 78
Gig 79
Barnardo Boy 79
Elocution Lesson:
    Hot Cross Buns 80
Love 80
Brothers-in-Law 81
Ballad Singer:
    Chichester Street 81
The Round Pond 83
Walled Garden,
    Irish Street, Downpatrick 83
Remainders 84
In Passing 84
Survivor 85
Welsh Funeral: Carnmoney 85
The Garden of Remembrance 86

The Girl 87
The Milkman 87
Going to Church
    One Morning 88
High Low 88
Birthday Poem 89
The Hole 89
A Word in His Ear 90
Reunion 90
The Traveller 91
The Astoria 91

**NOTES FOR
THE HINTERLAND** (1983)
Ballyshannon 95
Post-War 95
The Grand Central Hotel 96
Conveyancer 98
Mortgage Redemptions 99
Sancto's Dog 100
Time's Present 103
Helston 103
After the Broadcast 104
A Death in Maryville Street 104
Sketches of Boz 105

A WATCHING BRIEF (1979)
Out in the Country 115
Reprieve 116
Postscript to Ulster
Regionalism 116
Latecomer 117
Self-Generation 118
The Island 118
Managing Clerk 119
Nursery Land 119
Christmas Eve 120
Theatre: Lunchtime 120
Eurydice 121
I Spy 122
Immigrants 122
Coffee at Crumble's 132

Allotments *136*
Heroes *137*
Philanderer *137*
Baptism *138*
Sound Sense *138*
D-Day *139*
Runaway *140*
Retribution *140*
The McKelvey File *141*
Armistice Day *145*
Fire Bomb *145*
Impostors *146*
The Law Courts Revisited *146*

VERIFICATIONS (1977)
March *153*
Knowing My Place *154*
Kew Gardens *156*
Smith *157*
Daisymount Terrace *158*
The Johnson Girls *159*
Stringer's Field *160*
First Funeral *161*
After Hallowe'en *161*
Portrush *162*
Downpatrick *163*
Ballyhackamore *164*
Quail Holdings *165*
A Sad Day's Rain *169*
Lucy Gray *170*
Family Group *171*
The Eiffel Tower *173*
Tuesday *174*
The Ards Circuit *174*
Uncle Alec *174*
Jean Armstrong *175*
Stranmillis Road *176*
The Ordeal
   of Clutey Gibson *176*
Tom's Tale *178*
The Trap *179*
The Riderless Horse *179*

THE GARRYOWEN (1971)
Glenarm *183*
Independence *183*
Roger Casement's Rising *184*
Synge in Paris *185*
Poem for John Boyd *185*
Memories of Chinatown *186*
Those Glorious Twelfths *188*
Sheepdog Trials *189*
The Arcadia *190*
Contemplations of Mary *190*
Folkminder *193*
Night-Fishing *194*
Family Album *194*
The Garryowen *200*
Brendan Behan *201*
Second Letter
   to an Irish Novelist *202*
The Golden Boy *203*
In Drumcliffe Churchyard *203*
Premonition *204*
The Summer's Gone *204*

**SPEECH FOR THE
VOICELESS:** *Poems 1947-70*
I Won't Dance *207*
Holly Tree *207*
Autumn Voyager *208*
Spring Breaks the Heart *208*
Child's Funeral *209*
Death of a Mahatma *209*
Death Dive *210*
Another Autumn *210*
Leaving Lisburn *210*
The Dogged Past *211*
The Healer *212*
The Backward Glance *212*
Jimmy Kershaw *213*
Music for an Anniversary *213*
Words *214*
One Who Got Away *214*
One of the Fallen *215*
Dylan Thomas *215*

Crocus 216
New Words
    for an Old Tune 217
Liverpool Boat 217
Homecoming 218
Belfast 218
Postscript 219
Return 220
Star 221
Dinah Kohner 222
A Song for
    One Who Stayed 223
The Moment of Truth 223
Flower Piece 224
Song for a Turning Tide 224
The Last Length 225
Paddy Reilly and Others 226
October
    and the Leaves Again 228
Elevoine Santi 228
La Servante
    Au Grand Coeur 229
Les Plaintes d'un Icare 229

ELEGY FOR THE DEAD OF
THE PRINCESS VICTORIA
(1953)
Elegy for the Dead
    of *The Princess Victoria* 233

THE HEART'S TOWNLAND
(1947)
Calendar 237
Autumn Rises 241
In this Their Season 242
Advice in Spring 243
A Carol for Christmas Day
    and Every Day 243
The Song Creates All 244
Portrait of a Poet 245
Elegy for a Dog 245
Thor 246

The Death of a Cyclist 246
Manifesto 247
White Death,
    Green Spring 248
Heartholder 250
Directions for a Journey 250
The White Bird 251
My Father Had a Clock 251
Treefall 252
Memory of a Girl
    with a Red Scarf 252
The Dead Prince 253
Virgin Country 253
The Heart's Townland 253
Forrest Reid 257
A Song for Victory Night 257
Interlude in May 258
The Upland Field 263

FLOWERS FOR A LADY
(1945)
Elegy for a Sixth-Former 269
Early Casualty 269
Elegy for a Noncombatant 270
Enniskerry 271
St. Stephen's Green,
    Dublin 271
Letter to a Boy in Prison 273
Epithalamium 273
Letter from the Mournes 274
Lines Written near
    Downpatrick after
    an Air-Raid 275
The Monk 275
Paul Robeson 276
The Dog 276
The Hounds 277
North-Antrim Prospect 277
The Island of Saints
    and Scholars 277
Sixes and Sevens 278
The Orator 278
Dublin to Belfast: Wartime 279

Memory of Sand 279
Portrush 280
Flowers for a Lady:
    First Elegy 280
    Second Elegy 283
    Third Elegy 284
    Fourth Elegy 285
    Fifth Elegy 285
    Sixth Elegy 286
    Seventh Elegy 286
    Eighth Elegy 287
And Like Cuchulain 287
All the Fugitivies 287
Two Songs 288
Saint Francis and the Birds 288
A Wreath for Shoon 289
Jonathan Swift 289
Elegy for a Mad Girl 290
Letter to an Irish Novelist 291
William Blake Sees God 293
The Drums 293
Cuchulain 294
The Journey Home 299

Easter 1942 308
Poem for Today 308
In Ireland Now 309
In the Meantime 310
Train at Midnight 310
You, Sitting
    in Silent Rooms 311
A Cry 311
The Poor Mad Girl's
    Love Song 312
Soliloquy of an
    Old Nationalist Woman 313
The Visitor 314
Prayer for a Young Man 314
Plaint of the Working Men 315
The Guest 315
Evening in Donegal 316
There was Sun Today 316
Song Towards Spring 316
Prelude to an Epitaph 317
The Pattern 317
The Girl 318

**SWORDS AND
PLOUGHSHARES** (1943)
Lines by Slieve Donard 307
Rain Towards Evening 307

RUSSIAN SUMMER (1941)
Russian Summer 321

Notes & Index 323

Preface

In retrospect we move from here-and-now to then-and there: from what we call the present to what we call the past; both of which, the long and the short of it, seem contemporaneous within the context of a lifetime.

Reading backwards from 1955 to 1943, and beyond, has involved a journey through remembered or part-remembered, perhaps remembering and part-remembering, existences: other ambiences in which the poet moves from the first person, the *I* of the early lyrics, to the second or third person; from the oblique *You* to the objective *He*. Throughout, there are continuing reminders that poems are never finished, only abandoned.

I was born in Belfast, during the Troubles of the 1920s; and I have lived there or thereabouts throughout my life. But behind the northern-Irish dimension a northern-English connection exists through my mother, who came to Belfast at the age of 11, with a pinafore and a Durham accent. The Jarrow Hunger marchers have claimed equal access to my streets step by step with the annual orange and green parades.

My first three collections were published in London during the years 1943-1947, when I identified with the anti-war poets, and subscribed to the political anarchism of Herbert Read and Alex Comfort.

During the 40s I was active in the literary awakening in Northern Ireland. In particular, I was co-editor of Northern Ireland's first poetry magazine, from 1948 to 1953, and assisted with other magazines and compilations. Radio played a considerable part in the encouragement of local writing; an ambitious production of my 'play-for-voices', *The Angry Hound*, was broadcast by the BBC in 1952.

For a time I was attracted to the concept of regionalism— associated as it was with an ideal of decentralised authority—until I recognised the danger of prescribed narrow boundaries fostering a reactive mini-nationalism.

Concerning content and style, I found a companionable voice in John Millington Synge's preface to his *Poems and Translations*:

I have often thought that at the side of the poetic diction, which everyone condemns, modern verse contains a great deal of poetic material using poetic in the same special sense. The poetry of exaltation will be always the highest, but when men lose their poetic feeling for ordinary life, and cannot write poetry of ordinary things, their exalted poetry is likely to lose its strength of exaltation, in the way men cease to build beautiful churches when they have lost happiness in building shops.

Many of the other poets, such as Villon and Herrick and Burns, used the whole of their personal life as their material, and the verse written in this way was read by strong men, and thieves, and deacons, not by little cliques only.

In re-reading the poems written over a period of fifty years, in the main I have respected the thoughts and emotions of the younger poet, but not always the manner in which they were expressed. Several poems have been excluded from this collection; others, to a varying extent, I have revised. In this I was encouraged by Joseph Hone's comment on W.B. Yeats. "Like the she-bear to which Virgil was compared, he was for ever licking his cubs into shape". And by John Unterecker's happy snapshot of the poet: "In 1930, anticipating a projected 'Edition de Luxe' of all his work, he wrote a joyous letter to his old friend Mrs. Shakespear, the mother of Ezra Pound's wife, 'Months of re-writing! What happiness!'"

The over-all canvas is one's lifetime. Here and there refractory poems will have second thoughts and adjust their appearance, while others will continue to amble unconcernedly through the anthologies. In the end—like the bottled messages children in the poem cast on the open sea—they are all abandoned to life.

Roy McFadden
1 July 1995

Introduction

You will not find the poems of Roy McFadden in *The Oxford Book of Twentieth Century Verse, British Poetry Since 1945* or *Poetry in the Forties.* That is not because he is Irish. You will not find Roy McFadden's poems, either, in *The Sphere Book of Modern Irish Poetry* or *The Penguin Book of Contemporary Irish Poetry.* Maybe that is because editors copy each other in preference to seeking the less-known.

Roy McFadden is by no means a newcomer. Routledge published his powerful first collection, *Swords and Ploughshares*, in 1943. It seems to have been mislaid among more metropolitan ventures. Yet *Swords and Ploughshares* deserves a place beside other work that has lasted. The title is appropriate for what is in fact a war book. Its vision is minatory; its verse is prophetic. Roy McFadden sees his native mountain, Slieve Donard, in terms of another Ararat. His 'Train at Midnight' strides by "their green/Tatters of flags". War prevails in his decisive rehandling of ballad form, particularly in one of his best early poems, 'An Irish Peasant Woman Summons Home her Absent Children'.

This is a ballad form, more intricate, however, than the term would suggest. It approaches an apotheosis of the ballad.

However, equally potent was the influence of Yeats, and for a long time this proved counter-productive. The vibrant oratory of the older poet was, in many ways, inimical to McFadden's Northern temperament. One result of this was what seemed to be a struggle in his verse, between inherent character and acquired style.

Flowers for a Lady (1945) and *The Heart's Townland* (1947), perhaps because of this struggle, show something of a romantic instability of tone. Indeed, after *The Heart's Townland* McFadden published no major collection for twenty-four years. That did not help his reputation when his contemporaries were, for the most part, building on their early successes. In this interval, however, McFadden's *Elegy for the Dead of the Princess Victoria* came out in a limited edition (1952). This, while it could do little for its author on the public stage, signalled to an intimate group of admirers a compassionate scope that augured well for the years ahead.

The bitter circumstances of Ulster decreed that Roy McFadden remain a war poet. His developing ability to write of domestic circumstances has, however, enabled a human face to emerge from behind the Yeatsian rhetoric. *The Garryowen* (1971) possesses, as a collection, an unforced authority lacking in the earlier books. It is craftsmanlike all through, but 'Glenarm', 'Roger Casement's Rising', 'Premonition' and various poems in the sequence 'Family Album' are especially poignant. A sense of time passing, illustrated by vignettes of children, is carried forward into a sequel, *Verifications* (1977), with equally effective evocations of children growing up.

Good poem, girl; your mother thinks
That line which puzzles me identifies
This fractured province begging for
Paternity and style.

The later verse of Roy McFadden has a distinct narrative voice: disillusioned, but never cynical. James Joyce seems a likely influence. *A Watching Brief* (1978) is unified by its running theme, that of a lawyer going through the forms and ceremonies of a lawless city. Here, McFadden's experience as a working solicitor enables him to put a finger on pulses that Yeats, for all his sublimity, never touched. The key poem has, almost defiantly, a Yeatsian title; 'The Law Courts Revisited'. Nevertheless, the poem itself is substantially and sardonically McFadden.

The side courts closed, Queen's Bench and Chancery—
Counsel gone
Back to the burrow of their library,
Litigants home
To chew the frayed ends of the argument,
Cleaners' time
To mop and scour the day's sufficiency
Of crumpled claim and counterclaim,
Stubbed out or smouldering plea.

The metre is what can only be described as a calculated slouch. The majesty of the law is reduced to cud regurgitated and cigarette butts cast aside. McFadden's present is set against his past, when the speaker "though half a lifetime younger, seemed the same". There is evidently a past even farther back: "The marble names of your profession's dead/Sentenced at Ypres, the Somme and Passchendaele". But nothing has really changed. One's content to queue behind tight bottoms and shoulder-length hair, but McKelvey,

an interlocutor who appears in several of these poems, chides
"don't be foxed .../ By an updated style". The same tone concludes
the poem with a tart epigram:

> Keep handy in your briefcase
> A summons & a shout;
> Not everyone who comes here
> Is certain to get out:

—ending wryly on a colon, one notices.

In *Notes for the Hinterland*, a mini-collection contained in *The
Selected Roy McFadden* (1983), this inwardness with the law has led to
a remarkable renewal of tactics in a sequence based on the life and
works of Dickens. Here, McFadden, for all his Irishness, shows
himself able to penetrate into the psyche of this most metropolitan
of all novelists.

> His clients were
> Characters with impediments,
> Eccentrically
> Knotted and private; yet obliged,
> Language's litigants,
> To remonstrate. He covertly
> Ran to the stairhead, dusted the office chair.

This detached and ironic tone is characteristic of McFadden's
later phase. *Letters to the Hinterland* (1986) contained wry but
compassionate portraits such as 'Old Mr Kershaw' and 'The Colonel':

> We peer enquiringly to where he's unfurled
> But watchful by the rubber-plant,
> Plotting new strategies perhaps, or still
> Exterminating Germans; or perhaps—
> Allow for wounds behind the uniform—
> Just being old, and lonely, and afraid.

Roy McFadden has crowned his life's work with the most recent
collection at the time of writing, *After Seymour's Funeral* (1990). In
some ways, this is his best: a remarkable thing to say of a poet in his
seventies. The compassion remains, and the technical control; the
wryness has, to some extent, evaporated. Take the very first poem in
the book, for instance, 'Bed and Breakfast'. It is life itself, as either

inn or hospital.

Daybreak recalls, informs the furniture;
While, Sotto Voce, silhouettes repair
To church, with book and handkerchief, to pray.
Sir: do not put down innocents today.

Morning's a woman who comes in to pull
Back curtains, open up the vestibule;
To put out aspidistras in the sun,
And tell the resident gong the day's begun.

You'll make yourself at home, love, here; but know
To keep your baggage packed, prepared to go.

As surely as 'The Old Fools' by Philip Larkin, but less wordily so,
this is a poem about making friends with the necessity of dying. It
occurs in a collection that is the book of an old man only in the sense
that the statement could be true of the *Last Poems* of Yeats. As
McFadden's best critic, the playwright and producer John Boyd,
said of the *oeuvre* at large, this is "a distillation of his imaginative
experience from childhood to maturity". For McFadden, recollection
is not a nostalgic but an energising process. There are character-
portraits: 'Jack Yeats at Fitzwilliam Square', 'Detail for a Painting',
'Mr McAlonen', 'Pim'—"A prompter in the wings, a telling voice"—
and, most evocatively, 'After Seymour's Funeral' itself. We may not
be too far here from the archetypal ceremony of Paddy Dignam at
Glasnevin. Here, the lawyer, who knows the intimate details, blends
with the friend who is also a shrewd observer.

They tidy papers, retrospectively
Put lives in order. I have made out Herbertson's will,
Spoken of books to Mullan. Monaghan
Has named a college for his manuscripts.
They are busy editing their yesterdays,
Tailoring tall tales for mythology.

I watch their evening stumble into night.

McFadden is a past master with an apprehension of the present.
He sets before us the trait that a lesser man would find trivial but
that, with McFadden, becomes characteristic.

Abruptly, I think of him then,
Tweedy and windblown, with the laughing dog,
Alive in summer, at Glencree, among
The young trees near where Joseph Campbell died
Pitched on the hearth, the passing postman warned
By the cold chimney, smokeless in the wind.

That bitter-sweet decade; those elegies.
The barren peach-tree on the garden wall
Urgent with blossom when the laughing dog—
Now only I remember—stopped, and died

Such powers of self-renewal at such an age argue a very
distinguished talent indeed. The talent shows no sign of diminishing.
In this collected volume there is a section of new poems amounting
in dimension to a book. We find curious vignettes, such as 'Miss
Purdy in Old Age' and 'Miss Walters', and turn to evocations of the
law such as 'Prior Title' and atmospheric pieces like 'The Low
Glen'. There is no overstatement in this verse, no lushness, no
posturing. But it is misleading to define by negatives. In the end, the
precision of the vocabulary marks out the man. There is no better
poet living in Ireland today, and few, precious few, elsewhere.

Philip Hobsbaum
16th February 1996

THE HUNGER-MARCHERS

Poems 1990-1995

NEW YEAR'S EVE

On New Years' Eves, before the bells
Usurped the air with lofty promises,
We'd open windows to the frost
For celebrating sirens in the lough
To play in midnight like a famous guest.

Then, as we pledged to the night air
Our breathless resolutions, hurrying bells
From ten townlands converged to fling
Out arrogant defiance to the dark
Void, to finality in everything.

Looking back now, this New Year's Eve—
Beyond the wasted, nihilistic years,
Back to the certainties, when death
(Always so far ahead) was still a part
Of all-embracing Life, an indrawn breath—

Recalling moments when the bells
Repealed, reprieved, prompted new promises,
Tonight no citizens will fling
Open dramatic windows to the dark
With sirens wailing where they used to sing.

MAGEE'S NURSERY

Look at the stars, she cried
As the trolley overhead
Sputtered and sparked on the wires,
And the tram shrugged forward towards the glimmering town.
Beyond, in the dark, the nursery was all ears
Listening, as Magee
Pottered on paths and tugged at greenhouse doors.

Now, in the hinterland,
Distilled from place and time,
A child in silhouette
Defers the promise of the beckoning town,
To linger in the presence of the late
Hurrying nurseryman
Firming the moment in the crumbling light.

THE LOW GLEN

Acknowledging survivors, here
And there identify
The yellow brick of lingering terraces,
A pardoned tree, an unadopted lane:
And greet, incredulously,
After an interval of fifty years,
The unmolested glen.

Half-light resigned to a green gloom
(Forgotten, edged aside,
When life's containing cupped hands fell apart)
Deflecting recognition in your gaze,
Your eagerness of stride
Across the glutted ferns and rampant roots,
Hides a remembering face.

Defer to that long solitude;
Do not presume to tell
Or ask about your common absences:
But, like that tree entranced by the thin stream,
Spilled ivy on that wall,
Enter the green unfathomable eye
Of a continuing dream.

ANOTHER PLACE

Whose frontiers confiscate appearances,
Where passports are what's scripted in the hand,
A turn of phrase, the kindling of an eye;
Which no one visits in his proper mind:
What is it, forward base, or sanctuary,
Or a fantastic trip to Tir-na-nog?
Where destinations smack of parables:
Joy's Haven, Vale of Voices, Quicksands Here,
Caverns where purblind wishes live on air:
A castle with a stairway lovers climbed
Half-intimate, half-strangers, when she played
Her music for them, coaxed her cats to dance;
While clocks below the watchful balustrade
Cried out like birds against imagined dawns.

MISS PURDY IN OLD AGE

She was the lady with the plasticine,
Chalk, sand-trays, coloured wool,
Lavender-scented, with beguiling hands.
The Senior Infants wallowed in her smile;
Miss, Miss, they cried. *Here, Miss, love me, love me.*

She was the song, the poem and the prayer,
A Vestal Virgin who
Tended and groomed their lives' incipient flames,
While her abandoned apron sulked at home,
And unlit kindling wilted in the grate.

And now, at eighty, under attentive trees,
Miss Purdy promenades
Past prattling leaves competing in the breeze.
Here, Miss: love me, love me. She looks ahead,
Hitching her stride to fall in step with God.

TIVERAGH

Those summers when the poet and his wife
Held court for fact and fancy in the Glens,
Weekend disciples in the regional
Heartland, the poet's down-to-earth romance,
Found myth and symbol everywhere, like whin:
Bowed to the magpie, asked after its spouse;
And made much of each trite or stock response
When sweetened by an idiomatic phrase.

Climbing the mist, sun wiped the colours clean
On hill and glen; at loanen-heads an eye
And ear awoke to challenge us; gruff fowl
Dispersed like scattered grain; and, solemnly,
A child absorbed our pleasantries, and turned
With wondering eyes to mark the way we went.
The glenside, under an opalescent sky,
Absorbed our own child's-gaze of wonderment.

Proclaiming how the local carpenter
Inscribed his pieces for posterity,

The painter sold his pictures on demand,
Without a dealer, to a passer-by,
The poet raised his stick to eulogise
The customary and traditional.
But I was listening to a desolate cry
Across the fields, after the huntsmen's call.

THE WHITE RABBIT

    Waiting, alert,
    Expectantly—
While the foreboding, fretful countryside
Huddled behind the dark, holding its breath,
Joining the listening silence on the road—
    He sat in solitude,
    Ready, it seemed, to wait
    In patient confidence
That I was on my way, however late.

    The headbeam held
    Him blazing white
Out from the uncaught darkness of the road:
So vivid that belief and disbelief
Glazed, mesmerised by that enormous stare;
    And time, yes time stood still
    As distance shortened to
    The thud under the wheels,
Then ran abreast as if absconding too.

    Who, what, chose me
    As friend or foe?
Cats, dogs, command me. Dead birds break my heart.
A week or so from now the question will
Be blandly shrugged off as rhetorical.
    So write it down, now, while
    The sweat's still on the car,
    Life shudders in the wheels:
I was the death he watched and waited for.

A DOG, AN AFTERNOON

Warm on the summer grass
He sits observing me,
Full of the moment, free of yesterday,
Unapprehensive of the longer run,
His tolerant gaze relaxed, affectionate.

Now. Hold the moment fast,
In perpetuity.
Now everything is in its proper place,
Houses and gardens, the wide brow of the sky
Above the hill; leaflisp; a curdled call.

Before he turns away
He holds, and he's contained
By this warm comprehending moment, now,
When everything stands still: for ever now,
Forever being what is made of time.

AN EXHIBITION OF THEMSELVES

Timeservers, bent on immortality,
    McKelvey hazarded,
    Shouldering off contempt
For careful faces hanging on the walls;
Whose intimate corruption was, he said,
(Despite kind notices, the apt degree,
    Sweet medicine for doubt)
    Old age's pimp and tout,
Incontinent, if closet, vanity.

It's said the Old Gray Poet, grumbling that
    The latest portrait showed
    Him quaint and querulous,
Commissioned softer, kinder artistry.
At his age; fancy that, McKelvey said,
Peering to probe the likeness and the date.
    Though he's keen to befriend,
    Take note of how the hand,
While firmly on his heart, is guarding it.

Old lovers in their clandestine affair
    With self; and, mounted higher,

The self-appointed Gael,
Got-up, posed to impress—*like* (Herbertson,
Curtained by smoke, confided to his briar)
A salesman leaning in across the door.
The farrow eats the sow.
Well-heeled performers now
Step over the poor scrubber on the floor.

Throw open a *salon des refusés*
For nose-twitch, uncouth head;
For bitten nails, the red or rheumy eye:
For warts, McKelvey said.

HERBERTSON AT FORTY

Though *apparition* is too light
For fourteen stone
Of fixed opinions buttoned tight
Not condescending to a chair,
Standing alone,
Sounding the fathoms of the lecturer:

Yet, while the rest of us can free
An hour or so
To paddle in a shallow sea
Of lecture and lukewarm debate,
He's gone, as though
To make his point he's chosen not to wait.

THE HUNGER-MARCHERS

Throughout the house, residual books
Left from my father's library
Memorialise those early years
When life, believably perfectible,
Beckoned with promises,
And courteous futures held out welcoming doors.

Dated in his punctilious hand
1911, '12, they've earned
Shelfroom not just as literature—
Small, florin classics, once so proudly bought,

Brought home as honoured guests—
But also for his resolute signature.

Sheet-music of my mother's, notes
From singing lessons, recipes
For moral and material good,
Minutes of meetings in decrepit halls,
The lonely public voice:
Their presence is a quickening of the blood—

As when the small boy piper led
The hunger-marchers from the north,
Dancing ahead on bandaged feet;
And hope lined kerbstones, craned from windowsills,
Clapped liberated hands,
And children's cheers like flowers decked the street.

PROXY

Roads under glass, abandoned nests in the eaves.
　　Snow's vigilantes fell in step,
　　Seconded, say, personified,
And kept abreast, discreet on either side.
　　'The answer's not,' I said,
Begging the question of alternatives,

'Just intimations', as the snowflakes fell
　　Silent, aside. 'It is to hold,
　　But never wholly comprehend,
Or wrench a meaning from a cruel end,
　　As the locked stone is bound,
Containing and contained, never to tell.'

If I presume, for that's the word, to stand
　　As proxy for the tongue-tied dead,
　　Or, in the longer term, to be
A leaseholder deferring to the fee,
　　Their voices underlie
My words, their hands direct my faltering hand.

5 ANGLESEA ROAD, DUBLIN

In conversation with friends—
When we lift the clasp of the mind—
Truants from ruled-off times
Insinuate through talk's interstices,
To re-emerge in reminiscences,
Strut through familiar themes.

So once-upon-a-time
And ever-and-a-day
(Those famous contraries)
Join hands to underline an afternoon,
Prompting our gestures, timing an aside,
Mouthing soliloquies.

Behind the silences,
The creaking of a chair,
The auditorium
Extends beyond a passing afternoon
To endless afternoons, whose wings are filled
With actors roused from limbo back to time.

CONFIRMATION CLASS

December walked the ringing roads, to where
Want preached remorseless sermons to the stones.
Before the others came, before
You broke ranks to interrogate
The cleric brandishing his creed,
You bent your head to hear
The empty chancel hearkening to God.

Agnostic, and a true believer still;
Mythmaker, and no less iconoclast—
Finding my journal of that time,
That boy's ingenuous chronicle,
A retrospective looking-glass—
I read, and eavesdrop on
A listening silence, an unanswering voice.

REMEMBERING ORPHEUS

He improvised,
Harping and singing through the listless woods,
    The introverted fields—
O whistle and I'll come to you, she'd said—
Coaching her silent mouth, his straining ears,
    Towards the first brave word,
Shocked like a bird out of a covert nest.

Once, in a dream,
She came, perturbed, but radiantly laughed,
    Telling him to pursue
His given life, not drown in silences.
But, wakened to a tight-lipped vacancy,
    He could not countenance
Masks that he knew would perjure or blaspheme.

Then—all his airs
Discounted by an airy nonchalance,
    An echo's mimicry—
Putting aside the bloodless elegies,
He broke from myth, unmasked the metaphor,
    And urged his quickening flesh,
Remembering desire, to harry hers.

This time she came,
O so uncertainly and painfully
    Between darkness and light—
The body swollen, racked with birth or death,
In travail—that a countervailing voice,
    Jealously in command,
Said no, and closed the frontiers of the dream.

MISS WALTERS

Those passionate years, unknown to history,
Picket her street. I stand still to recall,
    On the familiar road,
Miss Walters dying slowly in the war;
    As if, I often said,
She'd paced death with the *Wehrmacht* in retreat,
Clutching throughout her undiminished hate

For England-outside-England: in Ireland,
And all those random places coloured red
    On pre-war atlases.
Pro-German, consequentially, she snubbed
    Tales of atrocities
As Tweedledum defaming Tweedledee;
Said liberty stopped short of the dole-queue.

Those passionate, uncompromising years
Accost me at the corner; and again
    I stand in no-man's-land,
An unsaluting citizen, whose flag's
    A protest in the hand:
Saying since death became a way of life
Little has changed to clean the canker off.

She hated the right things, selectively.
What she excused, she oversimplified.
    Whether from love or hate,
In answer to the anger of the streets,
    She lent a voice to put—
Strictly, at personal cost—the ultimate choice
Of life or death, each way a sacrifice.

Gone with the rest; my somnolent memory
Her only lifeline from the past. And yet,
    In this parenthesis,
Her voice is raised again in argument,
    An undiminished voice
That calls up answering echoes in the man
Stopped here, reminded, love and hatred gone.

IRISH STREET, DOWNPATRICK, 1886

Parleying figures pass the time of day
Unhurried in the street.
Windows incline to listen, not to look;
Corners turn back, or wait.
'Frozen in time,' you say, 'they're sure to hold
Names, dates, all those responses that I seek.'

They stare out from the frame, inquiringly,
Gazing ahead as if

Towards a future where we vaguely stand
Watching the photograph,
Frozen in our own time, anonymous,
Blurred at the edges, features undefined.

You could imagine one of them declare
That we, so far ahead,
Must have acquired by now passwords and keys,
Have come to learn indeed
Life's ultimate meaning, being free to chaff
And quiz Almighty God, standing at ease.

These likenesses of vanished citizens—
Tenaciously secure
In infinite sleep, housed in forgotten ground—
Held to the light appear
To mark time, as it were, prevaricate,
And cover tell-tale footprints left behind.

THE GARDEN SEAT

Bringing the garden seat out once again,
I say it seems no time
Since last September, when summer lingered, and leaves
Hung back on wide-awake trees;
And, reached by the kindling sun,
She wondered if, at last, she should come home.

Glimpsed on the seat, alone, seeming to hold
Court with the garden trees,
Eavesdropping ivy on the garage wall,
Fawning grass at her feet—
A captive audience—
Perhaps she tried to bridge old distances

As trees and flowers endeavoured to repair
Gaps in the patched-up years.
A border brought her childhood to her mind,
Roses her wedding day;
And, busy in a breeze,
The hedge recalled her father with his shears.

What she withheld from us she trustingly
Revealed to them, as if

Diverting her prognosticated death
Into their ambience,
Where an eternity
Is sunshine on the wrist, a flickering leaf.

I leave the seat to greet the kindling sun;
And, in a small aside,
Ask that her confidants, the courtly trees,
Ivy, the avid grass,
The garden standing still,
Accommodate the fact that she is dead.

BURNS NIGHT

As they came in by Dumfries town
They were a comely sight to see:
The Fencibles, the Volunteers,
The groundlings of the Infantry;
And, taking makars in its stride,
The Cinque Ports Cavalry.

They played the funeral march from *Saul*
Along the road to the kirkyard,
And mounted on the coffin's lid
His military hat and sword;
And he kept pace with pipe and drum,
As straitlaced as a laird.

Beside the grave the Awkward Squad
Fired three damp volleys overhead,
And from the dripping cypresses
Black corbies shook their shawls and laid
An elegiac shadow on
Cock Robin lying dead.

Well in their cups that night they roared
His bawdy choruses, while I
Sang to the baby on my breast:
O wha my babie clouts will buy?
What maudlin memory or myth
Will tent me when I cry?

CLASS OF 1926

Like windows on an Advent calendar,
Young faces peer out from the photograph
Into a promised land;
And, brightest of them all,
My brother, eight-years-old, acknowledges
Life like a trusted friend.

What moves me is the thought of how the years,
Unknowing and unknown, old history now,
Stood neutral by his desk
As, fisting the penny pen,
He wrestled with the letters of his name
To put above his task.

Then everything was named and self-possessed,
Streets, hydrant-covers, lorries, churches, schools:
All held, so it appeared,
In God's unflinching eye.
The enemies—indignity and death—
Stayed tethered to the word.

He, being older and the first to find
The trick within the magic, the marked card,
The dead thrush by the fence,
The gardener's horny hand
Behind the shed, leaned backwards to defend
My right to innocence.

Now, with him gone ahead again—this time
Into the silence, the quiescent air,
It seems beyond recall—
The photograph's alive
With all the promise that is now his past,
Redeemed by his credulous smile.

McKELVEY REVISITS SCENES OF CHILDHOOD

Catching his breath, he swore, then prayed
Aloud in ecstasy. Among the trees,
From rediscovered windows, undismayed,
His eyes looked back at him; across
Two streets his young voice whooped and called
Out champions and accomplices:
And he drew back from the oncoming child
Behind the sad offence of being old.

AUTOGRAPH ALBUM

Turning a page you open up a door.
Here's Galli-Curci, in
The Ulster Hall in 1934:
Henry J. Wood conducting. ('A bad man,'
A neighbour said, implying mistresses.)
Trams hummed and sang outside the hall's applause.

Here Tetrazzini, on her farewell tour,
Signed with a flourish, slow
To say goodbye. Isobel Baillie: clear
As a bell, the neighbour said, sweet singer who
During rehearsals charmed birds off the trees
To settle at the window for her voice.

Tauber, McCormack, Dawson. Centre-page,
Kreisler, alone, aloof.
Larger than life, his voice crowding the stage,
Paul Robeson, black with sweat, with pride and grief,
Committed his dark songs to face the light,
Warning that it was late but not too late.

Signatures, greetings; an outlandish date.
After, fame faltered, died.
Ask, as you open doorways to salute
Their having-been, that they may be allowed,
Reminded by each given signature,
To capture echoes from the grateful air.

PRIOR TITLE

Over the years you come to know
Adjacent headstones and memorials.
At Rest. Till Morning Break. Called to the Lord.
Drawn to his graveside by the modest stone's
Plain lettering, what seemed to be a stern
Avoidance of the glib or gaudy word—
Simply *In Memory*; the name;
Solicitor: died 3rd March 1912—
I stumbled on a lifetime, a career,
Ended before my own began;
Ended indeed before his easy world
Collapsed and fell apart with the Great War.

Bow Street and Market Square. Belfast
On Fridays? Did he daily check his watch
Against the townhall clock? On market days
Hide typists from the farmers? And,
In summer, follow cricket in the park,
Slow evenings kicking heels under the trees?
The local court, the auction rooms,
Church, council chamber and the Orange Hall
Were forums for professional vocables;
The inner office, firelit rooms,
Farm kitchens, the confessionals. Did he
Watch hard men blubber over grudging wills?

Don't guess or speculate; instead,
Address the wonder of a life fulfilled,
The headstone long since weathered, years before
Life finally found time for me:
The interval between the death and birth
Past history now, of revolution, war,
A no-man's-land between our worlds.
So, unaware, but schooled in precedent,
I too trod Bow Street, glanced up now and then
To mark the time; addressed the court;
And sat at bedsides and in drawing rooms
Holding the parchment flat, testing the pen.

BELGRAVIA IN WINTER

I

White terraces,
Known previously in sunshine, shrug
Off snow from roofs and sills.
As window-boxes colour girlishly
In expectation of spring,
You whistle back flickering hoops, kites hissing on string.

Soon prying heads
From area-gardens will presume
To rise above their place,
Mews-cobbles muscle lightly in the thaw,
Hoof-polished, wheel-, heel-honed,
Keeping their counsel, pressing close to the ground.

II

Do not essay
Equation of the memory
With reappraisal, or match
Your audible footsteps with footprints glued to the ground.
But, leaving the mind ajar,
Lend sanctuary to all that seeks your ear.

And be as quick
To welcome and accommodate
Those obdurate presences
Behind facades, as you were to exhume
The lure of meadowsweet
From fields in waiting under Motcombe Street.

III

Facades persist.
But inside, claustrophobic ghosts,
Confined yet dispossessed,
Appellants, not for justice but for grace,
Catching the fanlight's eye,
Yearn for the mercy of a turning key.

You, in your turn—
Locked in your own predicament—

A picket marking time,
Extemporise petitions for reprieve,
Asking eternity
To temporise, and cut another key.

JUMP

Linger awhile, and lightly look
At flimsy pictures in a book,
Designs for dresses you won't wear
Next summer, here or anywhere.

Climb marble steps, or choose to rise
In the suave lift to paradise.
A window's handkerchief of sky
Says dry your tears and wave goodbye.

Does God perceive the City Hall
Like this, a white municipal
Tiered wedding cake, whose royal bride
Lacks a prince charming at her side?

O wherefore should I comb my hair,
Adjust my scarf, look debonair?
The flagpole will not dip its flag.
Step out; hold tight to your handbag.

MINIATURE

    Herbertson says
That poet's portrait brings to mind
A salesman knocking at the door;
    Perhaps implies
That those in business for themselves
Display *For-Sale* signs everywhere.

AFTER SEYMOUR'S FUNERAL
(1990)

BED AND BREAKFAST

Daybreak recalls, informs the furniture;
While, *sotto voce*, silhouettes repair
To church, with book and handkerchief, to pray.
Sir: do not put down innocents today.

Morning's a woman who comes in to pull
Back curtains, open up the vestibule;
To put out aspidistras in the sun,
And tell the resident gong the day's begun.

You'll make yourself at home, love, here; but know
To keep your baggage packed, prepared to go.

THE INNOCENT EYE

The cottages at Ballyhackamore,
For instance, or
Houses with names, before the builders came—
Demolished, vanished now—
Stage properties in an eternity
Of childhood rubbing shoulders with the scene,
Seem rather, in recall,
Actors, directors, sentient presences,
As time and place, in retrospect, stand still.

Vanished; usurped by structures no one loves,
No exile mourns.
But wait; for here and there about the town—
Behind veneers, façades,
On gable-walls at corners, or unmasked
By bulldozer or bomb—you may discern
Pale skeletons
Of family names, antique advertisements,
Obscured or elbowed-out before your time.

So, somewhere in the suburbs of the mind,
Landmarks remain;
And, if you're constant, the familiar
Timeless fraternity
Will hold your gaze against unaltered skies,
That shepherded the living and the dead,

When you were told
That the departed never travelled far
Beyond belief, or doubted their recall.

HYDE PARK

Memorialising trees
Interpret light to dark.
Ducks on the Serpentine
Usher like offspring consequential wakes.
Still, hands in pockets, pigeons steal the scene.

What memory filched, misquotes,
Challenges context now.
The retrospective view
Of parkland and the skyline's pokerwork,
If ever a quotation, now quotes you.

Take heed of that fabulous boy,
Immortalised in stone,
Trapped in a ring nearby;
Commanding shadows, adjuring distances:
His forward gesture pointing to yesterday.

THE DANCERS, SLOANE STREET
for Margaret

Unlike the statues round the City Hall—
    Hand on lapel or heart—
    They partner light and air,
    The diffident shadows of leaves;
Still-lives, exempt from the ephemeral
    Moment which they portray:
    As, time checked in its stride,
    They stand full-stretched like a wave
Apple-laden with sun before its fall.

Alone in their enclave, among the trees
    Hedged in a private green,
    Their slow grave ecstasy
    Takes, gives back solitude:
Yet, casual strangers, taken by surprise,

Observe them and rejoice,
And summon to the mind
Appropriate music; and,
Behind a cough, the notes materialise.

So many glances, if you think of it,
   May leave their signature—
   Like tatters on a bush
   Crouched at a holy well—
So, when you look, you may reactivate
   Head-over-shoulder eyes,
   Transient messengers
   Saying remember me:
Past, present, future stilled by those dancing feet.

THE HILL

Hard in the cold night air,
Their cries tumbled and rang,
Commanding, over the snow, downhill
To where I guarded my circle of light, enthralled:
Rang; and then, as it were,
Catching their breath, ran echoing back uphill.

Careless of frigid gloves
And starved, snow-heavy feet,
The girls laughed; and the flighty light,
Flirting with slides in their hair, obliquely glanced
At shadows miming love's
Flight and pursuit through trees in the trembling night;

Until the housemaid called:
When, whispering, they went in,
Their laughter thorned on an icicle;
And, yes, that music, suddenly aware,
Missed the connection, stalled;
And the snowball flinched in my hand, at the foot of the hill.

Prim mid-day, sober-eyed,
Restored the Newcome girls,
A shade withdrawn, superior,
To their milieu of stylish cars that took
The hillside in a stride;
The redhaired maid they'd brought from Manchester.

It never once recurred,
That cold lucid delight,
Swept up with childhood; not until,
Rooting through cupboards, limiting excess,
I saw again, and heard,
Those silhouettes, their voices, on the hill.

THE STUFFED FOX

His presence under the trees,
Rippling with shadows, combed
By amber fingers of sun:
For a moment he stands alone, testing the air,
Ears up, guessing the mood of quirky grass,
Joint-cracking stones in the ditch,
A bored shrub's petulance;
Rooted, yet tensed to spring, life honed to kill,
Peripheral, a shady customer;
The taut nerve of the place.

Now, dressed to kill, he stands,
A stiffened attitude,
Collector's *bric-à-brac*,
An undemanding pet for room or hall;
And, as they carry out the merchandise
Towards the sun-baked car,
I say: o countryside,
Predators, victims, acquiescent gods,
Shake leaves, crack twigs, bend grass, in memory
Of his immaculate stride.

A DEAD CHIEF

An old man, pondering by my desk,
Deferring to professional advice,
Suddenly kindled into poetry,
And cupped an ear in retrospect
To where, facing the class, he'd squared his voice
To grapple with Gray's *Elegy*;
Or hushed and rounded it
In reverence for *The Lady of Shalott*:

In a golden apple-county. Where,
Within a twelve-month (still, he'd have said, on course)
He came back to his parish and its dead;
And left, befittingly for one
With a chief's ticket, all his late affairs
Properly logged, shipshape; godspeed
Ahead, past distances
And voyages becalmed in his spent eyes:

Ashore with the buoyant dead. Where, yes,
Young apple-trees held blossoms in their arms,
Across the hedges, in memoriam.
But I hung back to hear the sea,
Where, after hectic nights and days of storms,
He'd calm the panting engine, climb
To sluice himself with stars,
And turn the wind's head with a gust of verse.

JACK YEATS AT FITZWILLIAM SQUARE

Just as, when books were scarce during the war,
    You bought, and set aside
    For less demanding times,
These second-hand, disowned originals,
But never found a proper time, till now,
    Dusting the shelves, to hunker down
With household names the house first came to know
    Years, no, decades ago:

So you reserved and shelved that afternoon
    Until another time
    Elected, overleaf,
To re-enact the scene; with you aside,
Prompting, or undemonstrative, above
    With the celestial audience;
Yet recognising the young actor who
    Purported to be you.

War in the North. In Dublin, undoused streets,
    The neutral tricolour.
    And, in Fitzwilliam Square,
The relics of old decency and style
Glimpsed through a window or a door ajar;

Where talk drew up an easy chair
In public places; and young Dedalus
Glanced from a passing bus.

Gracious, benign, the old man raised a hand;
Murmuring, bowed and smiled.
Egyptian cigarettes:
A choice of sherry, medium, sweet, or dry.
Throughout, sporadic knocking at the door:
Discreetly deprecating hands
Conferring some mundane necessity;
A murmured courtesy.

So, as when taking down a book you find
A letter interleaved,
Embalmed for twenty years,
And read, with hindsight, what's between the lines:
Discarding all the famous faces there,
Mature reflection indicates,
Within those giving hands, framed in the door,
A kind of metaphor.

CARRIE COATES

Unwilling to shake hands,
For fear of germs she said,
She rummaged in her skirt
For a man's handkerchief
To dust the hooded armies off the chair.

Raw meal and orange juice
Sustained her. She discerned
A light upon my brow,
And murmured that AE
Would have endorsed my juvenilia.

She brought them home like strays,
My mother, in from the cold,
To stretch their hands to the fire;
To muse, and prophesy.
And they were always old, obsessed, and wise.

A name in his letters now—
An eager girl, she said—

If pressed, she might have told
Whether her mentor saw
More than reflections in her broaching eyes.

Their close platonic walks
Among God's metaphors
Kept to the higher ground;   .
While guts and genitals,
Brute ecstasy and anguish seethed below.

Mick Collins, on the run,
Cut short the monologue;
Stubbed pencil-butt on pad
Jammed on his knee, and said:
Your point now, Mr. Russell, if you please.

A crone in a picture-book
Consigned to the gloryhole,
With old, discarded toys:
Nevertheless, she still
Cranes from a chair, intent on the heart of the fire.

THE UPANISHADS

She hadn't known, she said,
A solitary prayer
Before she went to school.
The Lord's Prayer, she declared,
Was something she picked up
In kindergarten, when
Peekaboo infants held—
Familiar, nonchalant—
Their *tête-à-tête* with God.

I taught you one, I said,
Of the Upanishads,
Put into English by
Shree Purchit Swami for
The poet William Yeats
To hammer out the words—
As Blake, so Yeats averred,
Hammered upon the wall
Till truth obeyed his call.

We send them out with a kiss,
A name and a handkerchief;
But fail to school them in
The qualifying smile,
The double negative;
The last stand not too far
From bridges still unburned:
And how to say *Gosh* when
All other words have failed.

DETAIL FOR A PAINTING

Posterity, I said,
Would not be troubled if he got it wrong.
A wall demolished forty years ago
Was not likely to haunt
Even a wistful resident
Turning his car where ivy used to grow;
The gateway in the butchered wall,
The pathway to the introverted glens,
No longer viable.

Nevertheless, he dwelt
On angle, line of brick and copingstone,
Roofshadow, stables mouldering in the gloom;
And held up each unsought
New adumbration to the light—
The cottage-flowers, the trees—as if for some
Adjudicator who would rule
Which revelation merited a place
On some celestial wall.

He worked to repossess,
Pursuing colour, shadow, angle, line—
As well as likenesses, an atmosphere,
A commonplace of joy,
An early-morning certainty;
Evenings agog, with perfume in the air—
As if, redressing place and time,
He could erase the avenue's dead-end,
And finally draw home.

JUNE BLOSSOM

Ramore Head, summertime;
Fort of the hinterland.
Breakers below, beating their linen white
On foaming rocks. Swing low, to indicate
The recreation grounds:
Grazing for bowlers, nets
For dancing butterflies. *Advantage out*,
Ah, too much green. The gulls
Wheedle, expostulate.
And, out of sight, reportedly ahead,
Apocryphally latent in the mist,
A word: *America*.

And, also down below,
Bleached by Atlantic gales,
That shack once opened up those blistered doors
To deckchairs and the groundlings on the hill.
Then a precarious troupe
Of summer troubadours
Suffered the sleekit drizzle of July:
June Blossom's Company
Of Laughter, Song & Dance—
A household, no, a boarding-household name—
Versed in the skit, the sketch, the monologue;
Seasoned professionals.

Upstaged by a hot sun,
Or fly, gatecrashing winds,
They played for sticky pennies, and the few
Sixpences from deckchair affluence.
They were a catchy tune
Drowning the gravel voice
Of gavel-thumping sea; a parasol
Flouting predicted rain;
A rainbow's amnesty.
So, when she walked out shopping in the town,
People stopped short, and lingered to engage
And memorise her smile.

SUNDAY-SCHOOL EXCURSION

She, whom boys pursued
Because of her blue eyes,
Her jaunty step and swinging hair,
He said: framed in the carriage window, blazed
And beat boys from the door.
And, ruefully remembering, said:
You were the chosen gallant at her side.

And thought me close or coy
When I incredulously
Smiled my disclaimer, and instead
Remembered races on the beach, and then
The cinematograph,
Biscuits and yellow lemonade;
Scuffles and giggles while the curate prayed.

But, unflushed until now,
The buoyant memory's
Of her companions whispering,
Wet-luscious-lipped from Tropical Delights,
How, in the wilderness,
God's outcast, excommunicant,
For want of manna, kneaded excrement.

NIGHT OUT

—When, like wafers of peat in the grate,
The conversation wavers and falls,
You summon to heel
Performances, pocket your anecdotes,
And covertly feel
For the hard ringed finger, mate of the sleeping lock.
—Then singled out by the night,
Resist new turnings, sounds in the stopped town
With its refuse of footprints, appointments, bereft
Greetings and gestures in doorways, looks leaning against walls,
And the voice that says go back, begin again.
—And, pledging another time, reclaim
The familiar shapes in the hall, a stair's *qui vive*,
The curtain drawn on the garden forgetting its lines.
And, stepping down shingle through shallows to shelving sleep,

Humble the heart, and pray,
After your fashion, your small talk bundled away—
Like an unknown guest at a party, alone with his glass—
For a distant nod from the host, an acknowledging smile.

IDYLL

Early October, say—
A premonition of frost—when trees
Were personal elegies; and new
Nights of shadows, close, peripheral,
Shunning the lamplight, hurriedly
Eschewed, it might have seemed,
Tremors of footsteps avenues away.

He listened too, he said,
During those breathless evenings,
Not for an anxious bark in the hills
Or upbraiding strands of laughter from Strandtown,
But for the tip of toes and tap
Of tell-tale heels, a lisp
Of skirt; the handbag rhythmic on her hip.

And when her shadow passed
(Itself scented, he swore)—lamplight
Unmasking vivid cheek and hair—
Then, catching breath, he said, he coveted,
Obscurely between love and lust,
Not the banality
Of flesh; but style: indifferent and chaste.

PIM

A character in corduroy,
    With knitted tie or silk cravat,
He said his father had known Oscar Wilde.
    Employed, sporadically,
    In bookshops, he'd dissuade
A customer from some expensive choice,
    And recommend instead
    A shilling paperback.
Pressed, he'd quote Baudelaire and Mallarmé.

Part-time performer at the Arts,
He was a born professional
In playing every character as Pim.
Not least, his private parts
In codpiece, scrotum-tight,
(*The Lady's not for Burning*) ridiculed
The bridle and the bit.
He gathered up applause
Like hothouse flowers he'd nurtured in their hearts.

And, annotating library's
Borrowings with his mandarin style,
Commending, reprimanding, he'd extend
Essays and homilies
To margins and fly-leaves,
Seducing errant readers from the text;
And, in that way, survives—
Attached to literature—
A prompter in the wings, a telling voice.

THE FOSTER TWINS

Tell how the Foster twins,
Equally beautiful,
Fair hair goldgrained, braided with sun,
Leading the little foxes down the hill
Past squiring hedges and obeisant trees
—Unblinking yellow eyes
Of cats lighting the leaves—
Stepped from a marvellous sky,
Braced on the slope against the tightening leash.

Not old enough to share
In casual ribaldry,
Mimetic gestures, elbow-talk,
I breathed in their magnificence like scent
Encountered in a garden late at night—
Not quite a moon, but light
Seeping back from the west—
When sudden ecstasy
Confronts, adjures, rejects, and backs away.

THE INVISIBLE MENDERS

Hailing the daily miracle,
Expectant on the stairs or at the door—
Invisibility made manifest—
He beckoned, as the raucous girls
Trooped from their attic down to the tart air.

But one was so exceptional
That her translucent skin, those brilliant eyes,
Insinuated signals of decline.
She's not long for this world. Aside,
The old wives ostracised her otherness.

She vanished. To another job,
McKelvey said; had married; or, who knows,
Perhaps the wagging heads had got it right.
Soon afterwards, her absence filled
And sank beneath those grosser presences.

When, after winter, she appeared,
McKelvey, hand on heart, behind the door,
Cried out *Persephone*; but, softly, said
The flush, the lowered look, implied
No one would make a job of mending her.

GALLAGHER'S DONKEY
for William and Mary Galbraith

Aware of us, she comes
Out of the covert air
With evening in her eyes,
Docile, ineffably resigned
To silences, acceptances;
And lifts her muzzle to the nudging hand

Clumsy with peppermints:
His gruff, even grotesque,
Token of love for her
Dependence and her diffidence;
While evening's bright perimeter,
Nearing eclipse, is at its most intense.

Securing gates, recall
That midnight, when we heard
From under the young trees
A cry wrung out of solitude,
Moved for a moment to surmise
God's voice is a harsh grief in a dark wood.

THE LITTLE BLACK ROSE

To whom shall I bequeath the wooden bowl,
Engraved with twelve wild roses, rimmed
    With Celtic lettering?
    How glibly I spelt out
The coded language of the parable—
Oracular, like something they had dreamed—
    While they stood, listening.

They chanted back the words. *It shall*, they said,
Redden the hills when June is nigh;
    And new affinities,
    A latent idiom,
Sweetened, and called out from the countryside
Beyond the gardens and the motorway,
    To stir familial trees.

But blood, stark on the street, cries louder than
A sentimental metaphor.
    A manic Irishry
    Has crudely paraphrased
Romance in monologues of bomb and gun;
And girls in black bring white clenched rosebuds for
    Red tumuli of clay.

I gave them Irish names; but I'll bequeath,
Salvaging words from rhetoric
    (The black, infected rose
    A captive emblem now
For self-ordained hot-gospellers of death)
What I inherited: a maverick
    Integrity; a voice.

END OF SEASON

The pierrots gone, an end-of-season sea
Sweeps up the summer's leavings. A derelict wind
Has requisitioned shelters on the hill
Where he, so lately, stood to view,
Behind the islands shipshape for the night,
The shrinking boats depart;
While, privately, his disengaging blood
Prepared its own goodbyes.

Romantic word that lacks a synonym,
O heart, recalcitrant heart: the scattering light's
Sharp ricochet from a dark afterthought
Catches a look-out on the hill,
Now you have turned a summer holiday
Into a pilgrimage
To where young children's castles on the strand
Held sway between the tides.

THERE AND BACK

  I walked out with my grandfather,
    Great with chattering hedges, trees—
Survivors since before the builders came—
Loopholes and coigns of nettles, buttercups
And dandelions, rampant, rural still;
  I with his past; my years ahead
    Latent for him in leaf's upcurl
And undermist of trees: o, hand in hand,
His fathers and my children ventured through
A child's slow afternoon, whose distances
    Promised, but said take time;
    And faraway catastrophes
Lazed on the sidelines, not as yet on call.

  The plum tree's vanished; but the hedge,
    Long in my keeping, quickens still.
Lamp-posts are gone, and most of Stringer's trees;
And, here and there, new doors, brash parvenus,
Fail to acclimatise; but everywhere—
    Laurel and privet, bread-and-cheese—
    Old dogged hedges prick up ears.

I hear the caught breath of that afternoon,
An afterthought of place surviving time;
And, conscious of the crowding distances
      Saying take care, beware,
      I call a child back to explain
The silence that contains my grandfather.

AFTER SEYMOUR'S FUNERAL

I

They tidy papers, retrospectively
Put lives in order. I have made out Herbertson's will,
Spoken of books to Mullan. Monaghan
Has named a college for his manuscripts.
They are busy editing their yesterdays,
Tailoring tall tales for mythology.

I watch their evening stumble into night.

—I loathe this decade, but I'll suffer it,
Sinclair asseverates, a cellophane
Sandwich in hand. Herbertson peers, inquires
For prunes in supermarkets. Monaghan,
The blackthorn gangling lamely in the hall,
Commends brown bread, and milk, and oranges.
Mullan reads Flaubert, eating distantly.

They reach out for survival in their words.

II

Herbertson pushed the button. Eighty years
Of Seymour shafted down
Into whatever name
You give to afterwards. His will being done,
He got no hymns or prayers, or obsequies.

Complaisantly,
Herbertson quoted Yeats, for Seymour's sake.
No spade on stone,
No turds of earth, contorted wreaths, or tears.
Someone complained
Down in the car park of the burning leaves.

III

Somebody, sure enough, was moved to say:
He drags a chair, to eavesdrop on the talk
Of Yeats, head-down with Landor and with Donne.
Across the city, sirens chorused round
Laconic murder in the street; who would
Commend *him* to whose hospitality?

Outside T. Just the Grocer's, decades past,
A younger Seymour smoothed his knitted tie.
The rain falls on T. Just and T. Unjust.
Grace, Thoreau said, not justice. Summer then.
Butterfly sunlight. The young year in love.
Peach-blossom on an old tenacious wall.

IV

White crosses on the lawn
Facing the City Hall,
The widow's ritual
Of camera-conscious grief,
Epitomise a town
Where death's a cliché and a way of life.

The river, underground,
Heaves shoulders for release;
Low-flying back to base,
Surveillant gulls pick out
Middens of rubble, and
A slumped abandoned bundle on the street.

V

Buildings, as well, are citizens.
In this bad town
They have shut up shop, closed eyes and ears; are dumb.
Touch wood and stone.
Linger in hallways; eavesdrop on the stairs.
Nothing responds; your whisper dies at your feet.
This morning, the buried river rose in the street.

While sun presumes, and gulls streel in from the lough,
A ruined terrace hangs a heavy head,
Glass whirs and chimes from ragged window-frames.
Today, the insurgent river took over the street.

VI

Though we believed, or tried,
The beggars have failed,
Staccato with crutches and cans,
To march on the town;
And screeching gates defer
To drovers herding acquiescent hooves.
Still, though we chose to stay,
The prisons suppurate;
Keepers harassed with keys
Salute, and genuflect
To totem flags and godforsaken spires.
You told us then; and we believed; or tried.
Wait. Wait a little longer ... They will come.

VII

Whatever doors there are,
Wherever bells to ring,
Inquire
What sleep, what absence or forgetfulness
Defaulted or betrayed.
We waited; but, alas,
Apparelled differently,
Others came by stealth,
Suborned the crier, commandeered his voice.
Like tolerated dogs, the poets stand
Sad-eyed with greed outside the butchers' shops.

VII

Glaziers' hammers in Ann Street
After the patriots' bombs;
Emergency shutters of hardboard
Pre-emptively at hand;
Buses burned in the depots:
A population resigned
To follow the ruts that tumbrils
Have totted like debts on the streets.

Wherever—here or there—
Whenever—now or then—
War, you declared,

Is the inverted self
Of mirror-images—
MacTweedledum against McTweedledee—
Whose glib apologists
Make altar-room for flags
Amenably with hymns;
And walk the road with hard
Men clubbing calloused drums.

While patriots infiltrate,
Plain citizens lack language to prefer
A proper challenge at the barricades.
Who, they could say, *goes where?*

Today, they blocked the bridges, the
Traffic festered in the thoroughfares.
Old, abdicating buildings close
Their eyes, hands at their sides, aghast.

While dust recoils
From the smoke's uprising, wounds
Of aching absence let
In profiles of sky and a quizzical eyebrow of birds.

They have tidied bricks into cairns where a terrace died.
Staying is nowhere, Serafico, now.

IX

Ask those who ladle out
Their lives in sonnets and pentameters
Who will exclaim bravo
In roofless space above the birthday stars.
Who cries out *Author* now?
And also ask to know
From addicts of applause,
The impresarios
Saying good show, good show—
The shadow-boxers and
The ukelele-men—
Who answers to the call
Of Reverence for Life
(Conceding Life's a cry
Italicised by death):

Whatever rootless space,
Agnostic or malign—
(The buried river's call)—
Engenders or consigns.

X

Abruptly, I think of him then,
Tweedy and windblown, with the laughing dog,
Alive in summer, at Glencree, among
The young trees near where Joseph Campbell died
Pitched on the hearth, the passing postman warned
By the cold chimney, smokeless in the wind.

XI

That bitter-sweet decade; those elegies.
The barren peach-tree on the garden wall
Urgent with blossom when the laughing dog—
Now only I remember—stopped, and died.

HANS CRESCENT

Forgotten phrases, images, recur,
And you identify,
Respond,
As if to messages
Flashed back from outposts in the hinterland.

The day's first-footed by the cavalry.
The Aston-Martin man
Unveils
Immaculate mannequins.
You watch for life in *Town & Country Dogs*,

Where, undeluded by dilating glass,
They gambol narrowly,
Informed
By warmth and nearness. Noon:
Alas, the window's bare; day's come to heel.

PARVENUS

Those who come late to words,
    McKelvey said,
End up possessed. You've noted how
They confiscate another's audience,
The sly cough followed by an anecdote.
    And you'll have watched hard men, seduced
    By personal rhetoric, pursue
Clichés, the drabs of speech, but, in their book,
    Mots juste for every parvenu
Who takes the willing victim by the throat.

Those who come late to fame,
    McKelvey said—
The tailored beard, the jockey cap,
The open collar and the loose cravat—
End up as prisoners of a posture; and,
    Stopped in the street, they'll hesitate
    Until they haltingly recall
Whose hand it is you take, as if afraid
    A chance remark from you might hale
Back disaffection from the hinterland.

OLD STYLE

She was extremely small; not more
    Than four-foot-six I guessed.
And she was also fabulously old,
A Queen Victoria in rusty black:
    Commanding a café table, or
Clasping her books in Donegall Square West.

Held high, a babe in arms, she said
    She'd witnessed Wellington's
State funeral. One of her forebears sat
In Grattan's Parliament at College Green.
    She'd peddled tea to pay her dues
And lived on air, to graduate from Queen's.

As later, when I knew her, she
    Lunched off a penny bun,
Saving a guinea for the library.

And, penny-pinching, resolutely skimped
    On tram-fares, and was seen to tramp
Enormous distances, shrunk in the rain.

    Despite her foreign languages,
        She said demurely—Greek,
And French (and English)—nonetheless, she cried,
She was illiterate in her native tongue.
    Each day, at noon, she'd meditate
On Ireland, closed and still behind her book.

    Descended from Ascendancy,
        She'd chosen to pursue
An unprotected path outside the pale.
Irish, not *Anglo-Irish*, she decreed.
    At noon today, compatriots,
One with a gun, gutted the library.

OLD KNOCK GRAVEYARD

These are our dead, he called,
Nodding concurringly,
Flaunting accommodating arms;
Then laughed to indicate
The mimicry. *These are our dead*,
He said again, and stroked
A stone with local names in copperplate.

But they do not belong.
Touching a stone, pronounce
Gelston, or *Kelly of Strandtown*;
Turn leaves aside to note
The dates, the lifespan and the text.
Those knowing witnesses,
Hoarding the years, the watchful trees, are mute.

Ours only in the sense
That *we* are the possessed.
As, fused by darkness, branches turn
Bright palms up to the sun—
Survivors and interpreters—
So, housing ousted lives,
We hold a door against oblivion.

MY MOTHER'S YOUNG SISTER

A *new decade*, the teacher cried,
Clapping chalk from her hands.
Then: *1930*. Someone laughed
Uncertainly; the rest of us were awed.

By 1939 we'd be
Coping with Life, she said.
Did I hold back a thought for you
Trapped in the Twenties, young Persephone?

My youth, not yours, is stirred again
By summer photographs,
Items of Twentyish furniture,
That outfaced decades you have never known.

But, in sleep's undertone, you came,
Sidestepping memory,
Vivid, vivacious; unperturbed
By futures come and gone after your time.

And I caught at your perfume, and
Half-heard the teacher say
You are a shade too old for him:
Above my head, as though *you'd* understand.

But such discrepancy in years
Death stands upon its head:
You, twenty-three for ever now,
My age careering towards my grandfather's.

You were a girl who hurried past
My childhood, with a dream's
Inconstancy; as if forewarned,
Time being short, you had to travel fast.

A SMALL INCIDENT IN TOWN

Rejecting her containing hand—
Defecting, breaking free—
He dared the artful dodgers (chance, mischance)
Idling at corners, weighing circumstance;
While, shepherding clouds, the sky
Swept on regardless, turning a blind eye.

Well-heeled insurgent on the run,
    Elbowing through the crowd,
He yearned for one upstanding citizen's
Conspiratorial concurring glance,
    Another solitude
Stooping to his, showing it understood.

    Then, as the traffic's hue and cry
    Smothered his way across
To exile somewhere off Victoria Square,
Morosely turning, he caught sight of her
    Eyes, vivid as a voice:
The motherland of her abandoned face.

A MAN OBSERVED STANDING BESIDE A GRAVE

    Frowning, as if he doubts
    The grave's identity,
    His face in profile lowers
    Over the laundered earth;
    Exhuming ages, dates,
    Reflects on family
Connections, disconnections, feuds, amours,
Some sudden death and compensating birth.

    Looking again, I see,
    Instead, what's obvious,
    That he's engaged in prayer;
    Set piece, or personal
    Avowal; a late plea
    For clemency. Or is
He standing up with all the headstones there
Calling on God to be accountable?

THE STATUTE OF LIMITATIONS

    A boy, hunched from the rain,
    Running to meet me, arms aslant
To house the young dog bosomed in his coat
From streeling trees and hedges, cradled it
    With such compassionate
Commitment (call it love) and wonderment

That, all these decades on,
   His future coffined with my past—
Your first sorrow, my mother said, when I
Put on my Sunday suit, with a black tie—
   The moment's poignancy
Confronts me like a scar, vivid, aghast.

   Why tell, or try to tell?
   Custodian of absences,
Attorney, self-appointed, I declare
An interest, here and now, in then and there;
   And speak up to defer
The statute running to bar absentees.

OLD TENNIS COURTS

A rueful connoisseur
Of relics—such as old
Forsaken tennis courts, usurped
By upstart, coarser grass,
Trespassing branches trailing elegies
Across where evening sunlight sauntered past
Tableaux of white and green—
He could, he said, relate
Their message to the death
Of (call it) elegance or style
In being, doing, art,
Quotidian once, he said, as sun or rain:
The actors glimpsed among attentive trees,
The picture's discipline.

From memory he restores
The blurred particulars;
Paints in the figures, white on green,
Engaged in play, the trees,
Branches inched back, showing a greener leaf;
The ambling sunlight lingering on the side
Suspending disbelief:
While I, toeing the line
Under the specious grass,
Address the hidden court and call
Upon a silhouette,
Rallying back to credibility,
To pair the faltering present with the past,
Contemporaneously.

FOR THE RECORD

Herbertson telephoned:
In need of someone old enough, he said,
To put back into context incidents
That happened in our time,
Which hearsay garbles and misrepresents.

A keen American
Cocked his recorder for the interview;
Unloaded questions. *You and I were there,*
I mocked; and Herbertson
Sagely concurred, and trimmed his smouldering briar.

Identity; degree
Of Irishness; the label on the jar.
Backed by his books, the old man underlined
I am of Planter stock.
A ring of smoke endorsed his nodding hand.

Planter and Gael. Estranged
From both the new grim Irish and the old
Colonial retrospection, I held forth
Over the scurrying tape.
When I was a barefoot lad in the English North.

GRAND OLD MAN

After a lifetime of neglect,
Honours, like conscience-money, dividends
Long overdue,
Slide from the table to the floor,
Prop open doors; or stand like jovial cards
Saying get well.

He mounts the medals, catalogues
The portraits, caskets and certificates,
The sculpted head;
Complains that freedom of the town
Does not extend to transport. *Erinmore*
Costs just the same.

And, taken in at last, aspires
To be a doyen among younger men,

Fount more than shrine,
Who hump his harp to parties, laud
His patience, prudence and sagacity,
His sturdy style.

But, late at night, in dishabille—
The metal fire cold comfort in the grate;
An empty chair—
He raises retrospective eyes
Up to an earlier portrait, done for love,
And tells it all.

WILLIAM COWPER

Being damned,
He stopped longing for meaning, or
Yearning towards the stars. The readymade
Pattern of life—he extended his hands—is here.

Debarred,
No longer banking on paradise,
He cashed each day's remittances
For instant use against immediacies.

It wasn't that
He'd bartered his salvation for
Pleasure or privilege; condemned,
Credulity obliged him to concur

And pass the time—
Winter without hope of spring—
Shin-deep in endings, torn-up leaves,
Composing hymns for simple souls to sing.

THREE COUSINS

I

The Day of the May Queen

Exile returned, disguised
With an alien accent and
A married name: Cousin,
Let me recreate and restore
To you the skipping-games
In the street, the swing, and the songs;
The sense of forever under
The streetlamp's widening
Benignly censorious eye and outstretched arms.

Never the queen, you sighed,
You were always a step behind,
Attending, adjusting her train.
Now—queen of your own domain—
In this forsaken town,
You're moved to abdicate,
And quicken step again
To bask in that other's shade,
Lady-in-waiting courting summer still.

II

The Kodak Kid

'Shy in my Sunday best,'
She said, 'I peeped to where
You read, chin propped on wrist,
Sleep-postured on the floor:
My age, and beautiful;
And unapproachable.

'A chemist's shop in the town
Displayed a cardboard boy
With camera, eyes cast down
As if in reading. I,
Minding that private view,
Posed in the street for you.'

III

The Other Grandfather

A shying horse; a flying rein.
Clattering yardmen ran
To lift the traveller in, and softly swore
As, deprecatingly,
Blood curdled like coarse spittle on the floor.
Dying, he dreamed back home again,
Across the river and its daffodils,
And heard, from the cathedral, through the whin,
Long spades strike stones, like bells.

Let's say an anxious child ran out
To ask the time of day;
The weathered saints on the cathedral wall,
The old saint's sepulchre,
Appeared to listen; and the prescient bell,
Clearing its throat, stood by to play
Its modest repertoire for funerals;
A young apprentice, dawdling in the street,
Hearkened for harness-bells.

You delve for dates. I speculate.
But I presumed to add
The name omitted from the monument,
After—what?—eighty years.
Though no one quotes a single incident,
One mortal word he ever said,
Yet, picture how, in passing, a young blade—
Ages before you set out in pursuit—
Cousin, inclined your head.

HOUSE UNDER CONSTRUCTION

Eleven or so, drifting on wheels
Under the cherry-trees, a mile
Or so out of my bailiwick,
In a parish of blossoms, pink and white like girls,
I skirted a spillage of sand, ladders aloft,
Hodsmen, like firemen, shouldering virgin brick:
Cavities, waiting to smile,

Addressing a prospect of doors and window-glass,
Appendant to coming and going, ingress, egress.

> *My* house. Not yet; but, marking time
> Assured of my advent. Had I
> Been told, would I have turned to look
For the stranger cutting the grass, tending the car;
Or for children, perhaps, under the cherry-trees,
Running, or drifting on wheels; the weathered brick
> Benign? Or, free to pry
Beyond to a cruel end, still marking time,
Have dared to sign the contract just the same?

THE ROCKERY

My father built a rockery
To mask the gulley-trap;
Embroidered it with snow-in-summer, and
Enclosed an underworld
Where I addressed a child's credulity
Not to the motive but the mystery,
A tongue-tied oracle;
Where revelation waited for a word
Which I had still to learn.

Pasts hibernate. Their dreams
Infiltrate memory.
A ladybird enamelled on a tree;
Evening; a gramophone
Heard by a child in bed while murmuring
Lawnmowers groomed the grass; my mother's voice
Rehearsing a new song;
Tweed and tobacco fragrance when I seized
My father's homeward hand.

Just as when, then, I stared full-eyed
Into the underworld,
The wooden horse abandoned in the hedge,
So, in these later years,
Retracing steps, I turn to houses, trees,
As if the suburb were a rockery,
Where childhood, closed inside,
Secreted like a helpless oracle,
Will not come out to tell.

THE BAR LIBRARY

The anteroom, McKelvey improvised,
    Is their forecourt; or, say,
    A neutral interface
    With actuality:
Where, nonchalant without the wig and gown,
    Their order's uniform—
    Plainsuited nuncios,
Fraternal, man-to-man, colloquial—
    They take in custody
Gauche inconsistent truths, so help them God.

Sometimes (he rocked the promise in his arms)
    You'll get a baby one—
    Lamb's wig, a too-big gown,
    Sixth-former's awkward scrawl—
And hold his hand in court, ventriloquise
    Words to placate My Lord;
    And later, in the pub,
Toasting a win or drowning a defeat—
    The fee marked on the brief—
Recoil from future judgments in his eyes.

THE SILVERMAN PLEA

The pleas were always taken first:
Succinctly, without argument;
Then strictures from the bench; the penalty.
We cynical conveyancers,
Used to a different discipline,
Said slot machines would cope as readily.

But that's forgetting Silverman.
His plea was *Guilty-but.* Impassively
Unrolling mitigating circumstance—
Reneging on admitted facts—
He'd finally insinuate
A covert case of injured innocence.

Behind the sweetening courtesies—
With great respect; If it may please the Court—
We read the blasphemous argument,

As he defensively arraigned
A wider culpability,
That facts themselves are seldom innocent.

MR McALONEN

The raincoat, bowler-hat
And solemn spectacles
Betokened a head clerk
In Ewart's or the Ropeworks, or perhaps
Some kind of major-domo, seneschal,
To family merchants in Victoria Street:
A liberal Methodist.
He played bowls in the park on summer nights;
At home, grew lettuces,
And made a pleasance from suburban grass.

Always dependable
To brave the elements
For meetings and debates,
He sat, impassive, inarticulate,
Impregnable behind his spectacles.
Good afternoon, for him, was eloquence.
Familiar furniture
At meetings, we moved round him, talked across
His woollen cardigan;
But marked his absence after he had gone.

So, when he took his stand
In Royal Avenue,
Stood up to witness *No*
Against the uniforms, the hangers-on,
The munching, acquiescent citizens,
He suffered insult and indignity
With such an unconcern
That, huddled with my protest on the kerb,
I shielded my small flame
Behind his unassailable aplomb.

EMIGRANTS

Some I recalled from when,
As if making their vows
Together, hand in hand,
They signed, and touched the seal
On lease and counterpart;
After I had explained, defined
The awkward words, and made a paraphrase,
Acceptably banal,
In substitution for the draftsman's art.

Since when, as vendors—names,
A stylish signature—
Knowing their way around
Life's heriditaments:
Vendors indeed—not just
Of *Chez Nous, Shancoduff,* they signed
Away the past like bits of furniture:
A springtime's muniments
Of title handed over with the rest.

If, as I said goodbye,
Or waved from the stairhead
To faces poised below,
Regret played a slow air
From under a hitched-up sleeve,
All that is past; for gladly now,
With terror's tumbrils uninhibited,
I guide each signature
On instruments that signify reprieve.

THREE CATS

I

A Certain Death

Those mornings when I came down
To darkness and cinders, there,
Its green gaze on the sill
For opening curtains and
The first act of the day,

The histrionic cat
Banked smouldering demands.

My daughter'd held a hand
Up tearfully in school
To save a kitten from
Death's casual orderlies.
It never licked a hand
Or favoured milk, or sang
Pursed by a settled fire.

Less pet than furniture,
Never identified
With anything except
Its own chair wigged with fur,
A somnolent judge that eyed
Family proceedings with
A cool reserved contempt:

It disdained me the least.
I gave her liver and
White chicken-meat, and then
Knelt conversationally
Caressing head and paws
Till mutilating claws
Punctured pretentious wrists.

Barn cat, uncivilised,
She trusted the vet's hand
And looked with faint surprise
At the bared needle, and
Nobody cried, but yet—
Whenever I come down
To flash the curtains back—

I look outside for her
Intent uncertainty,
Or listen to the tree;
And, unclaimed, hesitate,
Grief retrospectively
Dishonouring relief,
To activate the day.

II

Young Cat in a Hedge

The frightened cat in the hedge:
Not just immaculate fear,
But an outlaw's wariness
Of breathless bushes or
Hushed undulations of grass;
And, masked by trees, a rigid wind as it were,
The presence of the executioner.

The young fox-terrier,
Your earliest love, put down,
The sun wrenched from your sky;
And that barn-creature none
But you could pacify,
Bearing the needle's thrust with knowing eyes:
Include, among thrusting thorns, in this one's face.

For one and all now, kneel,
This time to repossess,
Manhandle back to you
From trespass and impasse,
A fox-faced kitten, who,
Across gatecrashing distances, weeps for
The length of a lawn with the door of the house ajar.

III

Satchmo

Life, or whatever, closed a door;
And, suddenly, with landmarks gone,
You feared your friend, the dark. Those nine
Lives, did all of them combine
To bow out with your uncontracting sigh?
This morning, fittingly, let no dog bark.

An epicure of silence, sleep-
Shrewd connoisseur of fireglow, sun
On rug and windowsill—o, let
Recalled warmth make a coverlet
For your last sleep under the rowan tree
Each time the garden turns to find you gone:

Or when, comrade of earliest days,
Playmate indeed, protector too—
Recalling, later, dignity,
Forbearance, love—faced by a tree
Beyond your climbing now, I bend to say
The garden grows in memory of you.

EVICTIONS
for Padraic Fiacc

Precocious refugee,
Between the ghettos' fires,
I stopped my tricycle.
A baby in a pram
Held out his penny flag.
I took it. In exchange,
I closed his fingers round
A wooden tomahawk.
On his side, and on mine,
The houses rocketed.
And detonating streets
Clapped reprobating hands:
Exclamatory, like squibs
Let loose on Hallowe'en,
Once thought to exorcise—
Out of the hooded dark—
Demonic messengers
Tending the torch's glow,
The flame's dilating eye,
Intent on holocaust.

THE LITTLE B.A.

My mother called him that;
One of a numinous company
Of unfamilial names
Still vibrant from her meetings. Then,
My father, marking his page, sat back
To smile at her mimicry
Over the warming pot, while her playback
Of lecture and debate offhandedly
Recaptured style and accent to a *t*.

Urbane and sociable,
Seldom forthright, familiar,
He found congenial ground
In crumbling Georgian premises
Downtown, in dead or dying squares,
Where, ready volunteer
With lectures on AE and Allingham,
He'd flex his elegant phrases, debonair,
Succinct and polished; and particular.

At séances, he said—
A casual fellow-traveller—
He was seduced, possessed
By female voices; sceptical,
He'd lisp falsetto to his friends.
You told me in the car,
After the funeral, of the irony
Of mutilating death in a wheelchair
For one so dapper and particular.

Do you remember a
Letter to William Allingham?
'You heard me speak of one
Lauret, a painter. He is dead.
His watchings, love of nature, toil;
O all his aspirations—I'm
So grieved; I don't like death, I tell you—dead,
Wiped off the palette, smudged out like a dream.
Four fir-boards. Listen; that's what's left of him.'

CAPTAIN THOMPSON

You may contrive, in talking to the dead,
To single out a captive audience
In some abandoned wall, a stranded tree.
    So, when I say thank you
    To Captain Thompson, I
    Will not expect to hear
Modest disclaimers murmured in my ear.

Because he took on board a twelve-year-old
Castaway from two centuries or more
Of clannish forebears, left in the spent town—

Numbering kith and kin
From headstones, or the vault's
Incestuous family tomb—
My father named his firstborn after him.

The old man's only love the open sea—
Passionate, self-consuming, unpossessed—
Aground, he'd trimmed his step to the river's gait;
    His trawling ear withdrawn
    To shallows only of sound;
    The weathered fist on the stick
Eased from the grip that veered past spitting rock.

Born to the craft of Irish Chippendale—
At home with wood, part of the natural grain—
Adrift, a lodger in his family's town,
    My father came to share
    The Captain's table, say
    Amen with him at grace,
And read the morning weather through his eyes.

An aunt said when my father left the town—
Eighteen: hard-collared, tie-pinned—and acquired
(That was her word, *acquired*) responsible
    Work in a city bank,
    Old Captain Thompson stood,
    Proud tears fierce in his eyes,
To glimpse a silhouette against the glass.

And when he died, she said, without an heir,
My father scorned to ask about a will.
Think of a sea-chest fit to burst, she cried,
    With treasure, maps and things.
    But what he gave, and what
    I celebrate today,
Spilled from a richer, rarer treasury.

Addressing wall or tree, I call to mind
Imperfect, re-created images—
The old man in the street, my father's head
    Clouded by window-glass—
    And shake out speech to find
    Such words of gratitude
As, scattered, may take root among the dead.

GONE AWAY

If I should knock the door and ask for me,
Who would peer past the startled householder,
Over those absent years?
No ghost for sure, from that forever time;
No cupboard skeletons, where candour could
Keep house without locked doors,
Where family entertained a neighbourhood.

Recall the hallstand's station at the door,
The hats and sticks, the mirror's challenging
Or recollecting glance;
The clothesbrush in the drawer with Sunday gloves,
Ancestral prayer-book, old, genteel like lace,
Surviving evidence
Of forebears in a legendary place.

Or say that you're the meter-man, and step
In with authority: nudging at walls
To peel off posthumous paint;
Cajoling carpets to resuscitate
Footprints from smothered wood; conjuring doors
To hark back in complaint,
Under the gloss, to unforgotten scars.

And ask the listening stairs to repossess,
Step at a time, a child climbing to bed,
When, late on Christmas Eve,
Beyond the flashing trams across the trees,
The churches counting blessings in their towers,
Faint sleighbells stretched a sleeve
Of reassurance towards his guttering prayers.

I stroke the hedge, *my* hedge, and turn away,
Back to accessible appearances;
And tell the passing thought
Survival's only in the heart and head.
And yet, if I could earn the missing word,
Such bidden beings might
Smile with relief: seen, seeing; hearing, heard.

LETTERS TO THE HINTERLAND
(1986)

2 SEPTEMBER 1939

At ease, basking in talk, as if
Respectful distances deferred,
Giving him time, the dandelion light
Already sentimental on the wall,
He stands forever graced by that afternoon:
Which I, looking for something else,
Thoughtlessly stumble on, as if
All the dead-and-gone had still to arrive
With ribbons and flowers, or wreaths under their arms.

34 TITE STREET

Houses, whose plaques commemorate
Poet, musician, painter, architect,
Tracked down and photographed
By zealous tourist, jealous devotee,
Continue, unimpressed,
Preoccupied with the domestic round.

Take, for example, 34
Tite Street, in Chelsea; whited sepulchre
In Oscar's heyday, when
Groomed, self-composed, he lingered on the steps
Adjusting his lapels,
Verse on his lips and bad boys on his mind;

And when, after they'd cornered him,
Right-minded and rampaging citizens
Sacked the exotic rooms
And plundered relics from the sacrifice
Of his magnificence,
While, further off, whores roistered in the street;

And when, abandoned, it shrank back
Into the terrace's conformity,
Toeing the building line,
From camouflage to commonplace, inside
The floors and stairs retained
Their spring for each new decade at the door.

Today, pausing to contemplate
The banished ogre's fairy palace, you

Stumble upon respect
For all those unpretentious premises
That, imperturbably,
Clean up the droppings after each demise.

STYLE

Bedside companion—
The lady nobly dying,
Murmuring I will see you there—
Soignée, articulate, you dignified
Goodbye for me as well:
Whatever distances you undertake,
May you arrive in style.

A friend had taken my arm
To indicate you in the street,
Pronounce with passionate concern:
Young poets, lacking confidence and style,
Require an older, educated love,
Thirty-or-so; intelligent: and, o,
Sophisticated, exquisitely heeled.

VICTORIES

Some still remember how
Caraciola in
The white Mercedes stormed
Majestically to victory through the rain;
And, later, Nuvolari, tanned
Under the goggles, lifting an elegant glove
Dappled with dust to greet the chequered cheers.

The district councillor,
Safe in the family car,
Switched the ignition on
And settled down to nurse the engine's cough.
Goodbye, they called into the dark.
All hell broke loose, they cried; and, later, he
Was spelt out from the fragments in the park.

THE DISAPPEARED ONES

Forcing the frames, the windows sang.
Seconds before the gable crashed,
Gulls, turning tail, dived back to sea,
The nervous suburbs barked;
And, brokenbacked, walls staggered, hand on heart,
After defecting stairs.

Now you, who strummed on railings or
Sheltered in doorways, climbed the stairs,
May hoist a black flag overhead
For vanished citizens;
And fasten, if you like, on your lapel
A black contorted key.

OLD MR KERSHAW

    Affronted and afraid,
The tentative greeting crumpled, pocketed;
    Perhaps alerted too
Against intrusion on a solitude
    That tended the torn stare
And turned his hearing to oracular shells,
I recognised that he was not all there.

    Slow to identify
The trudging stranger with the family friend,
    Respected, amiable;
Eyes following defecting distances,
    With the myopic gaze
Over his glasses as my father talked—
I sidled from his new, prophetic face:

    Too young and ignorant
To apprehend inside the guttering coat,
    The flaring scarecrow sleeves,
His huge intolerance of civilities
    Distracting him like flies
From explication of the mystery
And words to stem the panic in his eyes.

THE COLONEL

When I was a child he lived on up the hill.
His grass and garden paths were derelict.
Though almost dashing, he lacked elegance.
On milder days he sported on his arm
A wife who looked much older, wickeder.
And, though they had a vestibule,
They kept the front door shut against the street.
Remarkably, they'd neither child nor dog.
He seemed far too important for hallo.
His groomed moustache suggested the Great War.

When I was ten we moved across the town.
He stayed, with childhood, in the hinterland,
A character inside a nursery tale,
A giant, good or bad, secure within
A legendary ever-ever land.
So, later, when I came upon a grey
Clerk at a counter, stamping documents,
It was his alter ego that assumed
The guise of unassuming citizen.
Back home, the implacable hero swung his cane.

All through the war he harried editors
With forecasts of disaster. Never since
Has *Northern Whig* or *Belfast News Letter*
Been so oracular without his name
Beneath the hardboiled *Yours etcetera.*
He argued for relentless war
From Stalingrad to Ballyhackamore;
Included every German cat and dog
In massive extirpation. *The poor things,*
My mother said, in ridicule and rage.

Now, after half a lifetime, I observe
His distant figure, like an old masher with
His tilted hat, his angled walking-stick,
The shoes alas no longer glittering,
The strict moustache still bristling for salute:
Glancing at shops and offices
As if expecting to be summoned in
To overhaul the system, improvise
A firing squad to line up in the yard
And execute the latest dissidents.

Young cashiers at the counter in the bank
Think he's an officer (retired). *Colonel,*
The one with tinted spectacles declares;
He cashes monthly cheques made out like that.
We peer inquiringly to where he's furled
But watchful by the rubber-plant,
Plotting new strategies perhaps, or still
Exterminating Germans; or perhaps—
Allow for wounds behind the uniform—
Just being old, and lonely, and afraid.

THE HOUSE

The house was built in a dry summer
On a virgin hillside of grass
Under a motionless sky in bee-dazed air.
The girl smoothed mirrored hair to meet her love.

Autumn dulled to bronze
The summer's brasses, but
The soil remembered and stirred,
And in the captive garden
Burgeoning then she knelt down to embrace
A leaf's complicity.
And the alice-blue dress was stained
With the grass of that last summer.

Today, after thirty years
Of burnt-out summers, I viewed,
Aloof on a faded floor,
A woman dead; the door strangely ajar,
The wireless lisping, and the red
Metal lips of the fire implacably dumb:
And the hillside levelled and drained
To meet the marching suburbs of the town—
As though I had never breathed, in the dazed air
Over the rush-harsh grass,
The word of a young girl's name, the sky
Becalmed in her eyes and the sun putting gold in her hair.

THE DEN

She called it 'The Den', the name
Persisting from girlhood, when passion and languors vied
In albums and diaries.
In the garden, the nesting-boxes had names for the birds.

The outlook anthologised
Decades of borders, rockeries, arbours and
(Not wildly incongruous)
Field-flowers permitted to roam, indulged like a child.

In her hat with the veil, and her hands
Majestic with lace or chaste in diaphanous gloves,
She established herself in a world
Where china and chat discouraged the cry from the heart.

But, for unbelievers, The Den
With the crack in the ceiling and damp like a hand on the wall,
And yesterday's flowers in the vase,
Had the look of a room abandoned by children and love;

Where, remote from the window, with age
Uncovered in neck and hands, she discarded her day's
Coiffured appearances, and
Exhumed the cry in her heart, and said o my love

Let them scatter my death in the wind;
For the house will defect, and neglect to reflect or recall
The Den and its denizen, when
They have covered the crack and coped with the hand on the wall.

FIRST BLOOD

When you and Kernaghan
Fought in the cellars, it began
With formal insults, ritualistically.
Exchanges petered out, and counsellors
Demanded violence;
Squeezed back and shuffled to a square,
And roared on gestures hurled
Over the arms and shoulders like balloons.
It was a game:
A bout of shadow-boxing; pantomime.

But once when Kernaghan
Provoked Maginess where he stood
Foursquare against the latrine's steaming wall,
There was no pussy-footing argument,
Naming of seconds, or
A kiss-my-hand and pas-de-deux;
But unabashed mayhem:
Tapped claret ugly outside schoolboy slang.
And we recoiled,
Not yet conditioned to the acts of war.

SIDE WARD

The trouble is we never believe it,
That the moment of truth, in a manner of speaking—
Reserving of course our own improbable deaths—
Is always now. But we never see it,
Until the moment is past, and the scent's gone cold;
And then, as often as not, the retrospection's
A new creation nurturing itself.

You could specify each *then*; advancing
Examples of *you* and *yours*, the *you*
Being notionally constant, but the *yours*
Shifting from childhood to age, and suddenly strange.
And the mood, on reflection, is not
Nostalgia; it is regret: for the children who run
Out into the garden to play, and vanish for ever.

So sit in your shining cell, deferring
To hospital sounds and the traffic of trolleys,
To patients' petulance, the patter of staff,
The demented lady demanding her long-lost home:
In a white-faced room unkindled by living light,
Outfacing the moment now, the fact of your being
Assigned to a faceless man with a knife in his hand.

SHOP SOIL

Suspiration of leaves
Snatched from submissive fields
Assails your frontiers, infiltrates
Your settled suburbs; and, a child,
You stand for hymns at harvest festivals.

Headstrong chrysanthemums,
Unbending merchandise,
You say address a hinterland
Where each aborted journey waits
For redirection by the traveller;

Where fugitives converge
From extirpated lives,
Survivors from the dark,
Trailing lame roots of memory
Back to the daydream of the marigold.

INTERPOLATION

One reading, Rilke, is that life elects
For breaking those who come too close to it.
Chosen, you knew how hard it is to thole
In silent abnegation. Nobody
Sends thunder skittling through the clouds or claps
A hand of darkness on the midday sun.
Nor can we say to anyone *Forgive.*
The house we built in springtime tumbles down,
And hindsight excavates the running sand.
Eurydice is buried in the dark
In bright midsummer mourned by petulant trees
Shrugging off sunshine. Think how Orpheus—
Then silent as the grave, when all he touched
(Advised beforehand) turned away from him
As something separate, intended, pledged
To other meanings—looked into their eyes
And saw in them his own disfigurement.
When he persisted, they dismembered him.

DOCTOR SERAFICO

I

The Muzot Event

Unwavering guardian of his solitude's
Establishment
In fortresses moated by distances,
He ruthlessly
Discountenanced ambitious canvassers,
New loves intent on rearranging him,
Old loves with querulous wounds.

And studied, cultivated silences;
And, stoically,
Put up with disappointment and despair;
Was sceptical
Of hearkening trees and hurrying steps in the rain:
For the Angels enter unheard, their luminous
Presence immediate.

Waiting, he sifted, sounded out his words;
And disciplined
Structures and rhythms, the obliging rhyme,
Bold metaphors—
(You must change your life)—for metamorphosis
To statues shrugging off the sculptor's hand,
The outgrown scaffolding.

But when they came at last, his separateness
Seethed into storm.
Whole days and nights he worked translating them,
Groaning aloud,
Until the agony and ecstasy
Expelled the unforgiving miracle,
And he broke from the cord.

Then he looked round, restored to furniture:
Assuredly
Heard thrushes singing in the startling rain,
And, from the town,
An arching shout buoyed up and lightly held
High in the air until it thinned and fell
To silence everywhere.

Adjusting vision back to surfaces,
To round and rind,
He groped for speech like coins or peppermints,
A clutch of keys:
And when he ventured out among the trees,
He marvelled that the untransmuted scene
Could still seem probable.

Then he wrote letters, propping up his hand.
  —To the Princess:
At last, at last the blessed, blessed day.
  —To Kippenberg:
I didn't know such storms could be survived.
Reprieved, he stroked the rough patrolling walls,
And fingered the moon's caress.

II

After Muzot

Depleted then;
Enormously bereft:
He signalled from the castle walls
Deliverance from his solitude;
And, when they sent for him,
Bowed to applause.

They fêted him
In salons, but their praise
Was for accomplishments before
He cried out to the Angels. Thus,
No one commended him
For altering Life.

Garrulous then—
Head upon shoulder, hands
Italicised, extravagant—
He seemingly apostrophised
Celestial auditors,
Seraphically.

Discountenanced,
They shrugged, and turned away;
While, fettered to his monologue,

Eyes mesmerised by distances,
He fretfully recalled
Incredible wings.

III

Marthe

Perhaps he followed her.
But far more likely it was she
Accosted him with casual impudence.
But, anyhow,
Their lives collided; he retrieved,
As you might say, her crumpled handkerchief.

Footloose at seventeen,
She bit on rinds while he
Suffered the sweetness for the core.
Fastidiously,
He waived her body for her mind,
Which opened up, he said, to his hard verse.

Street-singer Orpheus!
His letters to the dear Princess
Intrigued her, convalescent in the sun.
She marvelled how
A little girl, catching his sleeve,
Could coax his solitude to follow her.

After his style, he found
A *pied-à-terre* inside her heart.
He, who loved roses, bought her violets;
And suffered her,
On tiptoe at the gutter's edge,
To fasten her quick choice to his lapel.

IV

An Honourable Death

Seeing his death
As life's associate,
As sleeping-partner or co-parcener,
Quiescent, reticent—

He pictured his dying as
The gradual dissolution of a room,
The slow recession of an afternoon
From books and furniture;
A congregation of friends,
Voices gloved in the dark,
Attending and participating in
A modest ceremony of goodbye.

How different then,
When, surging up in him
Perversely in the common residence
It tunnelled through his veins
To burst in sibilant sores
Whose incoherence lacked interpreters,
Whose mouths decried impervious presences,
Inert, inflexible wings.

But he persisted; still
Electing to command
The rhythm of his dying: to endure,
And honour his commitment to the end.

TELLING

You too, he said, have seen
Styles come and go, modes, fashions change.
The match's head
Flared into transient flame; contentedly
He nestled in companionable smoke.

The reddening core engaged,
He shook the smouldering splinter dead,
And said that all
Variety of manner is a sheath
That flight makes, or the rocked wake on the sea.

POETRY READING

I know you. Having climbed the stairs
Of elderly buildings through the years
To public meetings, rallies, conferences
For culture, justice, peace,

Here at the top I recognise
The same decrepitude:
Cracked ceilings, decadent walls and cupboard-smells,
And, underneath, mouse-furtive silences.

And contemplate resemblances
In tentative faces at the door,
Muted or caricatured in middle-age:
Life's nonparticipants,
Spinsters and tidy bachelors,
Obliging furniture
For long-dead skivvies' loveless attic-rooms,
Abandoned or forgotten by the town.

I know the poet too; or did,
When he was young and adamant,
And living called for more than livelihood.
But, grown professional,
Paid for the act, the one-night stand,
More than the verse commands,
He works the system of establishment,
Whose imprimatur is his business-card.

He finds marked pages in his book
For prefatory paraphrase.
They listen secretly, or elevate
To high grey windowlight
Aspiring or despairing eyes,
Drugged by the monotone,
The trudging traffic of his images,
A substitute for summer in the blood.

Closing, he makes an actor's bow,
One hand adjacent to the heart.
But hungry voices remonstrate, and he
Reads out another page,
An encore, if you like, for love,
Then smiles, and deprecates.
Chairs back and bark; and hasty hands applaud.
They line up for the plastic autograph.

He packs his bag, shrugs on his anorak,
And shuts up shop;
Then softly goes
Back to the safe street where he parked the car.

OIL PAINTING: THE MANSE AT RALOO
i.m. James Steel

Late March perhaps was breaking
Disdainfully into spring, unable
To nip in the bud the catching laughter of leaves;
Or autumn itself had turned
Its coat, defecting to hare-lipped horns
As winter blazed a trail for quickening hooves:
When you
Turned and composed your last look at Raloo.

First leaf or last, you guessed
Next year some tolerant branch would bend
To others' April or October thoughts,
And the same stones submit,
Still sentenced to parenthesis,
To the same wheels honed by identical ruts,
While you,
Boxed in a frame, reflected on Raloo.

Now, decades after you turned
Away from unanswering angels and
The easy virtue of the countryside,
Your picture hangs on a wall
With views of Carnlough and Glenarm,
Without a hint of how the colours bled
When you
Cried out for affirmation at Raloo.

AN ATTIC IN HOLBORN

A window-plant grasps at the crippled air
Reprieved from the rancid town; a chair
Condones the abdicated coat;
The candle's tongue-tied in cadaverous wax;
Torn manuscripts curl scattered round the box:
And, white as his face, the valedictory note
Is his receipt to fortune for his lot.

Below, life rustles in the waking town.
Light scales the curtains; windows yawn.
Thumped mats fawn welcome. Stubbornly,

A voice rehearses fragments of a tune.
A drayhorse kicks up saffron sparks from stone.
And gulls cut inland from the estuary,
Where tethered sails fret for the open sea.

GIG

Reaching to autograph fanatical hands,
You stand perhaps where I
Gormlessly missed the dolly-catch,
Young watchful wolves in a ring.
The hoods have spared the Methodist church hall.

My son, my brother also trod those boards,
Young croupier of applause,
Ace who outplayed the shuffling pack;
While I, dealt awkward hands,
Failed to conform, and never followed suit.

BARNARDO BOY

Trousers too loose, too long—
Toulouse, Toulon, in school vernacular—
Cuffing the kneecaps, head cropped to the bone;
Rough and recalcitrant
In class and yard, he was peripheral:
A kind of gypsy; Jew who'd married out.

Though he was tolerant
Of blackboard quip and badinage,
He kept a cutting edge on his resolve
Not to be cowed or conned
By circus discipline: the paper hoops,
Life tamed to tied or studied attitudes.

And unaffectedly
Declared his manhood, or perhaps it was
An indication of his innocence,
When, surreptitiously,
Under the sloping counter of the desk,
He showed himself to shiny big-eyed girls.

ELOCUTION LESSON: *HOT CROSS BUNS*

Flapping a flaccid hand—
(Imagine a handbell
Cuffing a cardboard street;
Add a castle cocked on a hill)—
She skirts the china dog
Matter-of-fact on the hearth,
The standard lamp, the what-
Not, and the paper shell
Of a fan in the summer grate:
While, miming her, the boy,
Watching his language, shapes
To shake his spurious bell,
His words to consonance;
Small fellow-traveller,
Agnostically aware
Of out-at-elbow streets
Incensed, incredulous,
The window sceptical:
Its outward gaze on bread-and-dripping lives.

LOVE

Now, after teatime, when the spoilsport sun
Abandons lawns, good evening hesitates;
Say like a traveller bent on distances,
Anticipating night. Or like the man
Turned at the gate as if to memorise
The ivy's scribbled geography,
Each window's narrowing leaden-lidded eye;

Who reaches down accommodatingly
To take her hand and squire her dancing feet
Askew up to the corner, murmuring
Familial phrases, educating her
In names of trees, and verbalising sounds
Of home-birds hunkering down before
Night twitches closed the curtains, shades the light:

Good hand in daughter's hand, the hidden one
Conspiratorial in pocket where
Pre-emptive murder threatens a by-blow;

His thoughts, observed for later, less concerned
With holed-up mistress quickening in distress
Than with the tart ambivalence
Of love turning a cheek for his goodnight.

BROTHERS-IN-LAW

Waiting for counsel in the hall,
You contemplate
A young man and a prison officer,
Attentive, affable,
Their heads together, shoulders intimate:
Then, unionists, separatists,
The handcuffs' wicked bangles on their wrists.

And say, within that context, they
Could equally
Be co-defendant, fellow-prisoner;
And both accomplices
Of that third party who goes home for tea
And passes time with friends,
After he's washed off judgment from his hands.

BALLAD SINGER: CHICHESTER STREET

I

Cheek by Law Courts' jowl,
The Variety Market stalls
For a further stay, and trades
Upon the Law's delays;
And, taking its own time,
Dallies, procrastinates,
But gets its business done
While the morning's fresh, and the sun's
Still rooflines short of the Sirocco Works,
And justices confer
Over a judgment, under their antique wigs.

II

She shrugs into her song
Of bright May mornings, lugs

The threadbare sentiments
Up off their knees to sing;
While, look, on the firemen's tower,
A young French officer
Steps from a picture book
And calls *To arms! To arms!*
Whereas, waxed water-clear,
The gallant engines stand,
Machines of mercy and
Manipulators of anarchic fire;
And shrewish women shop
Shrewdly around the stalls, closed to her song.

III

But: *here and there* you say
With wry inconsequence
To someone in your head,
Italicising words,
Continuing comrades of
Comfort from the war:
And here and there a petal. For—
As litigants congregate
Soft-footed in the hall,
Whose marble walls reflect
Contorted images
Of miscast actors nervous of the play—
Miss Primrose, virginal
In wig and gown, cravat
Chucking her chin, evades, declines, deflects
Advancing glances, here
And there, a petal, glad-eyed, thought-caressed,
From mid-term dainty solemn Dresden face.

IV

You enter; feign to cringe
Before the petulant head.
She redlipreads, lisps through the list.
(If you had waited, she'd have sung your song,
Shawled arms akimbo in the street.)
Leafs through the list, wrists intimate with lace.
(Abandoned to, abandoned in her song.)

THE ROUND POND

Later, you say, you will compare,
Not just with photographs,
Your recollections of
This place, already fiction in your mind,
But with those earlier memories of
Nostalgic stories told on evenings now
Themselves part of the dayligone,
The bittersweet
And legendary outback of the mind.

So, passive in the sunshine now,
You watch a steadying kite
Clean as a whistle shin
Up staggering altitudes, but note the man
Feeding the string, who, cat-eyed, covertly,
Is author and producer of the play,
A J.M. Barrie of the park,
Whose fantasy
Trails back at tea-time into his fussing hands.

WALLED GARDEN, IRISH STREET, DOWNPATRICK

That old walled garden, where
Among staid eighteenth-century trees
A cuckoo rang its flat ironic bell,
Seemed even then
Only a lull, a gracious interval
Missed, or dismissed by storm,
A pardoned pleasance where
Sun ivied on the wall
And breezes arched catfooted on the leaves.

What have you made from that
Windfall, or other intervals
Between recurring storms, while cuckoo-clocks,
Vox populi,
Proclaim false summers from constraining springs,
Other than keep ajar
Conclusions, premises,
Accommodatingly,
For white-faced revelation at the door?

REMAINDERS

On Exhibition Road,
Given dry weather, you are sure to find
Remainders spread like bait
On tables by the door.
Old masters sprawl, reduced, in modern dress,
Abandonedly, to lure
The hurrying eye, the wet inquiring thumb.

Out for a paper, or
A matutinal stroll round Thurloe Square,
Sidetracked, compulsively
You'll probe for treasure trove
Lost in the lurid jungle, seeking out
With credulous fingertips—
As always—the remaindered Holy Grail.

Embarrassed by old friends
In dishabille, the masterpiece recast
As story-of-the-film,
The television-play,
Nevertheless you're liable to find,
Among the cover-girls,
Forgotten poets, banished novelists.

Then heart and hands extend
With undiminished gratitude and greed;
You even count the coins,
Make shelf-space in your mind.
But they are all at home: originals,
Pursued decades ago
Through long-demolished shops, and bought for love.

IN PASSING

At the piano singing,
In trained contralto, songs
By Schubert, or stiltedly playing
Demanding pieces from her repertoire,
Familial like photographs—

Hardly so much it seems
A passive memory,

A locked parenthesis,
As, what was the word, interpolation, a
Laying on of hands—

She plays from memory now,
And looks with neutral gaze
From new-found distances;
An incarnation of light, absorbed, although
Comprising yesterdays.

SURVIVOR

In early summer snatched
Into whatever alien element
Or separate dream, she could
Given a voice declare
That all those unpermitted years,
Extended to others, have edged away like a dream,
Leaving only a pared phrase, a glance's glint
And flurried lipless cries
Sifted by weeds short of the open shore.

Tidying her hair,
One who survived declared
It was another world,
It was as if
Some other had performed her part;
Or more as if
She'd found a letter written long ago
Purporting to be hers:
Or even more as if
She'd come upon a shiny photograph
Of once-upon-a-time, and cried
Alas for a slip of a girl with her winning smile.

WELSH FUNERAL: CARNMONEY

Only the daffodils,
Young hardy trumpeters,
Stood up to the sleet's despite, the wind's harangue,
While, circumscribed by wreaths,
Stiff in his Sunday best,

Tom Davies held his breath as the spades rang,
Soil eructed on wood,
And the preacher reasoned with God.

The argumentative hand
Knuckled on knee to cram
The briar's bowl or pluck to brandish a phrase,
Conformed in a gesture of prayer;
And, backed by daffodils,
His valley-verdant, dark-down-under voice
Rolled from hills and dales
Of the wind, homesick for Wales.

Muscling in music then,
Propping up pits of grief,
They hewed from light-and-dark ambivalence,
Shouldering wind and rain,
Their paeans and laments;
And, exile's face behind the citizen's,
Myth-harried and myth-blessed,
Hymns of the dispossessed.

Ambivalent citizen,
Reluctant patriot,
I thought of Ballinderry in the spring
When Samuel Ferguson
Mourned Thomas Davis, and
Quickened like leaves to his greenfinger song;
And said: Tom Davies will
Recruit the daffodil.

THE GARDEN OF REMEMBRANCE

Grown old in sinecure,
The cenotaph's alert
Only when brigadiers and clerics, hard
Hats and jowls, municipal collars, the
Militia of establishment,
Pout in parade to lay
On Victory Days
Their wreaths of poppycock.

Dismissed, the ghosts decamp,
Bugles and flags at rest;

And statues turn back to the City Hall,
Where in the twilight, through kiss-livid lips,
Lovers nostalgically recall,
Only to lay,
Ghosts of their disparate pasts.

THE GIRL

Was there a girl; or did
You conjure from thin air,
One August evening, walking above the shore—

Striking an attitude
Against rocks straddling the strand—
A figure hearkening from the hinterland,

Stirring and stirred by your blood,
To still life on a coast
Where spume spits back the losers and the lost?

Or: young, inhibited,
Did you retard your pace
Short of the candour of an actual face?

THE MILKMAN

Quick apparition on the step,
Your small change clattering in his fist,
He hugged effulgent in his other grip
A baby that he seemed to think you'd lost.

Proprietorial delight
In parenthood was tempered with
Grief for an unremembered loss. Her throat
Ovalled a word too fragile for the mouth.

GOING TO CHURCH ONE MORNING

Apprehensive of bells—
Like children tumbling to tell;
Clashbags at the gate;
Ringmasters, breezy interlocutors,
Pre-empting rehearsed events—

Securing your smile,
Infallible father support,
Walking backwards to school,
The girl in her new white dress, her face like a flower
Wide-eyed, to a new roll-call;

While, beckoning down,
The saints in their windows trace,
With halo in hand,
Profiles of childhood peeping through masquerade,
Illuminating their vows.

HIGH LOW

When he is being pompous or afraid,
He hides behind his teaching-voice
And keeps his eye on what he's said,
Bidding his words beware. That I've observed.

But when a schoolmate, long since anglicised,
Called to astound him with his speech
And dapper culture subsidised
From rates and taxes, then the unreserved

Vernacular he'd spluttered as a child
Broke from his mouth, and rioted
Like dandelions in a field
Where access was an easement they'd preserved.

BIRTHDAY POEM

At fifty, I suppose, you'll count the change,
Number your debtors and your creditors,
Adjust accounts, write off old loves, and put
The reckoning in your diary. But, or yet,

You'll also scatter starling glances over
A set shrugged shoulder soldiering through time
Back to a time when, with so much unsaid,
Life was a girl always a step ahead.

THE HOLE

We were proud of the newsagent's calling ... Occasionally I was sent down—
great privilege that it was—to collect our copies of the 'Sixth' at the 'Hole' in
the Belfast Telegraph building ... Anyone who has held his own at the 'Hole'
will never be cowed by anything in later life ...
                           —Robert Greacen, *Even Without Irene*

Precociously out of his mind
With politics and sex and poetry,
He was obliged to stand

With hucksters assailing the Hole,
Jostling to catch the bales of trussed-up words,
The early-morning kill.

Young swain of literature,
He postured for his clap of thunder from
The mews's aperture.

If I had my rights, Yeats cried,
I'd be the Duke of Ormonde. Covertly,
Campaigners in *his* head

Hoisted him in above,
A young blade cutting loose among the straw,
Brandishing words like love.

A WORD IN HIS EAR

I gave him my word.
Intimations I said,
Releasing it to infiltrate
Beyond his public attitudes
Into a personal sanctum where—instead
Of late conferments: gown, certificate,
The pensioner's clock, municipal platitudes—
He cries out to an absent editor
For a last proof.

REUNION
i.m. Michael McLaverty

Within a fractured province; less:
Inside a town obscene with barricades
And rifles at the ready, bless,
God or Anon, before the picture fades

A congregation of four friends
Gathered to acclaim in separate ways
A long-loved book's rebirth, old hands
Renewing friendship with a wry surprise.

Before they crumble bread or spill
Wine's secret into glass, let glass reflect
Four faces singly stemmed, until
They share the wine's slow statement, and extract

From dregs and crumbs a sacrament
For two believing, two agnostic minds,
Each singular ingredient
Familial under the author's hosting hands:

As, after thirty years, the voice
Of that small masterpiece binds them together,
A four-leafed clover, to rejoice
That common ground survives disastrous weather.

THE TRAVELLER

Coming at evening—
Midsummer, with the mowers murmuring,
Handclap of shears;
Autumn's curtailment, when the gas
Mantles hirstle and cry at the shortening days;
And Christmas-time—:

After the blandishments,
The ritual exchanges, he remains,
A surrogate
Postman important with the news,
To nibble gossip like wine-biscuits, sip
At peccancies.

Socks uniformly rolled
Like gallant puttees round abandoned shins,
His bicycle
At ease against a window-sill,
He licks his pencil while you distantly
Call from the shelves.

Gleaming with medal-brass,
Its fetlocks feathered, the huge blinkered horse
Next midday heaves
The hooded cart from door to door.
Oats, dribbled from the feedbag, countrify
The dayligone.

THE ASTORIA

Outlandish frontager,
Confronting thoroughfare
With unabashed bucolic innocence,
Its old glass signalling
Back to the sparking trams;
Decades of privet, cemetery paths,
A tepid greenhouse, couped red wheelbarrows:

Shorn from the hinterland,
It mimed suburban ways;
Rubbed shoulders with the shops and houses, paid

Its taxes, and observed
The early-closing day;
But stoically, if absent-mindedly,
It kept its *thereness* like a stranded tree.

Abruptly it was gone.
You noticed first the lack
Of glass, then took in all the emptiness
Where bushes along the paths
Had made a natural maze.
Laid out along the slope the apple-trees
Were statues in a morgue, dead, falsified.

Hoarding and scaffolding
Thwarted a sneak preview.
But nobody was moved to entertain
A plea for pleasance when
That local Eden changed
Into a hothouse for exotic love,
Lettuce supplanted by a let's-pretend.

Sixpenny patrons, we
Embraced in the back-stalls
Sophistication and unnatural warmth;
Inhaled America
And Ealing's England, but
Translated them to Ballyhackamore,
Ecumenists of the vernacular.

Now *it's* succinctly gone,
The skyline engineered
For some anonymous shell; and, in your mind,
Circle and stalls line up
To join old greenery
Vegetating in the hinterland,
Where yesterday perhaps is still today.

NOTES FOR THE HINTERLAND
(1983)

BALLYSHANNON

Dear Mr. Allingham:
When you hear girls singing your songs,
Harping late at their spinning-wheels
These summer evenings,
Do you slacken your pace as you pass
The glancing doorways before,
Officiously,
Dusk shutters the town?

Pray Mr. Allingham:
Do you turn at the head of the town,
Stick elegant in salute,
An airy autograph,
And touch the brim of your hat;
Or do you elect to be,
Anonymously,
The singing, the song?

POST-WAR

Cold and clear are the words
That belong to bright March days,
If you think of mornings
When sky is gunmetal blue
And a terse breeze flexes its strength in the raw trees.

The hard years after the war
When life, in a word, was spare,
Were like March mornings
Cold-shouldered or cut by spring,
Yet with promise, in spite of the promises, sharpening the air.

Remembered merchandise—
Shelved childhood's packets and tins—
Trailed back from limbo,
Nostalgically labelled, and we
Reflected on pots and pans, matched saucers and spoons.

Under the cenotaphs
The poppies foundered on stone;
And over the bomb-holes

Pert window-boxes presumed.
They restored the excursion train and the ice-cream cone.

Then we dallied with summer again,
Making light of the rusting guns,
The snarled wire's venom,
The abandoned towers on the dunes;
And salvaged stray bullets for girls to give to their sons.

THE GRAND CENTRAL HOTEL

I

In June, examiners
Seconded from
The London Guildhall School
Of Music (Speech and Drama) commandeered
    The Londonderry Room,
And summoned elocution-anglicised
Provincials to pout London vowel-sounds;
    Posed as it were
    For kiss or medicine:

Where, testily carpeted,
    They diffidently
Surrendered up their lines,
Still fighting shy of their stepmother tongue;
    While, down-to-earth, below,
Incorrigibly aboriginal,
The pageboy squired his privileged reserve,
    Between the lift
    And the revolving door.

II

When officers and their whores,
Hotfoot for the hotel,
Forced you back to the gutter's lip,
You reckoned them as war's
Recruitment of the rubbish-tip,
And counted your contempt contemptible;

When, out of character,
You threw off diffidence,

And remonstrated in the street
Against the abattoir,
The flatulent bellow and the bleat
Of butcher's meat dressed up as citizens;

Reluctant activist:
What forced you to declare
Your single-mindedness before
A crowd you still mistrust?
It wasn't love. No; rather more
Distaste, and loyalty, and being there.

III

Those were the palmy days when affluence,
    With cash in hand,
Benevolently knocked at doors,
    A Fyffe-banana man,
Paid to give money to the provident.

Swanning in taxis past the river's sleep,
    Or rakishly
Riding the Jaguar, we lived
    It up, you should observe,
In gracious living as distinct from Life.

Upholstered corners intimate with drink's
    Complicity,
A world in a glimmering glass, to be sipped
    In purchased elegance,
A world away from the world and the shout in the street:

Where dainty legs and unembarrassed eyes,
    The delicate tilt
Of cigarette red from the lips,
    Concealed in masquerade
The idiomatic hatred of their streets.

IV

This is hostile territory now.
In Royal Avenue
Planners and bombers have united to
Wreck or eliminate

Taken-for-granted, only-to-be-missed
Familiar presences.
You miss the water when the well runs dry.

Here, where a millionaire
Hoovered the street at midnight, choked with sin,
God's drunken seneschal,
You ranged the library, stalked titles down
At Greer's in Gresham Street,
And through the lanes past where the stony head
Hangs, lidless, lintel-high.

Those boarded windows displayed waxwork boys
In blazer, cap and tie,
Models of uniform propriety,
Observed on Saturdays
When you descended on the bandying town
With florin or half-crown
Warm as a girl's hand urgent on the thigh.

And later, in the war,
When poets patronised the lavatory
Inside the grand hotel,
Disdaining public inconveniences,
We gravely buttonholed
With foyer-chat persons of consequence,
As if habitués there.

This hostile territory's symbolised
By the bricked-up hotel
Inside a cage to keep the bombers out,
Where soldiers document
The dirty tricks of violence, and you
From time to time attend
For leave to motor through Victoria Square.

CONVEYANCER

   I remember your saying
   That among our acquaintances
   There was scarcely a reader who
Was not ambitiously, however covertly,
   A writer also; who
Read just for love without a vested interest too.

I omitted to mention
The withdrawn conveyancer
Who, throughout my apprentice years,
Taciturn in his tent of blue tobacco smoke,
    Probed at ancient roots
Of title in shrinking lease and wizened fee farm grant.

Compulsively weeding
Through recitals and covenants,
He examined the drift of a field
Towards a ramification of streets and sites with red boundaries,
    Down to the last demise,
Where a brisker narration begins new chapters of lives and deaths.

You could say it was factual,
A sort of biography
Of properties shaping a town;
And their people coming and going, appurtenant, in a word,
    Till they claimed the ultimate word,
Unanswerable at the end, in the form of the probated will.

Or again, alternatively,
That his reading was really romance;
For the parchment pages proclaim
A myth of ownership for ever-and-a-day,
    Whose hereditaments
Depend upon yellowing skin mortgaged to truculent time.

MORTGAGE REDEMPTIONS

Reserving judgment, let us say
The middle years
Like Common Law enhanced by precedent,
Preserve the freehold of forgotten fields,
Riparian memories of the culverted stream,
A perpetuity
Of springtime that outlasts each transient spring.

The parchment leases you prepared
At twenty-two,
Now, with the loans repaid, the sub-demise
Redeemed, revert to your remembering hands,
Your naive signature
A wide-eyed witness to the act and deed.

Lessees return, and look at you
Inquiringly,
Their families reared, sophisticated to
New styles and appetites and ennuis:
Compare their wounds, or credit-worthiness,
With yours; and smile
Acknowledgement that you have made it too.

They talk of semi-villas, rates,
Adopted roads,
Techniques of gardening and the pampered car;
Insurances, and then, perhaps, a will:
And sometimes, moved to impropriety,
Cough, and recall
Summers before the builder slew the trees.

SANCTO'S DOG

I

Come to the door,
Miss Anderson, with the lapdog slavering
Concern against your pinafore.
Listen for archers' bows in Stringer's Field.

Wait.

Call home your dog,
Sancto, the black Alsatian, silently
Skirting the children's frozen games,
The yellow eyes reserved for harder things.

Wait.

Joan Hamilton,
Run in your party frock with flying tails,
Hide in the entry from the kiss;
Fondle your hair back to its Sunday slide.

Wait.

Miss Pinkerton,
Mouth tight with pins, a needle on your breast,

Your pince-nez screwing towards the light,
Wear out your heart upon another's sleeve.

Wait.

You, redhaired maid
In the house in the culdesac, eavesdropping on dreams,
Coax him to talk in his sleep of girls
High-heeled in the evenings, dangerous in silk.

Wait.

II

Still in the family way,
The houses suffer life.
But alien tenants glance from windows, or
Usurp the trimmed prim privet's privacy.
The streets, the same,
Are taken over by exorbitant cars.
Just coteries
Of grown-up trees, prehensile, recollect,
Indeed encapsulate,
The cornered field before
They folded it and carried it away,
With all the picnic things
Of childhood, adolescence; yesterday.

Wait.

III

Startled, you say hallo
To Mrs. Robinson
Contending with the grass,
Say *All this time*,
And cautiously unflap the past,
Potentially a letter-bomb
Whose sealed constituents on release
Unite to maim.

And then, uneasily,
You falter and suspect,
And then become aware,

That she is not
The mother but the daughter, who's
Mistaken you (so like him) for
Your father; and you say your name,
With mild regret.

Wait.

IV

You, redhaired maid,
A fact of life still unmythologised,
Another listener minds the dreams
You flirted with beside the moonlit bed:
Calls Sancto's dog
To pad the pavements to the light's arcade,
Where, silhouetted, he informs
The absences of their identical lives.

Wait.

V

It must have been
Before the hedge was grown, because,
Small as you were
And cautioned to stay put,
Nothing obscured your anguish from the street.

Wait.

Hand on the door
Of the anonymous car, its strange
Driver alert,
She called anxiety
And reassurance, but still made to go.

Wait.

O where was *Vote?*
You were too small to follow. She
Would disappear
Round nameless corners, and
You'd stand for ever, holding a laurel's hand.

TIME'S PRESENT

I promised you I'd buy
A silk dress and a box
Of King George chocolates
Embossed with his golden head.
My father told me how,
At the tobacconist's,
Rutherford Mayne threw down
His first week's sovereign
And named the dearer blend.
But I'd no chance to pay
Out of my bright new pounds
My grown-up compliment;
My father bought the flowers
We laid upon your grave.
Time past's time's present now.
The sleek dress and the box
Of gorgeous chocolates,
Shelved in the gloryhole
Of broken promises,
Acquire, interpolate,
Though self-bespoken now,
New, mythic presences.

HELSTON
i.m. James Thompson McFadden

Some wait. Some travel distances.
But *it* is never late; it is you
Who one day will be late of where you are.

Imagine next year's Floral Dance
With only the ashes of his company,
The burnt-out hospitality of his hearth.

But now, with a seemly stateliness,
His body lies on a shrouded bed,
Intent upon itself, careless of life:

And yet, with a curious courtesy,
Tolerant of their plans, resigned
To wait for the conclusions of their love.

AFTER THE BROADCAST

Uncertain of your timing, you
Kick at the final paragraph,
   The margins streaming
Like lane-tapes signalling,
The clock adjudicating on the wall.

Then, ventriloquial, overhead,
Official voices tidy up
   The wavelength for
Big Ben's sonority;
Father of millions, bursting with the news.

The man behind the window thumbs
Approval, or at least reprieve;
   And, tension broken,
The studio unwinds,
Unflapping pockets, cigarettes and words.

The lifeless microphone's ignored
By voices it materialised;
   No longer focus
For speech and acting eye,
Invigilator of page-hushing hand.

Outside, bland traffic in the street
Insinuates that no one stayed
   At home to listen.
Your unprojected voice
Sticks in your throat; the number's still engaged.

A DEATH IN MARYVILLE STREET

These little palaces,
Doomed in a street of executioners,
Perpetuate
With yellow facing-brick
Gracing the exits and the entrances,
Remembered terraces
In hinterlands, before the pestilence.

Diverted by patriots' bombs,
The brusque car frets and simmers to a halt;

And you, perforce,
Study and learn by heart
A two-up and two-down, the trite
Delph at the window, while
You pare in your mind indifferent fingernails:

Till, loose in the captive street,
A girl runs like a frightened fugitive,
Not *to* but *from*.
Rejecting a questioning hand,
Cries out abandonedly *She's gone!*
Horror rather than grief
Weals in her wake as she makes for the sealed-off town.

SKETCHES OF BOZ

I

The blacking factory

On his twelfth birthday,
Quick, eager and delicate,
He was sold to a rotting house
At Hungerford Stairs.
In the cellars, garbage rats
Plundered, and spat decay.
This, he had heard them say,
Was to be his station in life.
The birthday boy
Prayed to blow out the present like candlelight.

On later birthdays,
Famous, caressed and proud,
After the greetings and gifts,
The kisses and smiles,
Gargantuan dinners with friends,
Fierce walks through the bootblack streets,
He would sit in his room alone
And, pale in the candlelight,
Listen again
To the dungeon under the boards of his carpeted mind.

II

The appraisal

His father swore,
Addicted to debt like drink,
That all his goods, wherever situate,
Of what
Ever nature or kind,
Did not,
Vested or in contingency,
Exceed in their totality ten pounds.

The Appraiser viewed
A youngster, steadying fear
With dignity, exhibit stoically,
Perforce,
Meagre habiliments:
Wrote off
Their shrunken value, and ignored
The ancient watch precociously chained to his heart.

III

Ellis & Blackmore

Small for fifteen,
He wore his soldier-cap askew,
Assertively, and
Was eager for words, a scavenger
Among the alleyways
Of badinage and repartee,
A connoisseur of unbelievable names.

Up at his desk,
Fingering out like Braille the carved
Initials of boys
Of earlier tenure, scheduling documents
Red-ribboned for the courts,
He'd pilfer an expensive phrase
From pompous parchments and sententious wills.

Identified—
The boy from Ellis's—he had,

Professionally,
Access to famous names, a right
Of way to privacies
Behind the postures and parade.
He infiltrated, scribbling on his palm.

His clients were
Characters with impediments,
Eccentrically
Knotted and private; yet obliged,
Language's litigants,
To remonstrate. He covertly
Ran to the stairhead, dusted the office chair.

IV

Hungerford Market

Dandified gallery-man,
He straddled and upstaged
Hungerford Market; aired
Success like a new cravat;

While, features varicosed
And ridiculed by sweat,
A toiling journeyman
Shouldered a somnolent child.

Recalled from truancy
By the backward-looking boy's
Somnambulistic stare,
Young Boz bought cherries; and,

Ambition's appetite
Nailed back to the bare board,
Extravagantly fed
The unrelenting mouth:

While the father, bent with his load,
Eyes lashed to the dragging street,
Tholed grit assaulting his throat
And the cobbles shipwrecking his feet.

V

Mary Hogarth

Perhaps, noting her bosom's hint
Of womanhood, the tilt-of-her-head's implied
Assertion of self, he feared
The morning when she'd come down
And fail to recognise him; pass
The paper and the time of day
With language alien to their intimacy.

Affronted by her naive death,
The bluff perhaps of his equivocal
Ménage à trois, in a phrase,
Abruptly called, he put on
Her ring proprietorially.
Young, beautiful, and good, he said:
At seventeen, immaculately dead.

Her ring, *his* now, the symbol of
An otherworldly bigamy that made
The best of both worlds, grew
Endearing on his hand;
And he could openly refer
To his undying love, acclaim
His angel, without compromising fame.

VI

48 Doughty Street

      Surprisingly,
The first-to-be-told, the famous Gad's Hill desk
      Is just a chattel, stained
And grained with blots of discarded, overspilled words:

      While, curiously,
The public reading-desk, his one-night stand,
      Though cornered, winded and worn,
Has him up reading fiercely through the halls.

Young, confident and flash in Doughty Street—
      Doughty indeed—

Signing the lease, he hungered for
The freehold to redeem the Marshalsea.

Not yet a mortgagor to affluence,
    He boyishly
Breezed through these rooms, impatiently
Drawing the curtains, stirring up the fire.

    Then, hastily,
He made his move before the lease ran out,
    Success, security,
Pursued by the Appraiser at the door.

VII

Maria Beadnell

She brought it on herself
Writing out of the blue,
Chancing her arm; and he,
Enraptured, no less culpable,
Was not slow to embrace
The chance to make the fiction actual.

He had transmogrified
His love and her disdain
Into a masterpiece;
Had locked her fast in literature.
Then, not unnaturally,
He fell in love with what he'd made of her.

But when she took his hand,
Silly in middle-age,
He fumbled for his pen,
The acid for the caricature;
And, passion petrified,
Ushered her back again to literature.

VIII

Miss Ellen

Miscellanies
Of True Romances tell how Older Men,
Bored by their wives, pursue

Trite slips of girls. There's no
Fool like an old fool; mutton feigning lamb.

Nevertheless,
They're not just armchair lovers, for if they
Abandon dignity,
They quicken step and glance,
Brush up their smiles and titivate their dress.

Inimitable?
His story was the same, and not his best.
Like them, he falsified
The books of middle-age;
Cooked-up a lyric from the turgid prose.

They say that she
Dissembled at first; but who can counsel how
A small-part player should
Perform when beckoned out
To play the lead in some Great Man's Amour?

If she had said:
What do you want; what can I add to your
Understanding of life?
He might have said: *Yourself.*
More poignantly, perhaps: *Your ignorance.*

IX

The public readings

You will remember how he made a fire
Of all the correspondence of the past;
And how, irreverently,
The children roasted onions in the ash.
The wife by then
Had been discarded. Soon the boys would go.
Only the dear girls stayed, like furniture.

And how he worked to prise the characters
Free from the burden of the narrative;
And then promoted them
Into a one-man travelling puppet-show,
With all the strings

Tied to *his* fingers, or like a lassoo
To rope in and corral the wild applause.

And how, actor manqué, he played the parts—
Exclusively, since *he'd* created them—
Of wry and passionate souls
Swarming and squandering in his halflit streets
And tenements;
And how, as author, he took curtain-calls,
And, solo, finger-blew the actor's kiss:

And, reckless of advice, plunged deeper in
The fog that made illusion credible;
Until, with *Oliver*,
He acted murder as reality.
The doctors marked
The rising tide of his abandonment
Menacing moorings and decaying wharves.

Infatuated with an audience
He'd made from lust for love: seduced, he craved
Uncritical love for him
Rather than for the semblances of art;
Distracted from
The solitary confinement in his heart
Of the abandoned, unforgiving boy.

A WATCHING BRIEF
(1979)

OUT IN THE COUNTRY

Out in the country
Was beyond the seventh green,
Where the villas,
Trailing behind, let fields
Run on to ruminate
Across the promising fairways.

Surprising mornings—
When, wakened by banding birds,
Terse, xylophonic;
School shelved with the bawdied books;
You railed the curtain back
To a new beginning—

Beckoned and chivvied
Over the new-pin grass,
Beyond a scotched mist
Soberly edging
Into a reticent haze,
Day's acquiescence:

Till, on the seventh
Dew-coruscating green,
Without forewarning,
The sun appeared pin-high
From over the stymie trees,
On the top of the morning.

It didn't matter
That no dog-walker saw
Mashie and putter
Iron out the bunkered fault;
Your unscored birdies might
As well be eagles:

For you played solo;
Partnered only by
A caddying silence
Attending on your game,
And following a style
That took your meaning.

REPRIEVE

Pharmaceutical antiquity,
Fumed oak and bevelled glass;
Brass plates with Latin sobriquets,
Framed letters on display;
A sallow sink in the dispensary:

And out in the disintegrating yard,
Behind abandoned plants,
Milk-bottles' collarettes of curd,
The roof-drip's rusty beard,
An outhouse with an eyepatch window board.

Over the years, he reckoned, he'd put down
A hundred, give or take;
And shrugged off any sense of sin
Merely for having been
A cat's-paw for some long-armed citizen.

But when the old tom broke the system, and,
Catapulting free,
Hissed acid from the bottle-stand,
Then his reneging hand
Opened the door to life as to a friend.

POSTSCRIPT TO ULSTER REGIONALISM

In Eighteen hundred and twenty-three
At Aughnacloy in the afternoon,
Samuel James Megarrity,
Unexciting like a prune,
Announced with unassuming cries
A son for the Megarrities.

In Eighteen hundred and twenty-eight
He learnt to lace his boots for school.
Sometimes early, seldom late,
Never brilliant but no fool,
He graduated to the rank
Of ledger-clerk at the local bank.

And there he stayed until he died,
Trustworthy, unremarkable;
Unpromoted, satisfied
To stroke each tidy numeral.
They said his funeral was as nice
As that of Mr. Alderdice.

But later audits brought to light
A guilty ledger from its hole,
Containing in neat copperplate
Abandoned verses resonant still
With fierce erotic fantasy:
By Samuel James Megarrity.

And now a man I know has won
A university degree
For his deliberations on
The Meaning of Megarrity.
Whatever Samuel meant, be sure
It wasn't Ulster Literature.

LATECOMER

Correct in the family pew,
He waited her arrival.
The genteel organ played
In soft anticipation,
Its echoes descanting
To thoughts of girly days
Faceted like the vase
Under the altar-window.

Advancing from the door
A slow colloguing stir
Announced her; and the man,
Alerted in the pew,
Stood for her coming. But
Slowly she passed him by,
Absolved from her young vows,
Heavy-lidded now.

SELF-GENERATION

But none of them can sing, McKelvey said;
And revelation's not
A pedantry of detail, but
A quasi-resurrection of the dead,
An orphic note.

The things I dig, he said fastidiously,
Are seldom if at all
Agri- or horti- cultural;
Raked midden heaps of corned mythology,
Or cloacal.

Their singular self-display, he said, aggrieved,
Owes less to poetry
Than personal psychology,
A nipple-greed to be the best beloved,
Indulgently.

Observe the banjos tighten, he enjoined,
In preparation for
The next award or sinecure.
Sold out at festival and one-night stand,
The self's a whore.

THE ISLAND

Brown as the sand they shaped
Into castle or fort,
Running with captured sea
To vanishing river and moat,
Children would pause, as if called,
And widely contemplate
The wishbone island, agog
With pirates, or hazy with sheep.

But I've been there. No masked
Sheep or pirates stare
From stones; but, underfoot,
Small brittle bones explode:
And, turned around, the town's
Imagined presences
Hide behind sheepish masks
The skull's piratical grin.

MANAGING CLERK

Custodian of procedural lore,
Queen's Bench and Chancery,
He was the system's go-between,
Its diligent messenger,
His daily round the Law's periphery.

His gossip was professional
And always pertinent,
Painstaking and particular,
Like pleadings, or a well-
Drawn affidavit grinding to a point.

But never, vexed or candid, did
He cross-question the Law,
Or scrape authority's veneer
To see what stuff it hid;
Or interpose a why before the how:

Adduce in Registry of Deeds
Candle's epiphany;
Or, in the Probate Registry,
A caveat that bids
The will beware of seeming to be free.

NURSERY LAND

Nurseries,
With inbred essences
Potent like the stifled spring
In a scent bottle in my mother's room,
Which, at a twist, rushed to reprieve
From dark desuetude
Wild violets;

Old pastures, where,
Redolent at doors
Of greenhouses with yellowed glass,
Amber tomatoes, brittle lettuces,
Sandwiched undertone of cucumber,
Hint of geraniums,
Those salad days:

Spelt for a child
The nostrils' alphabet;
Love-letters for the middle years,
When genii of perfume bottles, faint
Outcasts of summer palaces,
Long dispossessed, drift back
To our domain.

CHRISTMAS EVE

Apprehension of night
Shouldered them like a coat
In the pub's bleary light,
The drink's seductive heat
Lullabying their eyes;
A Salvation Army band
Trite and sublime
Heralding Christmas beyond.

Throughout, he saw
The interior scene from the fringe
Of his own hinterland,
Though party to the ring
Of the caped table; just as their talk,
Close and elliptical,
Would recur in retrospect
Public like opening doors'
Street-lash on intimacy,
Alarming the mind's small hours.

THEATRE: LUNCHTIME
for Joseph Tomelty

Sit down; I won't be long, in quick aside
He mouths over a hand
Gagging the jealous telephone.
Yes; two up front. Collect
The tickets by half-seven or before.

You join him in the office; box indeed:
And glance at photographs
Of showy profiles on the walls,

Blown-up, like self-esteem;
A writer's playthings, creatures of his words.

Yes, yes, be early; every house is full.
Goddammit, he declares
Across his hand, a gramophone
Would be more like it. Yes—
Back to the palmed-off phone—half-seven sharp.

Well now, he says, yourself; and, sighing, leaves
The sweat-bright telephone
Off-hook with programmes on a chair,
Until the undeceived
And knowing operator rasps at him.

EURYDICE

What did she, retreating, lapsing back
Into the shadows, feel, beyond the grip
And grasp of him, who opened all her doors,
For whom her windows watched, when he let slip
Into the shadows her known shape and sound
That warmed his wintry self, disarmed his voice?

Did she, thinning to darkness, sadly throw
Thought like an anchor back to life when choice
It seemed clustered like apples and her marvellous days
(All albumed now with sunshine) ran ahead
Like shouting children, endlessly; when death
Was *it* affecting *them*, and all the dead
Were grouped with hymns and prayers?
                                Did she compare

Her bright and busy days, all meaningful,
All relevant as thread to needle's eye,
With that denying darkness, and from full
Heart and mind cry out that every branch,
Twig, stem and petal, pebble, and all moving
Creatures upon earth, yes, all of life,
In sanctioning, evading or ignoring
Her slashed and smashed-up living, began dying,
Their outlines dimming with each fresh concession
Made to the dark denying underworld
Whose open graves await each retrogression?

And did she, with goodbyes tight in her throat,
Turn again to him in daylight dying
Away from her, and finally demand
That he break into godhead by replying
With equal vehemence to her entreaties
And blow out darkness like a candle's flame?

And finally, did she, her daylight hero
Gone, bereft, alone, cry out her name
Sharply and clearly, once, at once defying
The speechless dead and rallying the dying?

I SPY

My English cousin was exceptional
First, in that he discoursed so differently
From the broad locution of my friends;
And secondly, and more remarkably,
Because he had an artificial eye.

Each night at bedtime, unaffectedly,
A fact of life like taking medicine,
It was removed and folded in the dark
Security of a silk handkerchief.

I never liked to pry; but fancied it
Was like a small glass marble you could minch
With much more cunningly than earthenware,
With twisted stripes and whorls like marmalade.

IMMIGRANTS

I

White Stockings

In other families,
Grandmothers were observed ·
Calling with baskets; or,
Distantly dominant,
They interrupted play
To hold imperious court
At Sydenham or Knock:

Intimate, or endured;
Inexorably involved.

But my own singular
Grandmother remained
Becalmed in bed; for whom
All time was bedtime, life
An interrupted dream;
While wicker baskets whinged
In bitter daughter's hands,
And up in the attic room
Grandfather canvassed clouds.

So when you told me how
She had been known as the girl
With the white stockings, when
She flashed skirts past the gate
After a startled tryst,
Not only was she blithe
And fleet of foot at last,
In recollection, but
Her lyric sang like a shell.

II

Homework

Mahogany fingers played
Out figures from the clay,
His concentrated cough
Clotting the intimate air,
Wrists agile and alert
For sudden semblances;
While, chin on table, I
Moulded up in my mind
This moment of recall.

Hands in skint pockets, he came
In from the down-and-out town,
Set cap and fag aside,
And counterfeited from
Our common idleness
A sort of holiday:
Until, for an afternoon,
Rejected skill took hold
Of renewed, importunate hands.

III

Luna

Voyeur; monocular
Scanner of continents;
Jarvey of tides, renowned
Promoter of stratagems:
Indifferent godparent.

The first of them Belfast-born,
Pretty and hard and frail,
She had little time for the quaint
Coon-song of memories,
For programmes and photographs,
Rumours of uncles and aunts
With small crescendos of speech,
Far off in the English North.

Fast, she danced against time
To wireless and gramophone;
At the Plaza thrilled to the drum
And throbbed with the saxophone.
Family and neighbours said
That one would dance on a pin;
But sure you're a long time dead
She'd say with a downward grin.

Kiss cousin's more than aunt's,
She could collude with a child
In cute complicity;
But also squandered like smiles
A spontaneity
Of generosities; spun
Transient love affairs
With a child's covert concern
And tiptoe confidence.
With each return she filled
Doors with glad entrances,
And left appended to rooms
Her scented signature
Long after her heels had tapped
Insouciant goodbyes.

Negligent elegance
Lounged in her honeymoon home,
Novel and modish, where
Furniture mannequinned
And posed on rug-pert floors,
A stylish dishabille;
And, the size of a handkerchief,
The cossetted garden bloomed
Busy with colours like
Her screen's embroidery.

Perhaps the day of the peke
And poodle had still to come.
She charmed and muzzled a wolf
(Terror of girls knock-kneed
On roller-skates, and boys
Discreet on bicycles)
Whose leashed gale swept her on
Scooped like a winded leaf,
Avid for chaos on
The innocent Belmont Road.

Did she give you a drink of milk?
My mother asked; and guilt
Suffused me like the cough
Staunched by her handkerchief.
The piano lid was shut,
And the flowers died in their vase.

She waned in the sun; and hard
Bone-lines darkened her skin
Like the ribs in her parasol.
She died in a stertorous room,
Lamented by gramophones,
The tap and swirl of her blood
Spinning off from the dance
To a final stillness of wax:
Her brave beginning's end
My grave new underworld.

IV

Lizzie

She was the plain one by the time
    I'd mind enough to judge.
But, crowded in a photograph
Of smocked schoolchildren, she's perplexed
    By beauty like a blush.

Uncle, toy-soldier Churchill wrecked,
    Uncles who went to sea;
Americans who didn't write,
The pretty aunt, the bitter one:
    She was poor Lizzie.

Married to a widower,
    She skivvied for his brood
Glued to her heels like tinkers' gets,
Substitute family, secondhand;
    Late honey for stale bread.

There was a scene at our hall door,
    And Betty Haddow hissed,
'Look at the beggars from Strandtown';
And, afterwards, my brother said
    I should have acquiesced.

We make impostors of our lives
    With each colluding breath.
I too put out of countenance,
Restore her faded photograph
    To young Elizabeth.

V

Lefty

He curbed the geordie whinny, and
Punctured his speech to simulate
Safety-pin mouths, and laboured at
Clichés like passwords to secure
An audience in pubs and halls,
Where talk of change was something more
Than a clutch of pennies after the round.

He preached, pitched against Sunday bells,
Deliverance at the Custom House
For cap and muffler, busked the bread-
Lines of loafing desuetude,
Fished their sour canals, and charged
Their dormant depths. O brave new world,
Theirs for the asking when they got
The questions and the answers right.

Marriage and children. But beyond
End-terrace and the job, pub-talk
Consumed his evenings, and ideas
Became quick chasers after stout,
The hard truths half-ones in the hand;
And counter-revolution shelved
The showdown for another dawn.

The gospel palled and petered out.
The revolution was referred
Back to the drawer. Dawn crept back
Into the dark, where challenges
Are introverted against light.
He tossed his cap over the bridge,
Acquired a suitcase and a hat,
And sailed away to affluence.

VI

Geordie

Before his accent cooled
And adopting pavements prompted his feet,
He packed his skill and sailed
Away from myth and counterfeit,
Marred matrix and cracked mould.

He watched the suburbs drown
In the steamer's unlamenting wake,
While marauding mist in the town
Defaced the consort's watchful clock,
And mauled his marble queen.

He married prudently;
Worked diligently at drawing-board

With blue-prints for the sea;
And scorned to slacken the taut word
To tact's tautology.

But when his son was born,
He bade the gantries burst in sail,
And slipways slickly turn
Their young ships back to Hartlepool,
With bunting for his bairn.

Old-fashioned for his years,
My cousin would interrogate
The nearest thing with ears;
And sometimes would invigilate
The conduct of the stars.

So when that letter with
Black edges signifying grief
Unfolded his young death,
The garden laurels caught my sleeve,
Importunate like a wreath.

I thought, uncomforted,
That now, perhaps forever, my
Uncle would turn his head
From the dead son he glimpsed in me;
Resentful, and betrayed.

A decadent decade
Slipped self-willed towards the holocaust;
And hunger on parade,
The peace pledge and the clenched protest,
Were merely an aside.

He watched his promised land
Rusting beside an idle sea;
Till, mobilised, he planned
Ships for a famous victory
His dead son might have manned.

VII

Florrie

Her windows snaps of others' lives,
    Doors tradesmen's entrances,
She was her mother's nurse, nursemaid
And midden for paternal needs,
    Moods, and indifferences.

Belfast flatness caught and sheathed
    The geordie kiting lilt;
But she preserved a haughty hint
Of dangerous steel that could engage
    The dagger to the hilt.

Her anger was a brush that stoked
    The shovel of her scorn,
And transgressors like calling-cards
Arrested in the vestibule,
    Dropped pleasantries stillborn.

On visits with my mother to
    Grandmother propped in bed,
Grandfather beckoned me to brave
The flight up to the attic room,
    And plot stars overhead:

Or, circling round sororicide,
    Steered deftly to the yard;
Showed where he saucered moonish milk
For fly-by-night anonymous cats
    That sprang to sip unheard.

Pencils, paper, rubbers, paint,
    Up in the house's head;
And, down-to-earth, below, my aunt
Recriminating; and, between,
    The pale forgiving bed.

And yet, the urgent words that came
    Out of the medium's mouth
Were not from homesick parents, but
'Flora MacDonald of the Clans',
    Her petname in her youth.

VIII

Prodigal

Hesitant in the hall,
He measured glances covertly
With his withdrawing self
Glassed in the mirror; left his key
With personal imprint on the shelf,
And hung up his identity
Now old hat on the wall.

American promises—
Amputations at the wrist,
And compromising tongues
Assuming accent like a boast—
Blurred in sentimental songs
Genesis like a palimpsest
And lives beyond redress.

He served the promises.
Would send for wife and son he said
When times got easier
Or he got harder still instead.
But promises were lazier;
And suddenly his wife was dead,
Without a new address.

The promises came good.
He married Annabella Lou,
And reared a family
Indigenous to spit and chew;
While back home, transatlantically,
The first-born never quite outgrew
His jettisoned childhood.

Out from the album he
Walked in unannounced, and called
Me by my father's name;
Stayed awkwardly for tea, and told
Little of himself at home;
Confused, refusing to be fooled
By changed topography.

I thought of pubs down town,
A close comparison of notes,
Sad hearse succeeding hearse,
Of three decades of broken dates;
But he was knowing and averse:
Before he went back to the States
He said he'd find his son.

IX

The Raloo Sermon

I have a pen-and-crayon drawing done
In Newtownards Union by my grandfather
Of an elderly eccentric man
Uncomfortably upright on a chair,
Hand concealing face as if to pin
And keep his thoughts intact, particular:

And on the back, in his neat draughtsman's hand,
Notes for a bitter sermon on being old.
I asked for bread the text accuses; and,
Resisting speculation, I've recalled
Only the scraps of table-talk that found
Their way down to the toy world of a child.

Clever, but: said Mr. Dickinson;
Frustrated artist, one or two would try.
But I watched for a small vivacious man,
Dapper and wise, blue eyes, moustache, bow tie,
Who lauded my precocious efforts to
Create a system; nurtured reverence for
Life beyond living; who, concerned, could go
From church to synagogue; adventurer.

The jigsaw pieces, hearsay evidence,
Unpatterned crazy-paving in my mind,
Are stepping-stones demanding diffidence.
But intuition, white stick of the blind,
Is a divining rod that taps out life.
Was there a cottage beyond mouldering gates,
A sad green fire of twigs, the final leaf
Torn from the sketchbook for the sermon's notes?

Squiring a cousin to Dunmurry manse
With gifts and greetings from America—
Uncharitably glad to have the chance
To flaunt his missing eighteenth century—
I made acquaintance with the minister;
And then, since he had known my mother's side,
Mentioned the bleak notes of my grandfather.
I heard that sermon at Raloo, he said.

COFFEE AT CRUMBLE'S

That blindside table by the wall,
Uncompromised by pledging eyes
Or speculating stare. Require
Coffee for one; no sugar say.
Two red-lipped concertinaed butts
Dunged in their ash; one broken match:
What elegant legs shone here before?

The room resolves for your review.
Lady shoppers pecking cups
In petulant truancy from stress;
Students encamped behind their beards;
Anonymous *habitués*,
Young Ulster Club, or YHA?
Do not connect with roving eyes
Of slippy-tit beside the Gents;
His covert glances violate.

Attend. Observe triumvirate
Of coffee-culture, biscuit-chat,
Hogging the corner-window. Yes;
Coffee here, no sugar. Stir,
And, unobserved, assimilate.
Better equipped, you may project,
O years ahead, an incident
Hoarded absent-mindedly,
Preserved against its transience.
Where's that bugger off to now?:
Buck Gogarty, when jackdaw Joyce
Stole off with an epiphany.
Astir, unsugared, contemplate
Those moving lips you cannot read.

Derry's walls; *tut* Derek Walsh,
Presiding, sipping briar stem;
Dan Armour, forward, hands alert,
Anxious with an anecdote;
And Maynard Chatterton, at ease
In soft and settled self-esteem.

Doyen columnist, he stands;
Uncrumples; settles waistcoat; peeks
Through window past the City Hall,
Scanning the small print of the street:
Leans back, exclaiming. Derek Walsh,
Accelerating sip to sup,
Extracts and brandishes his briar;
And Maynard Chatterton inclines
An eyebrow to denote concern.
O rush of lips you cannot read.

> *Exude habitual*
> *Contempt for City Hall,*
> *Uncouth municipal soul*
> *Made architectural.*
> *O elegant widow of*
> *35 or so,*
> *Endow me with your love,*
> *And your investments too:*

The poet, passing Crumble's, said
To fame and fortune in his head.

—Poetry in our midst, Dan Armour cries.

—What poetry? says Maynard Chatterton,
Grey bristling bard in their immediate midst.

> *Who scuttle between trams,*
> *Winged exile bound to earth;*
> *Condemned pedestrian*
> *By accident of birth:*

He struck an attitude between
Dan Armour and the marble queen.

—You mean? calls Derry Walsh, wet pipe at ear.

—Be patient, boys; he's just gone into Moore's.

—O yes, I'm with you now, says Derek Walsh:
The Swan of Lagan. Cygnet, I suppose.
He has a pregnant look, Armour avers.
A literary rebirth is at hand.

—Another one? shrugs Maynard Chatterton.

—Who's got the frankincense? crows Derek Walsh.

—What's wrong with commonsense, chides Chatterton.

'Now Mr.—o yes—the anthology.
We've had it costed. There are two or three
Items we might pursue if you've the time,
Now that we are partners, hah, in rhyme.
Breasts is a word which, in its proper place,
Is inoffensive—well, like *arm*, or *face*—
But *urgent breasts* I judge a trifle strong
For poetry lovers down in Annalong':
Says Mr. Thomas (No-Relation) Moore,
As realistic as he is demure.

Deflated, thwarted, Armour turns
Back to the table; crumples; speaks.
(O pearly speech denied to you.)

'Now *heaving bosom*; if I may presume,
Would not alarm a tactful sitting-room.'

—May I presume to sit beside the ghost
Of William Butler Yeats?

                    —What is it now?
Chatterton injects a jealous note.

(Unprincipled, insinuate
The skivvy's pence beneath the plate.)

—You've heard it then, shines kindling Derry's Walls.

—Enlighten *me*, gloams gloomy Chatterton.

'Or *panting bosom*. No; perhaps that might
Suggest a pent-up sexual appetite.'

Sip, puff, and sip again. —O, a First Night
Down at the Abbey: I was all toffed up;
A complimentary ticket; in the stalls
With the renowned intelligentsia—

—Pat, Tim and Cully; Mick and Joe, says Dan.

(Catlick your coffee-cloying lips.)

—Well, (sip to gurgle) as the lights went down
Some character observed my Yeatsian
Snowy thatch, my brow, my spectacles,
And sent a rumour flying that the old
Man had returned to castigate the play.

'Or simply *bosom*. One word more or less
In *vers libre* (does it?) hardly signifies.'

—A likely story: Maynard Chatterton.

(They lack apocalyptic lips.)

—A bloody hefty ghost, Dan Armour swears.
A resurrection of, what? 16 stone.

(Epiphanies procrastinate.)

—That poet's never coming.

                    Chatterton,
Spoon tapping, clapping coffee-cup, intones:
—The Lagan's mudflats do not favour swans.

(Prepare your exit to the street.)

—Another wild goose then? skirls Derry's Walls.

—Or plain domestic fowl, plumps Chatterton.

(Whose thighs will glimmer from your heat?)

ALLOTMENTS

Between the wars,
At Belmont and beyond,
Ex-servicemen and jobless artisans
Salvaged and tilled,
Stanzaically, inhospitable ground;

Where bicycles,
Heavy as mangles, propped
Against a lean-to, sported lemonade
Bottles, strapped,
Each white or amber with its milk or tea.

On their hillsides,
Wavering in the sun
Of a shimmering afternoon, or clipped alert
In early frost,
Their shadows semaphored back to the town

Whose animal crawl
Advanced into a climb.
But, with the war, the villas stopped; cement
Mixers became
Statuesque, like mines from the Great War.

Then spades became
Weapons for victory;
To dig as patriotic as to kill:
The system claimed
Back as its own the outposts on the hill.

After the war,
The guns and spades were stored
In flag-stained churches, and the mixers churned
Out citizens
With garages, whom no one semaphored.

HEROES

Protected by a proper distance,
    So it seems,
They could entertain
A stature and a style known but impersonal,
Like children's stilted shadows in the sun.

Unruffled at the crease, or snatching
    Lapse at slip,
Cantering into bowl,
Or running, head-in-air, pinpointing the hooked ball,
They were standoffish, like their photographs.

And even at the pits, when racing
    Drivers paused
During practices,
And lifting goggles to rekindle sombre eyes,
Scratched autographs, they were a race apart.

Where you from rainy terraces or
    Promenade,
Watching the fly-half score
Out in the corner, then, all on his own, convert,
Might claim him as the cousin of a friend:

Now all of them are friends; and even
    Marathon
Runners ambulate
Rubbing intimate shoulders through our living rooms;
And we cringe from the footballers' embrace.

PHILANDERER

In middle-age, young girls seduced his mind.
Behind the careful banter lay
The anger of his lust;
His flirting gestures were the ploy
Of a despairing fist:
And he was calculating, being kind.

A married woman took him seriously,
Overt accomplice, who forsook

Her journey for his stroll;
Confused the jacket with the book,
Conspiracy with style;
And, outgrown petting, pledged fidelity.

He ran away, not with her, but from her
Too compromising honesty;
And she, stung to disdain,
Packed off his whispering letters to
An expert to explain
Smooth characters that lacked a signature.

BAPTISM

i.m. John Gibson

So the child in her father's arms was blessed.
But he wept over her, a slight
Bundle of beginning, guessed
At more than known as yet, as light
Opened eyes in the windows. Right
Enough, the sun had joined them as a guest.

Hold that image, you in the stark
Recesses of the formal scene
Upright with sanctioned symbols; mark
The man's pale broken face between
The blessing and the blessed: but lean
Against your isolation in the dark.

Should you turn to an open door,
Your child in your arms, and nominate
A candidate for something more
Than tied responses, then submit
To your being guardian of the gate,
Alone, against the midnight visitor.

SOUND SENSE

Lucas used to gloss his party piece,
MacDiarmid's 'Watergaw',
By stressing how *its chitterin' licht*
Conveyed the stuttering flight
Of water fowl skimming a river's breeze:

Till finally a plastic Scot complained;
Translated *Rainbow*. But
He hardly faltered in defence;
Just veered, and took his stance
On sound suggesting more than language meant.

Sam Bell it was who raised a somnolent head,
Insulted back to life,
Bitter from heavy reading and
The need to comprehend.
Tit, *fart* and *willy* were the words he said.

D-DAY

The family grown, his pension was enough
For careful husbandry.
Waspishly he swept aside
Gnats of accountancy,
Released to write his masterpiece for love.

He groomed his desk, dusted with deference
The touchy typewriter;
Discharged and fuelled fountain pen,
And tapped the paper square:
Adjusted to celestial audience.

But it was not compelling. Undismissed,
The centipedal street
Occluded with occurrences,
While he, irresolute,
Contended with the self's recidivist.

Tweed hat on forehead, written off, he stole
Out to the urgent air;
Reviewed the beans and lettuces,
The slugs' gelatinous spoor;
And combed and petted the ecstatic soil.

RUNAWAY

Alone with the sad dog in the shocked house
(No hope, no point in hoping) with grief's arm
Across his throat, and upstairs madmen loose
And stumbling towards the stairs, he broke and fled,
Dog at his heels, out of his hammering head
Into the clockwork streets, the air still warm
From vanished sunshine, like an empty bed.

Tonight, years after, present absence flings
The street-door open, and against a wall
His shadow's an apostrophe, then swings
Into the darkness of a moon-missed street,
The city coffined by his tapping feet.
What is this echo, ghost of grief, that all
Composed appearances revolt, retreat?

Tell personal grief that life's an accident,
Moored flotsam blown from death's closed continent.

RETRIBUTION

Dabbling for baby crabs
In summer's rock-a-bye pools,
Or stirring languorous weed
In buckets of sluggish sand,
Did we cover or ignore
An upward bubbling eye?

At cricket on the lawn,
Whose laurel boundaries
Were packed with easy fours
Running to centuries,
Did we scamper from the dark
Umpire in the leaves?

Hurrying to the school
To aid bewildered feet
Wend down uproarious stairs,
Back to home's apron strings,
Did my quick concern attract
The bogeyman's revenge?

THE McKELVEY FILE

I

Canary on a Stick

Hunchbacked in the yard,
In curious company,
The Courthouse opposite
Pompous with symbols of
A euphemistic trade,
You huddle with the rest
Adjusting glance and voice;
Till, crookedly observed
Absurd on the empty mast,
An uncommitted gull
Sends memory hurrying back
To an ailing child's distress,
And a yellow bird that sang
Whirling on a stick,
Your mother brought you when
You too chafed at the light,
Dismayed by incredible doors.

II

Wednesdays

The strident bellman cried
Through the streets of the Old Town,
Little girl lost; asleep
In the witch's house with the cat,
Your mother whispered her name.

A warder nominates
Faces with latent names;
Uncalled, anonymous,
Still out-of-place, you blur
Into a commonplace.

Deprivation of *there*:
Under the stairs that night
Tense for the All-Clear;
Departure lounges, ears
Alert for the exit call.

But this time you engage
To be summoned *in* not *out*;
To bring back a good name;
For the crier and his bell
Halt tongue-tied in the street.

III

Wash Day

Official Visitors
Walk glancing past the cells;
And sit for interviews
In bright mahogany rooms
With chairs and windows. Then,
The dinner's better, and
The screws are tolerable.

IV

The Tattooed Lady

Now waiting has become
Another ritual.
After an hour or so
What you'd rehearsed to tell
Crumbles captive to
Interminable walls.

She smuggled things to say
On to her shopping list,
Tea, and table-talk,
Episodes, cereals;
But the woman searcher said
I'll keep your wee list, dear.

Examination-wise,
She used a ball-point pen
To brief her resolute arm
With an agenda for
A family dialogue
That would get past their walls.

V

Gipsy Inside

Like a leashed pup he sprang
In terror from restraint,
Fiercely pulling against
Authority's dead hand;
And, though the sheets were ripped
And knotted by his hands
Into a lethal leash,
The grip was that dead hand's,
As he flung out towards the light.

VI

A Hearty Meal

The murderer's wife was repelled,
Not only by the deed
But by his later calm
Acceptance of the meal.

Does the wife of a hanging-judge
Puke into finger-bowls?

Relieved of courtroom cant,
Punishment's violence;
Retribution stands
Charged in another court.

Their mirror images
Betray accomplices.

VII

Light

Cigarette lighters flash
Answering courtesies,
As waiting's brutalised
Beyond assuaging words.

A few declare themselves
In tribal ornament;

For others, loyalty's
A confrontation of walls.

Locked gates at either end
Discomfit differences;
The lighter's quickening flames
Stroke similar cigarettes.

VIII

A Salutary Sentence

Affectedly, the judge
Tips back the itching wig;
A vulnerable face
Adjusts to enmity;
An officer digests
Conviction with a smile.

The old lags of his words,
Like dog-eared precedents,
Come to heel at a nod
Of the wig, like a skull-cap now:
And sentence is pronounced
With alien vowel sounds.

Night's sport for barracking men,
Fair game now, youth goes down.
The officer clips his smile,
And counsel calculate
Their honoraria:
The judge returns to God.

A tunnel runs like a sewer
Under the road, to the jail.
Accept a watching brief,
And marginally note
A promise to engage
In savage sentences.

ARMISTICE DAY 1938

Every year in the Assembly Hall
We would exhume the dead
Protagonists of the Great War.
With marbled eyes McKelvey prayed
For unknown uncles killed at Passchendaele.

The blood-roll of the drums, the bugle's cry,
The curt succeeding hush
For masochistic memory,
Insinuated a death-wish;
And history sugared to mythology.

In my last year, the radio relayed
A nation's fading grief
Live from the London Cenotaph;
But my suspended disbelief
Was shattered with the silence when a loud

Dissident voice charged puppet-masters with
Rigging another war.
McKelvey broke ranks also, and
Came out against more murder for
Conflicting emblems cut from the same cloth.

FIRE BOMB

McKelvey watched from his baulked car
The corrugating fire consume
And lick the building clean; but for
The casual motorist hurrying home
He thought the fire might merely seem
Inclement weather.

Be careful not to generalise
In anger, he rebuked his thought,
And censure nihilists en masse;
Distinguish between this and that
Obscenity, each tit for tat:
Particularise.

He'd never loved his native town;
But now with buildings torn apart,

His generation's bridges blown
And future generations hurt,
He could not quench his smouldering heart
With cold disdain.

IMPOSTORS

I

Avuncular; clearly not
The secret visitor,
Only a man disguised
In wig and robe to sell
Pink- and blue-wrapped toys.
Yet he was the harbinger,
Before the holly, the tree,
And the spires of carols astride
The indulgent City Hall.

II

Anachronistic; speech
Bogus Ascendancy,
Prejudice and power
Discreet in wig and gown;
For a child on Christmas Eve,
Caricatured in dream
His silhouette will loom
Like a rampant highwayman,
Arresting the harness bells.

THE LAW COURTS REVISITED

The side courts closed, Queen's Bench and Chancery—
Counsel gone
Back to the burrow of their library,
Litigants home
To chew the frayed ends of the argument,
Cleaners' time
To mop and scour the day's sufficiency
Of crumpled claim and counterclaim,
Stubbed-out or smouldering plea,
And to restore

Its impassivity to the Great Hall—
Eight pendant golden lanterns inculcate
A humour that refers
You back to that same atmosphere
When you,
Though half a lifetime younger, seemed the same.
And you,
Alone in the russet light with just
The marble names of your profession's dead
Sentenced at Ypres, the Somme and Passchendaele,
Carved on a wall's reflecting apple-sheen,
Fraternise, and hesitate between
A youth approaching from the lecture room
And your advancing self; contextually
Set in the italics of the mood.

                              *

Snap out of it, you hear McKelvey say.
Those were the days
When terror and confusion ruled
The Central Office, and apprentices
Cringed in with papers for advice and got
Red lugs from upstair despots. And
Some sedentary sadists in the Seat
Office peered at wills for pinholes, clips'
Rusty implications, and required
Affidavits of redemptive prose.
And:
That old warlock with the flaming face
And stick-supported legs, who jokers said
Punctually beat his passive clerk around
The clock to break the tedium; and, enraged,
Shouted Shut the Door when you'd just knocked.
In retrospect, material for a laugh.
No laughing-matter then, when you contrived
To cut through paper jungles to My Lord.

                              *

I am a social engineer
He said with some acerbity
In answer when you asked him what
A lawyer's special role might be.

But does he question what's amiss
With the machine he services?

*

But once in, what was it, a year,
Those upstair spiders in their offices
Prepared to meet their god when the Lord Chief
Stalked through the corridors. I tell you, Mac,
Even their pens clicked upright to alert
Till after he had passed. But—bear with me—
The sweetest memory is of '45,
Election Day remember, when we were
Part of an amazed majority.
Ecstatically recall
Their worried wirelesses
Bellowing news of Labour landslides and
Staunch Tory strongholds taken. Masterful,
I brusquely cautioned them for dallying:
Hurry along, or you'll be nationalised.

*

Litigation's disguised violence.
Was it McKelvey or yourself who thrust
Anarchic horn into the prim debate?
Then, goring heifers for the hell of it:
Every judgment smacks of blasphemy.

*

Give me facts, the barrister
Admonished, ruffling out his brief;
Beyond him, the gestating fact
Of his shot body on the floor.

*

Humanity's defaced by uniforms.
Cleric, soldier, policeman, judge,
And masquerading poet are
Insignia more than men; and note
The nomenclature too: for while
Gerard Manley Hopkins could

With all respect address his God as sir,
An ageing man in wig and gown
Becomes My Lord, as if
His elevation truly did convey
Him upwards to Jehovah, L.C.J.
Not all of them used politics to climb
On to a local lintsack; but
You've heard the talk of dogged canvassers
Travelling a circuit of constituencies
Seeking adoption, jaunty hat in hand;
Downing democratic pints in pubs,
Jolly with beasts and besoms on the farm,
Tin-hatted on the site or factory floor,
Clucking encouragement to battery hens;
And, unselfconsciously,
With party men in some provincial hall
Mothy with flags and banners, bend
Their eloquence
To an inelegant cause: a curious way
To prop a ladder to the judgment seat.

*

A late young barrister flops in
Down from the Crumlin Road,
Bound for a consultation or
His overtime's workload;
And earlier in the day you'd seen
New white wigs at the door
Being photographed while they were still
Immaculate and clean.

And you'd reflected on your prentice years
Without much rancour, though you gave too much.
Your main regret the limits of the job,
Where people sit as clients, losing face
In the transaction. But, opposed to that,
You never looked for presidential chain,
Or wore a bowler hat at funerals,
Or drank politely, or completely lost
Contempt for commerce once you'd learnt its style.
You sound like Hewitt, Mac, McKelvey says.

Sound poet, who picked out your crooked smile.

*

The ambiguity
Of seniority
Permits you to explore
Those upstairs offices,
Where, after thirty years,
Fresh idioms demonstrate
A new permissiveness.
In the Writ Office now
Bosoms and beards abound;
And one's content to queue
To stamp a document
Behind tight bottoms and
Loose shoulder-lengths of hair.
But don't be foxed, McKelvey chides,
By an updated style:
The power and prejudice are there
Still, even when they smile.

The Law is not so much an ass
As a bland crocodile.

*

4.30 now. The youth has disappeared.
You have translated him. There, overhead,
The eight jowled lanterns are your witnesses.

*

Keep handy in your briefcase
A summons & a shout;
Not everyone who comes here
Is certain to get out:

VERIFICATIONS
(1977)

MARCH

Stoned cheek turned again
The stone turned from the tomb:
Unvault spring
Like a lad
For your parish needs hoeing
And a weeding of snakes
In constricted land—

Although the houses are aghast
Mothers and children stay
Tears for another day
For someone who provided
Everyday:

Hold up your favour Patrick
Not like a riot shield
Or clerics with their bibles
Or perpetrator's hands
Guilty of blood on the tarmac
Vengeance on old sick walls:

From Downpatrick Cathedral
(Abashed by daffodils)
Pronounce a curse on snakes
Fused to ejaculate—

From Downpatrick Cathedral
(Three saints smudged on a wall)
Now that Easter flusters
From the shattered egg

Stained window-glass and rubble,
Chance another spring
With hailstones maybe,
Or perhaps daffodils.

KNOWING MY PLACE

I

In fortunate places
They worry only
About a prospect of rain—
Who's for tennis
Deckchairs and parasols
Shopping without
Barriers soldiers saracens
The person touched by strangers
War conditions with
The enemy inside—:
What private hate
Wrecked the Abercorn;
What itching hand
Gutted Smithfield?

II

In a wet jilting June
I review and assess
What I have made of half
A century, and guess
With trepidation what
I'll do with a bonus of years
A post-dated cheque
To be marked invalid perhaps
By a bilking bank.

III

I began in violence and
My age now coincides
With hooded murder and
My children know no other
Place or style
Than the bomb the fist and thugs'
Intimidation,
The tortured corpse in the ditch.

IV

The toad puffs and the snake smiles;
Cancelled faces kill.
I recall two figures poised
Between the sea and the shore
On the fringe of life,
In my early fatherhood;
Yes they
Had time and place to affirm
Or to be nonchalant,
To whom I sang old songs
Driving the car
Through strange townlands.

V

The toad bellows and the snake snarls.
Songs suspect now, the younger ones
Have seldom grasped
Bucket and spade without blood
Coursing like sea
From the Irish curse that wrecked
Picnics and destinations—
(Mitchel and Yeats; their cry:
War in our time O Lord).
May peace, I taught them to pray
From the Upanishads,
May peace and peace and peace
Be everywhere.

VI

I declare
That in this vicious town
Where the future drips on a line
Unhoused from the weather,
Where hooded men walk out
With cudgel and petrol bomb—
That along High Street
A river used to stride
Sails lintel-high in the air,
A semaphore:
Now culverted underground.

Expatriate now, I look
At the trees my father made;
Stateless, I look around
At the loss and the waste,
The desolate acres; and watch
My children stooping to lick
And stick down emigrants' labels.

KEW GARDENS

Queuing in Kew Gardens
For tea and sandwiches—
The English order freedom
Where we take liberties—
We trespassed upon sunlight
And unfunereal flowers,
And no one thought to ask us
To prove our names were ours.
Unthreatened glass in windows
Reflected as we crossed,
And the present had a future
Not completely in the past;
Where children ran and shouted
Against a bantering breeze,
Without a glint of murder
In an innocence of trees.

Over milky tea and
Discarded crusts of bread,
I swapped with a German widow
Our blitz for her air-raid;
And said sunshine seemed guilty
Like streetlamps in the war
In Dublin, while in Belfast
The dark went on as far
As the hills and the last siren
Straightening to All-Clear,
The kettle and the tea-cups
And the sip-away from fear.

Edwardian sunlight falling,
Like imperial grace,
On an afternoon of tea-cups,

I chose to reminisce
On mutual bombs and sirens,
Families under the stairs,
Rats blazing from the manholes,
Their Messers, our Spitfires;
On bankruptcy of empire
And fraudulent nationhood:
Then framed an awkward handshake
For words I'd left unsaid.

For I hadn't marred our wartime
Brisk reminiscences
With a provincial quarrel
Remote beyond the trees;
Or complicated teatime
With clever theory
That Belfast courted ruin
Chasing identity.
The killer wears a mask, and
The victim gives his name
To just another headstone;
The clichés stay the same.

And the waitress hurried on to
Set another place;
And children ran and shouted
Against a bantering breeze.

SMITH

May Johnston's shop has gone skyhigh;
Farringdon Gardens is burnt out;
There's no more petrol in the pumps.
Men of Ulster; behold, I bring you my son.

Sally Houston wore a ring
With five white diamonds; now engaged
With wheelchair and paralysis.
Men of Ulster; behold, I bring you my son.

Never troublesome, she said:
A good boy; helping, he was shot
Drawing the bedroom curtains, dead.
Men of Ulster; behold, I bring you my son.

Cuchulain warring through the North
Defenceless then from grief, embraced
And cried out over the dead boy:
Men of Ulster; behold, I bring you my son.

DAISYMOUNT TERRACE

I

From the school in the Church Quarter
Lately laden with books and tasks
My brother whooped downhill,
Fighting allcomers, back
To paraffin lamps and griddle bread
The Moat and the Church overhead,
And the Reverend Cottar poised
Pruning his sermon, where
The stream behind the houses stole
Pebbling his sleep.

Then Daisymount Terrace
Was beyond the tramlines
And the festering city's war,
And himself with his popgun lost
Between the opposing armies—
Where the stream had no name
But prattled with children among
The humped-up fields

And the cottages,
Gape Row limewashed, the gardens
Hunching up to the Moat:
Where old bent kitchen spoons
Could dig for giants' bones;
Dundonald a breath between
The ghetto's threat of eviction
And the virgin house with the garden
Cultivated and groomed
Outpost in a violent town,
By our father making our world.

II

Gardening I look at my hands
Veined like his, the stream
Still stumbling unnamed,
And myself also aghast
Between the opposing armies—
Slow to pluck weeds—
And Daisymount Terrace now
Lacks fields for a daisychain
For a mayor in a frightened town.

The stream stumbles unnamed
And a tithe
Of the Church Quarter
Enfolds the school, while I
Stammer downhill lacking
A shout from my brother
His keeper and sleeper
His brother grown in his place
With a father's hands and stance
In recovered forgotten ground.

III

With nettles in my hands
In an innocent afternoon,
My brother running back
With whose guilt in my hands,
The stream a gutter now
Silenced by traffic ground
To a red-handed stop
A rumour of bombs—
I listen hand at ear
For a mercy of water and
My brother's confident shout
In an innocent afternoon.

THE JOHNSON GIRLS

Gloved for church
The Johnson girls
Stepped down from the gate

A distant breeze
With scented honour cards
Hankies and lace:

Nonetheless there was common
Ground for the fence was broken
Their grounds admitting
A hullaballoon of boys when sun
Occurred like a holiday
The old trees neighing:

Nice skirted and clean
Prayerbooks in lilac hands
They whispered and walked
Reservedly from their estate
Down to a private pew
Under an elegant steeple:

While over the hedge's gap
Shadows steeple-jacked
The length of a monument
Under their dying trees.

STRINGER'S FIELD

This is no proper route for middle-age
Seeking the stirrups of a rocking-horse,
Key lacking door, superior car too big
For the meagre streets of Kick-the-can and Tig.

I have gone back too far. Then a townland,
Before the first death, brimmed and hummed with summer,
And life like loafing kerbstones stretched eternal
And The News was always the same from wireless and journal.

I have gone back too far. Then that white summer
Trite with daisies and the next-door girl's
Buttercup kiss through the laurels when we were seven,
And at night the streetlamp guttering up to heaven,

My robining boyhood under Stringer's trees:
Now, leafed back, reveals the kerbstones cold,
Kiss blown, ironic laurels unallayed
By my return to all I left unsaid.

FIRST FUNERAL

Uncles in bowler hats
Puffed out cheeks and sighed
Over the undressed grave;
And curious children neared
Slitting daisy stems,
Mild connoisseurs of tears.
But, two-faced, I kept back
My awkward posy for
My Strandtown Lycidas,
And played half-master of
The lowered flagging gaze.

I had no eye for the girls
On the Upper Newtownards Road,
Nor mind for repartee,
Alive to his bandaged head
And the wax wreaths ribboned in glass;
But purged my repertoire
Of grief for his sixteen years,
Discarded death's armband,
And broke my truce with their love.
The word's compassion; for
Everything that has lived.

AFTER HALLOWE'EN

It was a sort of ritual,
The morning search for firework shells
Acrid under the garden mist,
Till actuality returned
To the witch's broom and the turnip-lamp,
And the bleary candle-stump retired
To the fuse-box for emergencies.

Their dancing over, sparklers lay
Like hat-pins with occasions gone;
Monsters that made us all afraid
Gaped from fearful suicide;
And, o, the rockets' rush and fanned-
Out peacock pride lay lucifered
And middened on debunking soil.

But saddest in that disarray,
Aloof disdainful onanist,
Proud spinner sordidly threadbare:
Hard-hearted still, the catherine wheel.

PORTRUSH

Not my curt baptism in the cold Atlantic
Or the smug wholesome limbs
Snug in the dairy after
The dreamy drink of milk at the head of the town;
When sandals peppered with sand
And whitened with salt
Ground up steps to a swell of a town,
The blood alert—.

No; it was never the sand or the sea
But rocks strewn
Like ancient garbage, and gulls
Doggedly diving, and forgotten
Perfect amphibious shells picked up
From bereft weed and listened to
Like the lug of my father's Black Cat crystal set—

Nor I suppose the trite
Boardinghouse with the smell
Of cats, and bacon wreathing and purring
A holiday smell when windows
Were dolly-dyed blue, and the sky
Was high with cotton-wool clouds and the Blue
Pool stared opposite, apposite—

Nor even the patchwork quilt late and guilty
With fairy-lights staining the page, the rasp
And gasp of lamplighting waves retiring
That last late night from the guttering ebbing fortnight
And the gull-stained peppermint rocks:
For later, war in the clouds
Over the Skerries, stranding
Barbedwire against Germans,
Above the harbour holding
A girl in my arms I watched
A boat slip by in the dark

With a port red eye
Conscripted into a buttermilk night;
And, blood alerted back from sirened love,
I counted goose-steps back to the postcard town:
Myself at war.

DOWNPATRICK

I

The houses in Irish Street
Cling like clegs
And English Street
Steeples up to three
Saints on the cathedral;
But Scotch Street slopes
Away from the river
The swans and the island:
The Welsh it is said
Given Saint Patrick
Declined to reside
By river or steeple.

II

My father was born there
In a brisk town, the Quoile
Familiar with barges then, before
The railway came and Belfast
Killed crafts—Quail furniture—
(Lynn Doyle on the wireless: *Irish Chippendale*).
But the swans remained on the river
Icebergs or islands
A wish of water away
From the steam, the steel and the hammer.

III

The swans I remember and
The cathedral footed
And fêted with April daffodils
Glimpsed from the fretting train then,
When exhausted with refugees
From German bombs, it stumbled forward

To a waiting future of Irish bombs promoting
The grief of a girl
With one eye and an arm.

BALLYHACKAMORE

Only a step from childhood—
My mother crippled with baskets
Myself leafing *The Magnet*
Only a stoned crow's
Fright from the trees in Stringer's Field
Alight with the flash of trams
On the Upper Newtownards Road—

For Ballyhackamore
And the cottages
Still a townland
Went on regarding

Paddy Lambe's and its sawdust
Smart's Butchery with its sawdust
And the church with the iron bell—

Myself reading before eating:
It was the shop at the corner
Of Earlswood Road where my pennies
Tilled an exchange at noon
On Saturdays when Billy-Bunter-full
I stumbled home like the local drunk
Reluctant for the meal, head down—

I remember in my pram
A hard stare at me
I remember falling under
A dog's aggression—

I remember myself at school
Pee on the floor and the smell
Of rubbers and rulers and pine
Desks and sand in boxes,

And the clean
Plasticine smell of the teacher, blue trams
Flashing past windows and

The big boys who told you
Forbidden things—

Ballyhackamore:
Later my grief,
And my pocketed love.

QUAIL HOLDINGS

I

Irish Chippendale

From the unitarian churchyard,
Dovetailed in their vault,
Those ancient cabinet-makers
Prescribed the way he built.

Jealous administrator
Of family estate,
He banned his sister's love-talk
With the clerk in New Bridge Street.

He jostled the process servers
Spinning a coin for the brief,
And sent in word to the lawyer:
Quail of Irish Street.

From that girl's disaffection
My father got his name,
And his son never fashioned
Irish Chippendale.

II

Title

They could hear the cathedral singing
The length of English Street;
But the shuttered windows in Scotch Street
Constrained good money to wait.

She remembered him at his wedding,
Groomed like a foreigner,

And her sister matching his ardour
With the veil thrown back on her hair.

As they slipped the ropes from his mother's
Suddenly jealous grave,
She fingered the keys in her pocket
Like a new-moon's penny for love.

She cooled her hands in the river,
Pale fingers without a ring,
Aggrieved by his misadventure's
Ambiguous last fling.

Since he lay without an inscription,
Back in his mother's womb,
She gave his children her father's
Title to hearth and home.

III

Avocation

Gray Quail descended from English Street,
The cathedral humped on his back,
Top hat, frock coat and handkerchief,
Exasperated stick:
Weir opened early; that young lad
Would not be overpaid.

Aloft on the conveyancing stool,
He watched his uncle's hat
Diminish downhill, stick stuck out
Half parry and half threat;
And read injunctions on the walls
For writs and civil bills.

Assigned to pumice parchment skins
For lease and fee farm grant,
The white dust mizzling on to sleeves
Pressed by an anxious aunt,
He pounded while the watchful clock
Stitched half-a-crown a week.

Gray Quail encountered customers
In apron and top hat;
But yellowing sawdust mealed on floors
Across in Irish Street,
Bereft of craftsmen to inspire
Dead wood to furniture.

At six o'clock the lawyer's clerk
Laddered down from his stool;
Stepped out and breathed cathedral air,
And marvelled at the skill
In doors and fanlights in the street,
And at his man's estate.

IV

Great-Aunt Anna

She swore she would not lie
With the rectangular dead
Prim in the family vault,
Her idiom denied
The soil's anthology
Of local accents honed
On the parapets of speech;

But, bland as a lawyer's quill
Limiting lives and lands,
She planned like codicils
Spring flowers for her grave,
Self-will her caveat
Against the family will,
Stiff like the key she flung

Into the river's sleep
To spring a dilation of eyes
From the bridge to the church's wall:
And, blind to the dusk's unease
Hesitant round the town,
Bequeathed to the river a glimpse
Of posthumous daffodils.

V

The Lay Preacher

Coming in by the bridge they scanned
The incestuous parish, noting beyond
The comfortable fields, withdrawn
Tête-à-tête of trees and pet
Domestic hills, the muscular
River's curved maternal arm
Jealous and threatening like a wing.

His sermon blatantly contrived
More Blake than Bible; a scant text
The pretext for his personal
Scheme of minute particulars.
But the girl sat listening to the bees'
Muted organ music, while
Concurring breezes turned the leaves.

Smiles and hands in the porch; the trap
Glittering at the gate. The girl,
Holding his strap of books, moved on
Intolerant of involved goodbyes,
Sunlight catching the brooch at her throat,
And strayed to a family vault, glanced down
For the inscription; but the name
Was faint, and his step came at last.

Quails in their wood; and up on the hill,
Aloof in episcopalian ground,
The brash invader of their blood
Lay without their name or his.
But she composed her gloves and hair
As the trap flashed past the river's breeze,
Unaware that the man on the hill
Had left his blood for her quickening.

VI

Mary Quail

Come out of the shadows, Mary Quail,
Plain name in the family tree;
Who never wed, or made a will
To change posterity:

But died, I surmise, pretty young,
With never much to say.

Before I open up the vault
To an avalanche of bones,
Permit me quizzically to tilt
The mirror of these lines,
Or coax a tentative miniature
From the shared blood in my veins.

Brown eyes and pinned-up hair; a shawl
Against infirmity;
Pet handkerchief with lacy frill,
Trimmed bonnet in the pew:
And always, at your hands and feet,
A sibling's hint of me.

A SAD DAY'S RAIN

Midnight now. Looped fairy lights
Spill colours into harboured sea.

For half my father's lifetime I
Entrained with faces annually
To kneel at rockpools, breast huge waves.
With case and camera, open shirt,
Finding packed memories fall apart
With crumbling step on people-littered sands,
I pined in raucous boardinghouse
Behind my medieval face,
Disdaining blunt nailbitten public hands.

Now, charged with feat too near the brink,
Wet bottoms, bloody knees, I think
Of my drowned bucket and lost wooden spade;
And watch my son half-hunt a crab,
My baby daughter's ankles stab
Short waves that hiss and thin like lemonade.

Lost child, child-tethered father, watch
A catsharp coast; and turn to snatch
From soft nostalgia clawed and bleeding hand
Back into life whose cliffcrossed corpses all
Are captive in a shell's shawled call
That cups my blood to make a tidal sound.

Despite bedridden rocks that pile
Contempt on root and tendril, I'll
Still signal life from smudged tidelines of pain.
So when I paddle with a child—
Legs varicosed with seaweed, mild
Monsters beckoning to a fair terrain—
Going no farther, I withstand
Seduction of the shifting sand,
And gaze with children at a sad day's rain.

LUCY GRAY

Hard hats trotting to funerals
Consort with me
And share my spade;
And exhume
Good soil and
Remould it over
A shallow grave.

A family cat denied
Being a stray
Hearth and silk content
Of cushion and the right to stalk
Tail-high along unchallenged floors:

She was neither out nor in,
A silhouette;
And the spade
Will stand in its mud until

Bulbs heave flowers from her grave
Vacation of the windowsill
Her will to get in
Her need and greed for love
Her gentle lacking paws:

But when I paused
To cuff my eyes,
A robin lit
On the spade's handle,
Knowing,
Alert and free.

FAMILY GROUP

Cushendun

Short of the bridge
And the peat-tinged air
Maud Cottages' glass
Glancing like cats

Father-in-hand
Your tentative square
Sandals exploring
You trembled after

The gun's colon:
When wings declined
In a misprint of commas,
Sentenced to stop.

Letter to Putney

Recline your head
Upon an alien pillow,
Settle sheets and sleep
And wake up lightly

Far from your empty room
The elderly clock in the hall
Pictures benign on the walls,
The schoolbag in the corner:

But always remember that time
When car wheels panicked on ice,
Short of the school's
Whisper after the bell;

For, captive still
On the ice of a stopped town,
I fume and fret like the car
Denied its destination,

Still struggling to engage;
But now for my daughter,
I break a match in two
And pocket it.

Laureate

Good poem, girl; your mother thinks
That line which puzzles me identifies
This fractured province begging for
Paternity and style. As for yourself,

Pater familias self-styled,
I hunkered you up to the poetry shelves,
And listened to you charge at words,
Soundly intent to winkle out their sense.

You're shelf-high now; but I recall
Your accent and your terse footfall.

Excursion

Shaking your fist
Against lengthening distance
On a wet August day
Wearing a mackintosh
Outgrown by your brother
You swore
Like a sailor
The wind whipping
The bad words back
With the rain,
No more compelling
Than your sandals squelching
On a ruined holiday walk:

And quenched you shook
A watery fist
After dismissing heels,
Rain and tears
On the reflecting road,
That summer's gone
Disastrous afternoon.

Tain

Rathmullan's seven streets
Bulged to contain its cry;
I floated down a hint
That mad cows follow boys.

You hid anxiety
Behind a diffident frown;
Perhaps for ever now
Cows will appear unkind.

Your turn will come to say:
Challenge mysteries;
Test ambiguity;
Demand references.

THE EIFFEL TOWER

On Sunday mornings when the weather's fine,
You can pick out their slow uneasy hands
Breaking the bread they've brought, tilting red wine,
Wordlessly eloquent like a huge shrug.

For up above the café, like a lost
Inland gantry stands the birdless tower
Having for ships the stormy traffic and
For lough the harbourless sky. So, hour by hour,

They look up from the pavement's latent ground,
Thinning eyes, and coarsening mouths in awe,
Not of the bony sentinel they've found,
But of its fame, and all who have gasped up

Into the rootless sky. Then they go back
Into their parched townlands, where they'll confess
None of their disappointment, saying o
It is indeed a miracle; why yes
You'd twist your neck off looking at the top.

But, like a frightened mouse deep in the straw,
The small doubt palpitates. Nothing can stop
Shocked recognition of the tower's contempt
For bulging faces gaping at its thighs,
And for the cold blind face of godless skies.

Checking the spade above a squirming sod,
They churn black thoughts about the death of God.

TUESDAY

The shawlie always came on Tuesday
With a beaten smile and her child
And ate her dinner on the doorstep
Off a good plate my mother served—

I met her once elsewhere
In another street
And tilting schoolcap said
How-do-you-do-hallo—

And she
Shawled her child and wept
In Aston Gardens.

THE ARDS CIRCUIT

When Kaye-Don Kershaw ran the horse and cart
Delivering things, a bed, a chest of drawers,
The dog ran underneath short of the heels
Pacing the wheels with acquiescent tread.

When Kaye-Don stiff as candle in the hearse
Was pulled by two black horses to his grave,
Underneath in spite of spit and curse
The dog persisted, pacing destined wheels.

UNCLE ALEC

Hospital blue
No public wound:
He saw
Cowards lashed to a wheel
And lashed until wounds mouthed
In the Dardanelles—

Churchill cigar a haze
Turning papers—

On a stool in a snap
My uncle sat
In hospital blue

My brother myself beside
With frozen grins.

Letters years later
He emerged
From Purdysburn
Where looneys yelled
And tore their hair—
Which I visited as a child—

And married and got a child
And I saw Kent and his café
And London and the lights
And my uncle wearing flannels:

But he cried out from his sleep
Distressing wife and child
For the soldier on the wheel
And seaside shells exploding
The hospital and himself,
Torn between
Clothes and uniform
A cup and a spoon
And what to stir
And why.

JEAN ARMSTRONG

When I was eleven, in the Scouts,
I sold programmes at Friday-nights'
Orchestral concerts. Jean Armstrong
Clutched her penny until hot
It warned me when I handled it.

She sent a postcard to Kilkeel
Where we were camping, and until
The tents came down, the guy-ropes pulled,
I kept it; then let pieces fall
Short of the bus, behind a wall.

Next week the Scoutmaster came up
With mocking eye and twitching lip,
And handed me the pasted card
With all her words rejoined on it.
My lanyard lusted for his throat.

STRANMILLIS ROAD

Leaves offcourse,
The river's trespass bright
On Ridgeway Street;
Your narrow room above
76 the shop:
Drummond Allison's war.

Then; but today,
Minding his own business,
A shopkeeper was shot,
Assassin's customer
Getting short shrift,
You'd say within earshot
Of 76 and our ghosts—
No leaves scuttling but
Flags like a stench in the air.

THE ORDEAL OF CLUTEY GIBSON

Cupboard Love

Clutey Gibson storming home from school
Drew up the string with key from letterbox,
Hunched in and slung his battered leather bag
Against the hallstand where his father's hat
Kept posthumous vigil; yodelled against things
Like thugs and burglars; inched his stockings up
And ran to suck hoarse water from the tap.

Mouth wiped across scored knuckles, he explored
Remnants of congealed sausage in the pan,
A crunchy rind of bacon frilled with egg,
Fried crumbs of soda farl. The clothes-horse drooped
Bandy and lamed with mended shirts and vests,
Stockings, trousers, drawers, and pale cast-off
Stuff from his father's day airing death clean.

With bread and jam he strutted scullery's bounds
Eating and snorting. Where was she at all?
Stained dish-cloths in the jawbox, freckled tea
In lip-rimmed cups. He yodelled cautiously,
Afraid of the hard hat without a face.

Where was she at all? The kettle stood
Severe and empty, and the scullery's space
Wanted her voice and movement. Soap was dead
Without her hands to mother it. Cold glass
Ranted from windows. Crust in mouth, he turned
To the tall cupboard, wrestled out the drawer,
Unclasped her purse and put a halfpenny in.

Wet

Half-day hero, hobnailing his flight
To mock and mow at girls and enemies,
He paused to breathe outside the Big Boys' Door.
Lugged back to smell of rubbers, rulers, ink,
Pine furniture, Clutey dissolved in fright,
Big fellows round him, that one at the board.

Clutey Gibson trailing bag humped home,
Shredding hedges, kicking ancient trees;
Then, elbowing past the door, he ran to her
Bent over washboard and the yellow soap,
And rinsed his shame inside her wet stopped arms.

Murderer

I heard him crying in the jakes until
He pulled the chain to flush the sound away.
I buttoned up and went back to the class,
Where that one laboured chalk across the board.

I knew all right; for yesterday he'd got
A present from his uncle, disembarked
With beard and foreign talk, and, bright as sin,
A vicious parrot swivelling eye in cage.

Clutey was frightened when he saw the gun,
Air-pistol really, butt mahogany
Stemming stammer of steel. We played around
Shooting at Germans, bushes, trees and things.

I don't know when he squinted up his aim
Against the skyline; but I saw it stop,
Hang silhouetted, then drop alien
Behind the laurel bushes. Afterwards,

Accomplices, we firmed the grave. And so,
Hearing the rumbling water and the chain
Clank against wall, I found it difficult
To suffer that one's chalk-talk at the board.

Evening Duty

When he was late he sometimes ran
Amok among the traffic, mocked
By bucking horns asserting right of way.

The apron made him womanish.
Bearing the weight he ran askew
Confused by bonnets and aggressive boots

To vagrant ground erect with cats'
Black mass seduction of his legs
For squalid leavings from the butcher's knife.

(Destroy them all, his uncle growled;
Ungrateful things while humans starve.)
As Clutey Gibson contemplated strays

Ravage anonymous flesh, the blood
On hands and knees seemed justified
By congregations still aloof from love.

TOM'S TALE

Saturday night
Steepled down from love to sinstilled morning
That time I loitered from Lissue,
Tight with a joy too vehement for shout,
And shadowed the road limewashed by a full moon,
Still short of Lisburn and the bolted door.

Do you know,
Thinking of her heavy kiss-tired mouth,
I stretched out of my clothes and danced
Flatfooted, yellownailed, in the moon's stopped sea:
And lay chindeep in buttercups, exposed
To the old green man in the moon, and sang
Snatches of love left at my mother's knee.
Then, sundayfaced, got decent, cut a stick, and turned
Down into Lisburn, back to frayed starched sheets.

THE TRAP

Although I brought the trap at ten o'clock,
He wasn't dressed. I waited while
Starved hens grubbed tealeaves freckling in the sun.
He filled the door: a big man, gnarled, and lamed
By lazy gutties; torn eyes turned
Round corners into private distances,
Away past my commission and compassion.

We plodded through an ancestry of lanes,
Past hawthorn adolescing towards the spring,
Dim fields still captives of the underground.
Short of the destination, the mare shied,
Veered towards a school of buttercups that spilled
Sovereigns and spellings for his working mouth.
I pulled her head, and we went gently in.

When rough men chained him and he made his howl—
Like grieving dog stoned from the darkened house,
Or buckling hare outraged in the hounds' teeth—
I ran back to the trap, got in,
And lashed the mare to Lisburn, reeling back
To cushioned chair, and my late sweetening briar.

THE RIDERLESS HORSE

The odds-on favourite won the race; but I
Watched a riderless horse, its jockey thrown,
Taking the fences and the waterjump,
True to its training but a dead loss then.

I saw myself in that loose riderless horse,
Fraying from cuffing wrists, but studding track,
Pounding alone between abandoned reins,
Its jockey thrown, still parched in a hard lick:

For, like that riderless horse, I ran alone
Along ordained conventional avenues,
Still kept in place by stable discipline
That throttles back the instinct to refuse.

THE GARRYOWEN
(1971)

GLENARM
for Margaret

Nobody told me then—
When I hung around Portrush in a wet July—
That you, 13, I steeped in my 14 years,
Were in Glenarm:
Scraped girlish legs in ferns; shrilling at sudden sea.

Who could have told me then,
Putting a ball towards a diffident hole,
Skimming skinny flints from the North Strand,
Despising dodgem cars in the brash arcade;
Bored by the boarding house, restless, and stretching
Beyond the gulls' complaint, and the finsharp islands
Only a handshake over the waves' last futile fuss—
That if I'd shouted, set a house on fire,
You might have noticed; curious, come to see.

Nobody told me then—
That loneliness is never an only thing;
That sometime somewhere there's an expectant hand,
A tentative harbour for unanchored sea,
And a destination printed in the sand.

I couldn't tell you then—
You in Glenarm, the glens spread like a palm—
Skirting the fuchsias' bells, past rhododendrons and
Moonclad magnolia trees, a haze of bees—
That a boy skirting disaster, aloof on a strand,
Conjured up someone like you in hope of a quick thereafter,
To be known perhaps in a house busy with children singing
      and spelling.

INDEPENDENCE

The sun itself was cheering, so they said;
On tiptoe in the sky, shouting hurray:
And all along the hot processional way
Laughter and songs exploded in the street
Where bombs and guns coughed blood the other day.
Dead patriots shuddered under the dancers' feet.

At last he came, his face like a black sun,
Traitor, terrorist, conspirator
Against an empire, now Prime Minister.
Silence hissed like rain as he stepped out
To say it to the straining faces there,
All ready to acclaim it with a shout.

But up there on the platform he looked small
And worn with study, exile, intrigue, jail,
Bewildered by the view inside the pale,
The years of hurt and work behind, the strong
Laws of authority now his to flail
To right or left, defining right and wrong.

And then he couldn't say it. There weren't any
Uncommitted words that could convey
Naked truths for Independence Day.
How could he *say* it when he *was* the thing?
He laughed out loud, and danced down like a spry
Enraptured child still fond enough to sing.

ROGER CASEMENT'S RISING

Good Friday in good Ireland. Risen larks
Soared from his footsteps and created over
His gaunt surprise, arresting place and time,
His journey's end. And made light of the darks

And guttering vicious entries in his mind.
Wet primroses and primfaced violets
All-eyed his watery rising on a strand
Of faceless shells turned from the shoreward wind.

He had no mind, smarting with salt and zeal,
For hired collectors of his private words
Indulgently put down soon to inform
And in the final judgment dock his tale.

Coy flowers, agnostic larks, ran down his fear's
Long spine of disillusion. In the end,
Disowned belongings, longings, quest undressed,
Were dirty linen washed by a priest's tears.

SYNGE IN PARIS

On the *Pont de la Concorde*, between the mad
Skeltering traffic and the pampered river
Trailing a violet scarf across the town,
He eyed from a jap of shadow, his book turned down,
The gurgling pleasureboat, the tittering girls
With pouting breasts and skirts fanned-out like shells.
Above, the flag of France, stiff, head-in-air;
And there at his feet, twin leaves in a trance like curls.
But, unimpressed, his brooding foreign mind
Schooled by Irish drizzle, sceptical
Of total sunshine, knuckled like a cloud
Over the city, trained in the ways of the wind,
Remembered flooded fields, breached harbour wall.

POEM FOR JOHN BOYD

The streets are strewn with footprints. There
Yeats walked beneath instructing trees.
Joyce raised his ashplant to confer
A footnote on those sunsprayed quays.
In that dim corner Synge would stare
At naked wall for half-an-hour.

Harsh leaves, the rattling footsteps blow
Across the windy town, and dead
Voices rise in a wave and throw
Salty words on heedless head,
Claiming, declaiming there is no
City outside the dream they knew:

That Ireland is a name they bred
In poem, novel, hounded play.
The declarations they conveyed
In dictum or epiphany
Were fashioned in the dream. The dead
Continue dreaming in the blood.

At best, what you and I can do
Is to perpetuate the dream,
Discovering footprints to pursue
The dreamers past the noisy stream

Of printless footsteps thrusting through
Each named but undreamed avenue.

What I wrote in Stephen's Green,
As a sadmouthed boy in a lonely place,
Deaths ago and births between,
Has swung into truth again, found grace,
As the spire's unsleeping cock is seen
Interpreting the storm alone.

MEMORIES OF CHINATOWN

Jackie Dugan

I

Under a streetlamp Jackie Dugan
Whipped his peerie-top alone—
Hoarse from yodelling out faint friends
Tucked up in sleeping houses with
Their greying grates, the tables set.

His father wore a uniform
Of navy blue with seams piped red,
Heels sparking steel on tramcars' stairs
Where he supported bag and bell.
His mother danced; came home at one.

II

He frightened me, for he was tough
And terse and tearless, unafraid.
He jumped from upstairs window once
Because he wouldn't wear new shoes.
They dragged him home and forced them on.

At *Kick-the-can, Relieve-i-o,*
He was the master in the ring.
I turned away from bedtime kiss
Each night he yodelled in the street,
Assassin of my innocence.

III

He mocked me, but I don't recall
A hard slap up the bake, or any
Other enormity. He stood
Outside my world and mocked me. Not

Because of my capped doctored eye
Or my weak stomach, or because
My speech was alien: but because
He lacked my privilege of love.

His mother taxied off to love,
Leaving his bed unmade, his plate
Unscraped; his kissless bedtime prayer
Unheard by skivvy clashing pans.

IV

From kitchen's soiled deserted door
Jackie Dugan stayed out late
Hunched in the lamplight, whipping top
With leather thong, intent, alone.

Heels scorched on stone hotwater jar,
I'd lift a guilty ear to catch
His last cracked yodel, and endure
The silent circle, top run dead.

Clutey Gibson's Eviction

Cordner Bell said Clutey Gibson's da
Sold penny pokes of home-made yellowman.
I ran with penny to his scullery where
He shredded *Northern Whig* and tented poke
Around his thumb to drop four pieces in,
Slipping my penny in a pocket where
Fat watch pokes out from real confectioner.

One morning, late for school with piece and bag
Under my arm, I hirpled round a pyre
Of Clutey's chattels dumped against the gate.
My high-heeled sister said that Clutey's da
Piled chairs and bedding on a red handcart
And, Clutey barking heels, humped towards Strandtown.

Bigamy

His cycle kerbed, the peeler found
The lad behind the door, the girl
Biting her flowered pinafore,
Hushed neighbours aching for a sound.

The lad went with the constable,
Cap wedged inside his pocket with
A blackened butt and one red match,
And helped to push the bicycle.

Neighbours stormed back to angry pans,
To housewifery and husbandry.
The girl stole in and closed the door
Against their straitlaced marriage-lines.

But no one chased the constable
To ask what harm the lad had done
In kindling love on her cold hearth;
Or who would be accountable

For her trousseau of cast-off love,
Her honeymoon arrested; shame
Shrouding her presence like a shawl,
Bare thumb betraying the frayed glove.

THOSE GLORIOUS TWELFTHS

At ten I saw exclamatory blood
On Earlswood Road, a cagecar and a beak-
Capped constable with crowblack gun. We went
To Portrush in July, the great event
Abstracted to indifferent gull and rock.

At twenty, reading law, I glimpsed a gun
Glint in the smile of D.I., former Tan,
War-hero who'd won fancy ribboned stuff
For gutting Germans. Dead Huns not enough,
He grilled half-baked dissenting Irishmen.

At thirty, pigmy family nudging knee,
Wedged in a village dazed by roaring drums

That drowned my destination; trapped by tied
Tiers of faces blinding stonedeaf road:
Inactive, voiceless, I chewed famine crumbs

Like those who willed another hopeless day
Eyeing the shrivelled root and the stopped hand.
Now forty, knowing men in government,
And collared curs that bark down argument
And foul what they must fail to understand:

If I rush children from the bloodsmeared drums,
My family back from history, and rein
Back white horse on the wall, the ricochet,
It is to turn a corner, or else, say,
A new leaf that will dock the nettle's pain.

Project an image for this place and time—
Aloof from cheers and flags, the maddened gun—
Of one embarrassed, guilty monument
Leaving its plinth in the establishment
To smuggle flowers to graves it can't disown.

SHEEPDOG TRIALS

Sheila and Roy and Mick: at Waterfoot
(Remember) they obeyed each whistled call,
Alert to each small signal; the pursuit
And herding in of sheep was gentle, wise
And moving to us watching at the edge.
They won again today the paper says.
And, reading, I remember hill and hedge
Shaggy with rain, the tea and sandwiches
Sold in a corner of the barking field:
And, in the foreground, you embracing him,
The champion, who, tolerant, would yield
Neither to hand nor word, but sat erect
In solitary pride; no, pride is wrong:
In ancient loneliness; yes, gazing out
Across the sheep-pens and the fuchsia hedge,
To where the hills evaporate in cloud.

THE ARCADIA

Old women wading, kilting skirts
Above the ivied veins, massage
Embarrassed thighs, and clumsily
Snatch water like a sign across the face.

Younger, akimbo, they were coarse
Matrons who jested while I wailed
Wet at the edge, their navy skirts
Tucked into knickerlegs or rudely held

Tumescent over fanning waves'
Screamed-at incursions: breasted-out
Like old ships' figureheads that rode
Disastrous storms they never knew about.

I chide my children to the edge,
Where faint waves shrinks from cringing toe.
They fear the claw and the quicksand,
Where I fled from the whirlpool lives ago.

CONTEMPLATIONS OF MARY

I

When he said *Mary*, she did not at once
Look up to find the voice, but sat recalling
Warm patches of her childhood, and her falling
Heartoverhead in love with every glance
Of admiration crowding through the dance,
Or in the streets bent back and almost calling.

Girls put on sex like flowers; tumescent breasts
Emerge like blushes, knowing, innocent;
The underflow of all their ways intent
On welling up with welcome for the guests
Who darken love's white threshold. All the rest's
Above, outside, like god and government.

So she sat on when he first spoke to her.
Hearing perhaps a new sound of command,
Like parent's tug at child's reluctant hand;
Did not at once look up and answer *Sir,*

But sat with memory her conspirator,
Downcast, and did not want to understand.

But he persisted. *Mary.* She resigned
Her meadows and her rainbows to his voice,
Inevitably now, without a choice,
Surrendering all the stairways of her mind;
Then, finally bereft, was empty, blind,
Until the word bulged up and broke. *Rejoice.*

II

Then she was different. Her past perfect years
Seemed like another woman's purse, all strange
In ordinary things, keys, compact, change:
And home no longer nested up those stairs,
Involved with tables, pictures, cupboards, chairs.

Everything was leaning out askew
Since it had touched, no hardly touched her, blown
A strange breath through her branches and the mown
And planted gardens of her private view,
Those yesterdays no longer *I* but *you.*

Was it her knowledge of the clouded womb
That crowded out her quiet corridors:
Her certainty of child? Or, like far doors
Slamming goodbyes, was it a shout of doom,
The dying of a world in her small room:

Her mind a skirt of fear ballooning back
To girlish unencumbered days when life
Required no definitions; sweetheart, wife
Made love, embroidered, lived without some lack
Of meaning like a rat at every crack:

Mary, still girl enough to twirl her hood
From birth and death conspiring in her blood
Against the bright truth of her platitude?

III

After the dying, tidying her room,
She pondered, wondered why he had cried out
In protest for his father. Was his shout

Indictment of the seed that filled her womb
Or plea for some known name to mark his tomb?
Now she was parched and hollowed out with doubt.

She had been satisfied the way things were,
Girl among girls, doing the usual things.
Then she had been exalted, hearing wings
Applauding through the galleries of air;
Came to know words that first had made her stare,
And talk to common people as to kings.

It never was her doing. She had been
Only the bottle for the conjured wine.
Involved with something magic or divine,
She had no axe to grind, no slate to clean,
Had never bothered with a party line.
Most of the things he said she did not mean.

Now she was empty. The last drop had gone,
And she was her own Mary, uninvolved
With parables or politics, resolved
To self, undedicated, pledged to none.
And just before the colours blurred, dissolved,
She closed the door on her disfigured son.

IV

I am the breath that stirred
Your bells to jubilance;
Conjured from cold distance
As surely as a bird
Immense obeisance:
I am the word.

My irresponsible
Dialogue broke down,
Was hooted, hissed and blown
Off stage in ridicule,
My sad forgiving clown
A love-crossed fool.

But I would blow again
My horn into your sleep;
Herd rational thought like sheep

Into a nursery pen;
Scatter my wolves to sweep
Doubt from the plain.

Yes, I would fill your page,
Your lines with poetry:
With liberating key
Empty the clipped lark's cage,
And give back wings to free
Ecstatic rage.

Mary, I am cold,
Bare on the brink of mind.
Open, and let me find
A place to grip and hold,
To thrust the exiled seed
In knowing mould.

FOLKMINDER
for Michael J. Murphy

That time in Cushendall
When sun tompeeped through slatted drizzle at the hills
Stretched like Pegeen Mike or Molly Bloom
Back to the tide's necklace, the wetmouthed *yes* of the sea:
Then birds flashed; and tutting hens fretted past foundering gates.
Summer then. Yes, fuchsias set red bonnets at the bees.

That summer in the Glens
When you charmed memory back to somnolent minds
Of painbright births, toil, copulation, deaths;
Exploring culverted streams, you groped for life
For love, for neverafter.
Summer then, quick gossip in the hedges.

What eyes snapped then I mind:
Your lovebright kitchen, glowing glancing children;
Small Winifred asleep, world clutched with doll in pram:
Yourself, burdened with silence, padding roads to poach
A shadowy thought from old polluted streams;
Yourself, goodman at home, inching buckets past
Her limpid dream, her waterpale limp palm.

NIGHT-FISHING

They drag the hidden net towards the shore
Nervous with shadows and grey attentive stones,
The village voiceless under a single star,
The sea quiescent, careless of the lines'
Whispering conversation with the shore.

The far boat creaks an oar, and a voice falls
Faint from the distance, calls, and veers to sea.
The wet lines tighten, strain; and life explodes
On to the shingle in fierce mutiny,
Riding the net in rainbow waterfalls.

Night's net hangs lightly on the countryside.
I walk back softly, with a poacher's tread,
Parting the silence, skirting the set alarms,
Around doomed dreamers scaling air to ride
Cold rainbows dying on a mountainside.

FAMILY ALBUM

ONE

Trespasser

May the small resolute shoes that guard the bed
Of my young son (intent in sleep) resist
No act of trespass for threats on a board.
Yet let them train those wild emphatic feet
To pass the prohibitions on the lawns
Of clipped conformity, the private roads
Shaded from history, the watchdog walls
Roaming the boundaries of the proud demesne:
Not putting heel where toe is for the sake
Of outraging the gamekeepers; but no,
Permit him, in his time, to walk straight on
To where the last forbidding sign says Stop,
At the map's edge; for there he'll comprehend
The final prohibitions, penalties
Of ultimate disaster. In the high
Air where all alternatives are clear,
He'll find the will to choose: to throw the map

And compass far behind and stride across
The line that shapes life, also islands lives;
Or else to turn, with equal freedom, back
Down to the city, carrying his love
A broken bird snatched from the end of the world.

Forebears

If you were to ask *Where are they,*
Those sunlit faces cornered in the album,
Kin I have never seen, who stumble through your stories?—
What should I say to your three alertly insistent years?
—That they were like us once, walked the same roads we travel,
    touched
Those chairs, that table, wound that loitering clock:
And always chose, preferred, the longer
Minatory lanes to the secure and sane
Highways of coming and going allied to things trusted and dusted,
That never show knuckles like snarls but suggest handshakes
    and flowers:
Evading the terrible answer that they
Are all and nothing, night perhaps to your day.

Children's Hospital

Because you are not here,
With your seven years, your need to know,
Your flattening curls, your new big stranger's teeth,
Thought-threatened forehead, life a watched bird in your hands—
Because you are not here,
I think of all the absences I've known,
The distances, the listenings,
And speculate on your inheritance:
Sadness, nostalgia, shadowy revolt.
My son, be no man's son and no son's father;
But stand against the sun, throw down your shadow.
And, in the meantime, hands and deeds curled, sleep.
Tomorrow is too soon, for yesterday's
A flat cracked photograph without a date,
And your horizons still are packed with sheep
And peeping shepherdesses telling tales.
—Sleep, unsuspecting surgeon's mask and knife.
Too soon, my son, there's no escape from life.
The sheep are slaughtered. Innocence must die.
You must grow to be you, as I, God knows, am I.

TWO

Feis

My taut small daughter on the stage,
Pink-eared, braved auditorium.
Behind a pillar, I could gauge
Little of how she had engaged
Adjudicator shredding thumb.

Her class came fourth. She was annoyed.
Behind my pillar I contained
The silent watcher, her forced words;
And shared a pink girl's broken joy
With paid professional restraint.

Too soon she'll put on adult dress
And mime the mediocrity
That affluence breeds in fake outrage;
Disowning what was washed and blessed
In modesty for grief and praise.

A girl once told me, pink with shame,
Her dying father took the dole.
Behind the pillar I restrained
Bravos, commiserations. Lamed
By greater griefs, I patched my soul,
And tholed the judge's shredded down-turned thumb.

Afternoon

Looking at a snapshot of me, eight-
Years-old or so, my daughter sees her brother.
And I whose childhood is a story to her
Ponder the far-off childhood of my mother
Run in another country with strange names.

The years queue up behind me this June day.
Uneasy in the sunshine I turn heel
To tease tense out of history, sense from play,
Now actor without audience, playwright
Without a theatre, singer without songs.

I tell her she is wrong; that boy grew up:
Her brother still plays games of right and wrong,

His sun and shadows slanting from outside.
Dismayed survivor of that eight-year-old,
I rein the impulse to go running back
Into the photograph, and stoop to scold
A little girl for dancing on my grave
Deliberations, when I could step out
And take her clouds and rainbows in my hand
And, eight-years-old, pursue life with a shout.

THREE

Grania At Three

1

Eager, querulous to be understood
In a world of double-talk, you primly walk
Out with your grandfather under elderly trees,
Chatting and chuckling with your leaves and birds,
Embracing clouds and windows lit with sun.
And now and then you dance around a tree,
Or chase a dwindling leaf, because you must
Run for dear life, knowing *to be* is free.

2

That Irish Grania was a flighty girl
Who made an old king conscious of his heart,
And cut off Diarmuid in his pimply prime.
But what have you to do with myth and moth?
It's time and your own time that will engage
Your reason, your compassion and your rage,
As now your small scuffed shoes dance round a tree
Anxious and friendly like your grandfather,
Who keeps his distance, letting the moment be.

FOUR

Taurus

Bull-like you charge. Then, swung up in my arm,
You turn your golden head, and smile, and charm
Pictures off walls. If I must apprehend
Your bullrush for the china, bear in mind,
Before glass breaks and doors swing loose and slam,
That in the English *Owen* is a lamb.

FIVE

Antenatal

Upstairs the baby quarrels with the womb.
The others are asleep, clenched, or abandoned
To skeltering funfair dream. Outside the room
A wind probes at the door like some forgotten
Father late for feast or funeral.
The wounded blackbird eyes its feathers fall.

What will it be, slow clock, a son or daughter?
Who cares, if it has four limbs and a head:
Cool eyes, hot heart, and the flint of ironic laughter
Equating crust of sin with holy bread.
The blackbird silhouettes a stony head.

Changer of nappies, god's lap, endless hands:
Let this brash ignorant child that dares presume
To stumble into a world where reason stands
Aghast at disaster or promised disaster, exhume
A laughing blackbird from the window's gloom.

Sing like a blackbird shawled on a white thorn
For every child striped like a refugee.
If death is a neverafter, then be born
With a late agnostic breath, death's enemy,
As the crippled blackbird sings, outraged and free.

Careless of name or nationality,
A child comes to the door, shrill girl, gruff son,
As yet unclaimed, anonymous refugee,
Turning to face a liberating dawn
And the assurance that the journey's done.

SIX

Probate

One hardfaced January day
My father walked out to his death;
Fell down like any tagless stray
Animal caught up beneath
Late scheduled wheels; stumbled, and left

His papers tidy, his affairs
Ready for probate. Son bereft,
(Suddenly father) he confers
On me his pipes and walking sticks,
That birthday scarf, the hats too small,
My mother's papers. Now I'll fix
The fuses, wind slow clocks, and call
On frayed relations, tend the grave,
Press speeches for occasions, stay
To hear pink chubby clichés pave
The road to hell or Stormont: pray.

Old God of lamplight, do not hold
Him guilty of his son; but let
Him enter heaven as foretold
By old believers. I would not,
To save myself like Joyce, have said
One word against survival, that
Sole meaning for the decent dead.
No, I would kneel and crumple hat
And cancel out myself for that.

Cold air, sweet dissolution, in the spring
A little girl, remembering
His presence with last Easter's egg,
Will stray on silences that beg
The honest questions she'll advance.
Forgive us most our ignorance.

Last Christmas

Christmas night. Full cars storm home.
Glutted with fowl and fun I close
On pinched moon and quenched houses door
That admits and denies.

Last Christmas Day my father picked
A slippered way through tumbled toys
And scrambling children, praised the fowl,
And lipped his final glass.

How do you tell a child to mourn
On Christmas Day except to say
From small cribs adult crosses grow:
God dies with each good day.

Unfathered father at son's feast
I close the door on Son's first day,
My father's last good day, to learn
His skills gleaned by the way:

Wrist plying crafty screwdriver,
Firm foot and hand behind a spade.
I bring to manger murder and
A craftsman slabbed and dead.

Christmas night. Cars screwdrive home.
The child is born, the father dies.
A door jammed on eternity
Permits, admits, denies.

THE GARRYOWEN

A Soldier's Song; the silence: then the roar
Of Lansdowne-Irish voices. (Who reflects
On Morgan, Cromey, Bailey, Moran, Kyle,
And Sammy Walker and Blair Mayne? The score
Will be forgotten in a little while.)
Stopped on the line, O'Reilly genuflects.

The scrummage labours over seminal ground,
While fledgling wings hang loosely for a sign.
Ecstatically, the undulating crowd
Climbs to a climax, tolerates the wound;
Implores, deplores, ejaculates aloud.
On, up and under, forwards; charge the line.

Irish for an afternoon they wait
For gory glory-o, the faceless men.
Close men from Belfast, Ballymena, loud
As uncorked Dubliners, and imprecate
Together in some sort of brotherhood.
Mothproofed, the old myths stagger out again.

The balls hangs like a sighted bird, and falls.
Lost causes rally on the emerald grass.
While clockfaced Fate knits destinies from time,
Who looks through game to life; hears ashblown calls:
Sees shamrock-favours bloom to climbing clouds
Above the cancelled world that missed the pass?

The symbols dominate and germinate.
Ball shamrocks like a bomb; the partisan
Applause gasps like the last transparent brick.
But mention also, in italics quote,
The language that survives the rhetoric,
Kyle's poetry of movement, his *élan*.

The barking journalists lift pints and vet
Form and performances. In Davy Byrne's
The Belfastmen with club conformist ties
Buy quick ones, nationality, and rate
Moffett and Mulligan, free kicks and tries.
Short of the line an offside bomber turns.

Let's talk of Championship and Triple Crown,
But not forget in toasting victory
What the final shout will be about.
Before you put the sporting record down,
Ponder an Irish remedy for rout:
The Garryowen, and the game set free.

BRENDAN BEHAN

A broth of an Irish boy no doubt
But don't mistakenly neglect
The learning and the intellect,
His knowing what he was about.

He died in headlines, gratified
To find an audience in death.
The air he breathed was public breath;
His monologues were amplified.

Condemned to play the roaring boy
Before the faceless firing-squad,
He won them over to his side
To shoot back at authority.

Some pace their lives. But he outran
Time-table and curriculum,
Leafing with an impatient thumb
Through recipes of god and man.

They'll say he failed to drown his drouth,
Like Dylan Thomas. Who's to say
What impulse prodded them to pray
At altars that required their death?

Though I am moved to elegise
His too-brief life, untimely death,
The air he breathed was public breath;
Headlines awaited his demise.

SECOND LETTER TO AN IRISH NOVELIST
for Michael McLaverty

Yourself unchanged, shy habits undisturbed:
After twenty years you still wring change
Out of the purse of knuckled prayerspent hands,
And fondle story's detail, poem's phrase,
As farmers clap a beast or rub ripe grain—
Because from ink and clabber they've come through.

Still *Sons and Lovers* you evaluate
A major novel of this century,
As when we first talked in a dying war.
But now I don't read Lawrence anymore,
My favourite book a street directory
That pages streets forever running home.

How to escape from a parenthesis
Back to the narrative and argument
Is not solely a novelist's concern.
I file at words like keys that might unlock
A sentence from curt brackets' manacles,
Space for the flexing of a paragraph.

On early breathgrey mornings you walk out
And finger frost, note cuckoospit and drawn
Threads in the hedges, introverted trees:
Then, at the altar, hear unaltering word
That needs no key or confidential file,
No laddering wall or jarred heel's certainty.

I travail over clabbered clout of ground
Whose sanction's not imposed but must be worked

Up from graves with delf and bone and snarl;
And riddle shard and soil, and scrabble for
Absolving evidence for cornered gods
Thorned in the hedges, hung in decadent trees.

If, unabridged, we fish in the same stream,
You celebrate, I walk heel-brightened streets,
Squinting at dates on buildings, searching for
The architect behind a bricked-up door;
Evicted tenants in demolished streets
Who served their sentence in parenthesis.

THE GOLDEN BOY

That time John Kennedy came home,
Blown out of history,
Cuchulain moved aside to house
Him in mythology.

IN DRUMCLIFFE CHURCHYARD

If that old man had clambered from the hearse,
How many could have said they'd read his verse
With more than the cold glancing of an eye:
That hardfaced mourner from the Ministry?
That poet drooling for the next review?
They might have felt an irate poet's shoe
Applied abruptly to posterity,
And heard the voice that mauled authority
In play and speech before rant from the dead
At drunkards putting sober men to bed.
A passing horseman pauses casually
As they conduct his bones to Irish clay
For Irish worms to pick at. But he'll write
His signature elsewhere, beyond the trite
Observances of country and of creed;
Endorse the tree on which Cuchulain died.

PREMONITION

You can never be alone again.
Here now, in the silence, you can sense
The prowling dog of loneliness slouch past
From room to hall, rousing a restless ring
Of questions like sloughed-off abandoned leaves.
You say lie still, or open doors to find
Always before you remonstrating eyes,
Stairways of searching feet unstitching the dark,
The heart a clock regretting its lost chime.

THE SUMMER'S GONE

Regretfully I say goodbye to Cushendall:
To the tree-thatched road that marries sea and sky,
The minding hills, and the sudden sun-smeared morning mists
        that scrawl
Child-signatures across notepaper sky,
Loanens that rear like kicking horses, and the hard
Cough of a crow and creak of the cold unminding gull.

Bereft on a hill of thought, nostalgic, I regard
The shoresweep of my days in Cushendall;
And, at my desk, snatch suddenly at smell and sound,
Blown truant scraps through a lazy gap in the wind,
And wish for turf under my feet and all around
Infinity of cold and heartless wind.

SPEECH FOR THE VOICELESS
POEMS 1947-1970

I WON'T DANCE

I am of Northern Ireland: born
Behind a barricade, when trenched
Soldiers, without leave or pardon,
Shot snipers on the roofs from our front garden.

I am of Northern Ireland: born
Behind a shuttered window, when
Crossfire of hate and answering hate
Spewed out a corpse across our garden gate;

Where double-crossing streets misled
Wayfarers to dead-ends, and all
Our brief excursions ended with
The dead man on the gate or in the myth.

I am of Northern Ireland: born
To exile in a local street,
When only bullets danced at night
And death scared skipping children from the gate.

1966

HOLLY TREE

Red beads and bangles berries now
On Christmas morning in the Glens,
Where sunshine touches head and brow
With cold promiscuous innocence,
The holly tree, young evergreen,
Terse exclamation in the snow, 's
Local as accent or the lean
And sheepgrey skyline where it grows
Out of a hedge at Cushendun:
Thuswise continuing otherwise—
Careless of mythic undertone—
Than metaphors and similes
Of poets who aspire to find
A universe in a townland.

1947

AUTUMN VOYAGER

A leafstep on the road. You turn to find
That autumn's at your shoulder. Here and there,
Evacuated trees
Switch off to skeletons. The year
Is digging in; the sap goes underground.

Under cover of dusk the leaves run on
Like quivering dogs; and, though you're standing still,
Sensing the loanen's gloom,
You're moving too, against your will,
On towards their promise of oblivion.

They leave their dead abandoned by the way
Or trapped in lanes, where some small child may take
One in to interleave
A bible or a birthday book,
Its palm extended in what seems goodbye.

1949

SPRING BREAKS THE HEART

Spring breaks the heart, you said with a caress,
Your mouth parting the leaves. Now April is
Lathered with spray, agley like laddering sand;
While, shanghaied, all at sea, I take my stand
Lashed to a shadow, fending off high seas
Of bursting hawthorn, foaming cherry-trees;
Indentured still to winter, weatherwise
To the snare's snarl, a beaten bone's grimace,
Where new grass loots the winter's skeleton
And tendrils frame a skull's sardonic grin.

Spring makes its case. All thumbs, I fumble for
An affirmation strong enough to bear
The pull of opposites: full springtide and
Strewn castaways, abandoned on the strand.

1949

CHILD'S FUNERAL

Under the oaks at Ballymore
A name not yet engraved in stone
Goes to earth with myth and lore,
A name he'd little time to own
Surrendered back to silence now.
And those who turn away aghast
Know life's insouciance will throw
Too many futures on the past
For grief and outrage to outpace
Each day's remorseless commonplace.

But, heedless of the dying-fall
Of courteous bells, coincidence
Of clouds in a cortege, that small
And grave inclining audience,
Now, with his youth and manhood wed,
Wax flowers, to the underground,
Riddling and riddled by the dead:
There now, precociously, he's found,
Dark at the root of Ballymore,
The mould that breaks the metaphor.

DEATH OF A MAHATMA

There's nothing more, you said; no, nothing more
That violence can do to you or me.
Imagine how the terror in his blood
Stampeded from, not to, eternity,
Till, after leaning towards the heckling gun—
The bullets hitmen for an underworld
Of hand-at-mouth, sidelong complicity—
And then, concurring, he knelt down and curled
In prayer or blessing. Deprecatingly,
He raised a faltering arm to discipline
His dissolution in the open sea
Beyond the gunsmoke misting in the sun,
The dwindling figures waving from the shore,
The surplus bullet's posthumous ricochet.
Turning away, you said: There's nothing more,
No more that they can take from you or me.

1948

DEATH DIVE

That film you saw in childhood: the shot plane
Spiralling down to death, and all the time
The pilot's eyes unflinching till the ground
Finally raised an arm and shattered him.

Equally bear the plunge of heart, and watch
As resolutely till the open hand
Of darkness strikes, that final moment when
Your cry will be a plea to understand.

1951

ANOTHER AUTUMN

The brass and bronze of autumn, struck by sun,
Reverberate across the countryside.
The year takes cover, stones bed deeper still,
Nights hunch expectantly. And all the red
And yellow flags of autumn dip salute,
Now summer's gone with winter almost come,
For lives outlived by summer photographs,
Radiant only in a sleep-slipped dream.

Beyond a sheltering lane's respite, the elms'
Serene arcade, leaves like disconsolate feet
Trail past the backdrop of a hardening sky,
A silhouette of refugees in flight.
Stand taut and still. And let your senses fill
And fall with autumn, so that years ahead
You may recall the mood, this moment when
You held hands with the living and the dead.

1948

LEAVING LISBURN

The year disintegrates.
As autumn falls apart
And nothing now placates
Winter's advance, so, heart,
Surrender like the trees
To dispossession; say

Exits and entrances
Are hinged on a goodbye.
Now, as I leave the house,
The raftered road, the skein
Of countryside, let mouse
And spider intervene
With tooth and web to break
And drape all sign of me:
Usurpers who will take
Insidious tenancy
Of passage, room and stair.
Though I claim as my own
Both here or anywhere,
What has made wood and stone
More than the builder gave,
No rhetoric can assuage
The grief of going, stave
Off parting's equipage;
Or, irretrievably,
The key's redundancy.

1949

THE DOGGED PAST

Never content to pocket the past
Like a handful of change—the petty cash
Of pub talk, anecdotal chat—
I promise that those years persist,
Aloof but never far away:
Say like a dog, of whom in name
Only I'm master, mindful of
Those moments when I turn to see
Him slipped free from the trailing tether,
Stark on the street, and cry *That's mine*,
Meaning that *I* belong, as bark
Or whine and whistle collude together.
So, while I'm dozing by the fire,
Those fixed and unrelenting eyes,
Tugging the hem of sleep, cajole
Me back, and beckon through the door
To distances of unrequited cries.

THE HEALER

The healer bent to touch the dying man,
The inturned eyes, the incoherent hands,
Adjuring him to stand, take up his bed.
I make you whole, he said; and snapped the bands
Binding the feet and wrists. Another said—
Between the draining night and a threadbare dawn—
That he would stand as sanctuary from
Life's cold withdrawal of a brief caress.
But she remained inturned, away from him,
With deserts in her hands and journeys in her face.

1950

THE BACKWARD GLANCE

Saying her name, he turned and looked for her;
And she cried out, and guttered into night.
Not to look back and know that she was there,
To walk ahead alone, bringing the heart
To heel, was more than longing could demand.
O not to turn and say *Eurydice,*
Not calling, simply stating a command,
Would have endorsed what ordered them apart.

So, rounding on the dark, he leaned to catch
Glance, scent or phrase to guide her back to him;
Distraught, turned incoherently to snatch
Insouciant laughter, impromptu delight
Back from the crowded silences of death's
Establishment; and darkness hurried between
And quietly cut the channel of her breath's
Incipient cry suspiring up to the light.

All that is known. But ask the reason for
The cruel bond and crueller forfeiture
For that imploring backward look at her.
Does Death say: past reproof, reprieve, relief,
I am the outcast always a step behind,
The introverted shadow at your heels.
Back in your place, in your own time you'll find
Her beckoning from the breaking heart of life.

1951

JIMMY KERSHAW

Implacably, he snatched at uniforms
Affronting his terrain. They showed respect,
The postman, milkman, coalman; binmen chose
To brandish lids as instruments of war.

Beggars and canvassers chalked coded signs;
Midwives on bicycles withdrew their legs.
Smelling of aniseed- or brandy-balls,
Boys zipped up yoyos; peerie-tops ran dead.

When he was put away I eulogised
His candid hatred and his naked snarl,
The dedicated ambush in the hedge.
Old cats emerged, condemned to quietude.

MUSIC FOR AN ANNIVERSARY

Tell daffodils, intrepid trumpeters,
To play out to these introverted graves
Not some slow hesitant lament, but rather
Reveille to whatever dream survives
Under the polished stone. Who shall say whether

Anniversaries die when lives descend
Into the underground, tomorrows only
The jilted dates upon a calendar?
And play too for the sad, bereft and lonely
Who fret for evidence of an elsewhere

Of being with its here and now, its errands
And destinations parallel with ours,
Clutching the promise of eternity
Which some assert, and others seek in hours
Of study, love, intoxication; see

Pinholed for seconds, blurred before believed.
And perhaps conjure from the crowding air
An answering music—no, not *answering*, rather
A gathering of voices asking for
A resurrection that we may die together.

WORDS

Happiness, he pronounced as if
It was the name of a resort
Expensively accessible
To rentiers who migrate for winter sport.

Pedantically, he chose instead
Fulfilment through commitment, in
Fastidious disparagement
Of turnkey language such as *love* and *sin.*

The clocks stood back around the town;
For it was early evening, still
A time for words to strut and twirl,
Before the shadows closed in from the hill.

ONE WHO GOT AWAY

Among the gravestones with the family names—
William and Robert; Thomas, John and James—
She kneels again before her grandfather,
Begetter of the house still lowering there;
Recalls the swarthy hands, his brambly chin,
Mouth tart with insult, soft with Sunday sin,
Hard as his house outside, inside as warm
As sleepless fires aglow on nights when storm
Straddled the roof to thump a Lambeg drum
And warn the brethren of the wrath to come.
The builder lives so long as his house stands.
But she has only sunshine in her hands.

More than a text divides her from the dead.
Intuitive heart seduced by knowing head,
She high-heeled from the rut of the townland,
The soil disdainful of her bookwhite hand.
Fish out of water, feather shed by air,
She's alien now, an awkward visitor—
No longer native, aboriginal,
Indigenous as water in a well,
Root in a field or apple on a bough—
No longer *here,* but *somewhere, then,* not *now.*
The one who got away, who married out,
And made a certain virtue out of doubt.

In dreams, she'd stayed—between the suck of life
And pluck of death—tending and mending, wife
And mother, neighbour, cautious counsellor
Mouthing her grandfather's vernacular,
With half-shut eye assessing crop and beast,
Black-visaged clouds colloguing in the east;
Tied like a tree to her particular ground,
To add at last another weedy mound
Inside the jealous railings on the hill
After a decent Christian burial,
Taking her place among the proper names:
William and Robert; Thomas, John and James.

Nor fish nor fowl, they said. In drawing room,
Tipsy with talk, she hankered for the bloom
Of cloud on hill, the canter of a field;
But, back, familial, borrowed gumboots heeled
With muck and clabber, she'd rehearse again
Vocabularies, civilised, urbane,
Cosmetic accent.—Gone for good, she lets
Covens of fretful shadows, silhouettes,
Advance, foregather. Sleep unmoved, old man,
Dreamer or dream, while, marble-white, the moon
Withdraws its cold caress, a trailing sleeve,
And unremembering silence shields your grave.

1949

ONE OF THE FALLEN

A thrush lies frigidly on the starched snow.
Dying continents inspire no grief
Greater than this, the heart's immediate cry;
For death is big in every broken thing.
A stark, rejected bird has grief enough.
I write my grief for those I could not save.

1945

DYLAN THOMAS

Rejecting all accepted masks, he wore
His own persona like a dickey-bow;
And, scorning brass plates, business cards, played darts
With timesheets, tax-returns, was pleased to scrawl

The one word *Poet* for his trade and calling;
Played his hand dangerously, and kept his nerve
When, over-acting, he leaned back on wall
And made a brisk trade out of bankrupt stock:
Prepared to share a bottle with the world
Or glug a pint down in a rowdy corner
Littered with jokes like walnut shells; but always,
However marginally, self-employed.

Tutter of Ts, cross-eyed with rhetoric,
He is a silence now, around which, whom,
The clock tiptoes and cinders sympathise,
As, at this hearth at midnight, and beyond,
Tangled among the threats and nets of being
Merely alive, a voice reminds, remembers:
Recalls a tubby strutting, stuttering man,
Who, nonetheless, could stumble through the smoke,
The pub talk and mythologies, on cue,
And summon the bravado of his voice
To meet the sober challenge of his verse,
And, in the end, break into innocence.

1954

CROCUS

Through tough hardbitten ground
The crocus, seeking spring,
Emerges in itself
Epitome of spring.
So those who broke their hearts
Or minds for an ideal
Achieve reality
Of shape for the ideal.
The flowers upon the graves
Of those authority
Broke but could not bend,
Adduce authority
For personal testament;
While shriven skeletons
In ultimate undress,
Unleavened skeletons,
Are understatements of
Lives that extended Life.

1951

NEW WORDS FOR AN OLD TUNE

The moon is in the river where
I set the caged bird free.
My grief is in this foreign place
Far from a quick green tree,
Where I must guard each covert glance
Askance at liberty.
I will cherish his song; if life be long
I'll treasure his song for me.

The bird is in the woods again;
His song incites the tree.
My sorrow clouds the windowpane
Now that I'll never see
Insurgent wings across the moon,
His arrogant head held free.
Still I'll cherish his song; if life be long
I'll treasure his song for me.

My sink is full of helpless dreams,
And my cloths are folded wings:
And my heart is torn with loneliness
For the place where that bird sings.
Yet I can rise and wash and bless
Life at my apronstrings.
I will cherish his song; if life be long
I'll treasure his song for me.

I will cherish his song; where I belong
He sings a clear song for me.

1958

LIVERPOOL BOAT

Departure's in the air; and up on deck
The Old Year takes its last look at the town.
Now home is cargo, and the past's a dream
Equivocal in the night, like those gull-bright
Handkerchiefs that stammer out goodbyes.
Now home's cast off. The foam breaks in a wave,
As light and faces tumble. On the quay
A man sings *Auld Lang Syne* in staunch farewell;

And suddenly,
Above the exits and the entrances,
The clocktower signals midnight to the bells.

1947

HOMECOMING

The brittle relics did no more than claim
Tepid endorsement, for too many thumbs
Had made a guidebook out of history
And smudged the small print underneath the name.
Positioned pieces lacked the urgency
Of hate's evangelism in the drums
Ranting from windy corners back at home.
You touched your hat to plaque and monument
But kept commitment fastened like a purse
Against the famous patriot's famous tomb,
The epitaph in pet commissioned verse
That funked the warts beneath the unguent.

You need not travel to find history.
Its myths pollute the wells of the townland
And spatter maps with tribal boundaries;
And under every still or singing tree
Your recollection-in-tranquillity's
Of feuds obedient to a dead command.
So, tentative traveller, the journey lies
Always behind you; there's no certain track
To fullness that does not in time retreat
Back to the doors you slammed, the tugs and ties
You ran from down the liberating street
And on yourself turned a denying back.

1948

BELFAST

Streets end with sky-grey hills; and look, the gulls
Bring tang and tongue of sea into the heart
Of tipsy thoroughfares. Yes; here you'll find,
Cross-stitched as in our devious temperament,
The unrelenting wheels and the clear gulls.
Scrape soot away, and underneath the hand

An honest dignity of stone appears.
Look round a corner, and you'll find a field.
Stand still in High Street and you'll hear the tide.
And under the shine and colour of our shoes
You'll still find smears of Down and Antrim mud.

This city's more than brick and stone and steel,
Than oozing traffic and distracted feet.
Stand half-an-hour in Royal Avenue
And you'll hear accents shaped by field and shore.
This city's like a tree with roots that spread
Halfway across a field; still rooted deep:
And every window's but another leaf.

At times I fancy if we overslept
We might awake to find that in the night
The hills had marched along the Antrim Road,
The Lough had pushed a long arm across town,
And in the suburbs the trimphant corn
Had stalked through gardens with the zest of fire.
For we are not deceived by paving stones
Or solid miracles of brick and steel;
Wary, we know that, underneath, the soil
And water wait for us; remembering still
Our grandfathers' townlands: and overhead
Breezes break through with scent and sound of them.

1949

POSTSCRIPT

This evening in the gardens
I passed husband and wife
Intent and bent on trimming
The rough edges of life;
While I walked on the roadway
With your dog at my feet,
And called on waste and famine
To be your winding-sheet.

1950

RETURN

    Observe, I said; delete
All personal reference
From poem, prayer and talk.
But how can I with sense
    Look without plunge of heart
At church and Orange hall,
Roads mitching to the hills,
The bell-blessed school, and all
    The see-saw of the red
And yellow houses, when
They dunt and dint the mind
And tug at tongue and pen.
    Too often landscape verse,
Recording the thing seen,
Leaves out the seeing, and
All that makes grass green.
    The sing-song of these red
And yellow avenues
Contains my voice. And yet
Perversely I refuse
    To fit or to belong,
Pasted into place,
Indexed *regional*,
Another family face.
    Perversely maybe, yet
Aware of what pursues
The solitary man
Who leaves the avenues
    Of home for distant parts
Of spirit or of mind.
I realise that truth
Is often left behind,
    A backyard flower; and choose
To cultivate truth here.
With this for warning. Build
From what lies sure and near,
    But be assured that some
Will criticise the plans,
Some challenge title, some
Repudiate one man's
    Continuing heresy
Against the principle

Of uniformity:
Those gentlemen can kill.
    Be careful; keep aloof
From smiling citizens
With ropes behind their backs.
Personal history spins
    Its pattern from a thread
Still delicate enough
To suffer hurt from hands
Employed on coarser stuff.
    Why simulate regard
For ignorance and greed
Because a farming folk
Have ploughed and scattered seed
    On one damp hillside for
    Two centuries or more?
The Englishman, I said,
Confused with Irish names,
Who tries to fit all views
In decent English frames,
    Is not more out place
Than those of us who strive
To justify the fact
And act of being alive.
    Accept that then, and from
The pull of opposites
Rehearse the utterance
That life admits, emits,
    With violent night behind
And birth reddening the sky:
When time and place pinpoint
    To one identity:
    The individual
    Containment of it all.

                                                        1950

STAR

The star you prayed to, seeing it as God,
Asking it for life, tree-, window-high:
Last night I saw it move from tree to tree,
Bright and hard and foreign as the eye
Of some strange animal outside the walls

Of cultivated thought, repelling all
Approaches and reproaches, nothing there
That one could cling to, coldly animal;
No glint of recognition in that blaze
Of bladed light turning all prayer away
Back to the jigsaw pieces of the mind.
But I shall learn new silences to say
What's in my heart; will study disciplines
And intuitions that will probe and hook
That gaze that overlooks my life, your death,
The thing you prayed to, that childlike you took
For all that prompts and justifies our breath.

1951

DINAH KOHNER

Like my small daughter she went hand in love
Of parent, past the birdbath's shining eye
Outside the schoolhouse; entered bustling room
Alert with leaves, brash pictures on the walls.

My daughter's finger guiding my gloved hand,
I genuflect by birdbath to respect
Mercy of water for her quick concern,
The minutes mitching from my littered desk:

And think of Dinah Kohner; and neglect
Appointments, consultations, turning back
To front again that font or crucible
That imaged wings for her who chose to fly
With hope and bandage for a worldwide wound.

Remembering Dinah Kohner, I delay
My world of type and telephone, and scan
Her life explicit as a homing wing
Whose shadow raced reprieve for cancelled lives,
And promised famine dedicated bread.

1966

A SONG FOR ONE WHO STAYED

I linger in an unloved town
Where lovers used to hold
Court in the breathless dayligone
Around the marble queen,
Where strolling innocents could hold
Hands in an unloved town.

I look from under lowered eyes
Askance at city hall;
See introverted statuary
Identifiably
Kin to the killer in the hall,
With his unseeing eyes.

Survivor in an infamous town,
Last ditch of the has-been,
I look past the imperious frown
Of the municipal queen
Back to an almost might-have-been
Of my familial town.

But I'll give new dimensions to
Massacred terrace and
Abandoned street and avenue
If I continue true:
A kind of reinstatement; and,
Yes, a reprisal too.

1959

THE MOMENT OF TRUTH

Moments of truth are also the moments of doubt.
As when the wind, say, stoops and lays in your hand
A perfect feather, singular, selfpossessed;
And you, discountenancing omens, stand
Back to scold, and recall to discipline
The incredible you that hurries from the eyes
With welcome for perfect strangers who appear
From nowhere, past subtracted distances,
Purveyors of a casual miracle.
And moments of doubt are also moments of fear,
Until, acknowledging the messenger,
You bend to what's intended for your ear.

FLOWER PIECE

Before I go to sleep, I'll turn my hand
To crafting words, he said,
For what that choosing glance implied
When, seen over a crush of roomtalk and
Shorthanded gestures, laughing you looked round
And held your glance a second on,
Acknowledging, reciprocating mine.

Had I the words, he said impatiently,
Words I've already spent
On cool advice, hot argument,
I'd dust them down and wrap them up for you,
Like candid flowers composed in a bouquet.
Accept, instead, my promise to
Retrench, and husband worthier tracts for you.

In the event, the flowers he brought, he said,
Were those which florists fashion for the dead.

SONG FOR A TURNING TIDE

Whatever you are looking for,
My young man, said she,
I hope that you may find it
On this side of the sea;
For over there, there's lack not luck
For such as you and me,
My dear,
With songs of a green tree.

But there are better songs, he said,
That quicken branch and stem,
Like current coursing through a twig
From some forgotten stream;
Call out from covert crevices
Blind faces to acclaim,
My dear,
Life like a famous name.

Young man, she said, the bitter men
Have poisoned the green tree.
Whatever you are looking for
Need not detain me.

I'll take my heart to my own hearth
Across the severing sea,
My dear,
Far from the gallows-tree.

White bird, green tree, knee-clasped she sang
Out on the broken sea,
Sadder than all the bitter songs
Around the gallows-tree.
Whatever you are looking for
On your side of the sea,
My dear,
Find a lost bird for me.

                                                        1959

THE LAST LENGTH

Resolute, she ran out
From light into the dark,
An instant's silhouette,
Ignoring the frosty bark
Of smarting distances,
Into the muscling sea,
Controlled, autonomous,
That tied still shoulders free.
In pullover and slacks
Small figure all alone
She ran from pedants, hacks,
From grinding gramophone
Playing a threadbare song;
From hands that fingered knives
Instead of dressings; wrong
Admirers who had wives;
Leavetakings left unsaid,
The smouldering cigarette,
The narrow bed unmade.
Resolute, she ran out.

Pedant and hack, you say,
Tilted at life in a dream
While between sea and sky
Life left her like a scream,
And had no truths that could
Have called her back to her mind—

For in the moonless wood
God help us, we're all blind—
Back to the shrugged-off room,
The crumpled book halfread,
The matching brush and comb,
The lipstick pink and red,
The tremulous rocking-chair—
Things fashioned to belong—
When she ran like a hare
Into the huntsmen's song.

Let sour greenapple lough,
Dredging up delph and glass,
Eruct a watery cough,
Cradle her corpse, and raise
Her weed-veined face; exhume,
Careless of verdicts and
The obsequies to come,
An unpossessing hand—
That pedant and hack, you pray,
May intermittently
Hone the blade of her cry
From the width and depth of the sea.

PADDY REILLY AND OTHERS

Now that Ireland's dead and gone
We're the fools that carry it on.
We alone who chose to stay
As unbought voices may inveigh:
We are of Ireland; we belong.
We'll sing none but a local song.

We who stayed to work our sod,
Breaking earth to force a god,
Chose the rusty memory
Of Ireland maimed by history:
Recurring and familiar face
Of a great actor in bad plays.

Irish cynics, take a theme
To cure insomnia with a dream:
The poets' image of a state
Called Ireland broken off from Fate,

From tyranny of straightline thought
Upon whose twisted hook you're caught.

Voiceless exiles, venture out
From barricades of Guinness stout.
Cast curt curraghs on the sea
Because in exile no one's free;
And take up residence at last
In Derry, Galway or Belfast.

You who demand quaint reassurance
Of pension rights and life assurance,
The signed and settled guarantee
Of fame or notoriety,
A market for your stiff reviews
And your limp poems when you choose

To fire heroic couplets or
Pound through a dainty trimeter:
Bring home your hatred and ambition
To combat nuclear partition,
Surveying dissident paths long trodden
By Clarke and Kavanagh and McFadden.

Now that Ireland's dead and gone
We who stayed will carry it on.
You, grudging too much to be merry,
Your songs outsung by Margaret Barry,
Exiled poets, shoulder spade
Above the grave and mossy dead:

Unrolling stones that stayed and bred
While you with belch and gesture said
The same again, and staggered out
From barricades of Guinness stout
To exile in a lavatory
In Hammersmith or Coventry.

You who departed like MacMurrough
To jealous exile, mend your curragh.
Paddy Reilly: venture home
From Moscow, Washington or Rome.
We are of Ireland: the gouged face
Of an old actor seeking plays.

                                                          1959

OCTOBER AND THE LEAVES AGAIN

October and the leaves again, a time
When autumn looks through windows, waits for me
At gate and turning, so that everywhere
Among the dying leaves the elegy
Waylays my voice. But this time, now and here,

Surprised survivor, I can turn away
From sad departures, the regretful look
Over the shoulder, the heart-catching breath.
Now I can sit and quietly read a book
Because the mood is fact now, actual death.

Autumn no longer takes me by the hand.
Because they are ahead of me, the past
Commands less than at any time before,
With thought and feeling free to move at last
To overtake; and never anymore

Shall I stand listening to a leaf's footfall,
Lest I should not attend them when they call.

1951

ELEVOINE SANTI

I join the funeral
Of individual
And stateless citizens
Cut down by violence.
When men turn wolves, then I
Must learn how to deny
The pack's consensus and
The leader's barked command.
I will not serve. Today,
I tell you to obey
Is to give up your hands
As cats'-paws to demands
From that authority
Whose clockwork soldiery
Of lowing citizens
March against dissidence.

1947

LA SERVANTE AU GRAND COEUR

That maid was the heart of corn who irked you long ago,
Asleep now under her sod of trodden earth; and so
We'll bring her flowers now, for the dead have mounds of grief;
And when October comes, pruning the dragging leaf,
Crying around their cold deserted monuments,
O then the living, curled, encamped within their tents
Of folded sleep must seem to the remembering dead
Thankless and unashamed of the dream-tortured bed
That holds the friendless ones, old frozen skeletons
Honeycombed by worms alive within their bones,
Tongued by the vicious snow, while wormlike ages crawl
Into eternity. If they should dare to call
Who would respond; among the living, who would care:
Who'd bother to replace the tattered flowers there?

And so tonight beside a bright log-lilting fire
If I should see her sit there in the easychair:
Or, some December night, ice-blue, should find her curled
In a corner of of my room, freed from the underworld,
Watching with mother-eyes the child of the dead past,
What answer could I give, taken aback, aghast,
To that unworldly love, and her young running tears
Breaking from sunken eyes, the resurrected years?

1952

LES PLAINTES D'UN ICARE

Lovers of prostitutes are blessed
With cheerfulness and fat content;
While I am riven, broken, bent,
Pillowing cold clouds on my breast.

Stars that possess, command the night,
Glaring out of sunken skies,
Have taken from my gutted eyes
All but the sun's remembered light.

Helplessly following through space
The frontiers of the running air,
Burnt by that red anonymous stare
I feel my wings give up the race;

Broken by beauty, I'll not have
The chance to give my name to this
Final frontierless abyss
Spiralling towards me from my grave.

1952

ELEGY FOR THE DEAD OF *THE PRINCESS VICTORIA*
(1953)

ELEGY FOR THE DEAD OF *THE PRINCESS VICTORIA*

There are more familiar ways of falling out of life—
Sated malignancy, the stalking over;
The silly step and stumble; the tightening scream of wheels;
The pantomime obscenities of war:
And always, in parenthesis, the blenched
Hardening sleep of the dreamer drifting out to death.

Then this now. Arms of wind and water crunching
Life out of the ship, and battening down faces'
Squared incredulous mouths denying their own deaths.
O it can never be fated for us, this freak disaster;
Some agency has gone wrong, or lines have crossed;
The message is not for us, it must be for others
Less real less loving than we are, people we do not know.

Imagine a congregation of mornings rainbowed
With planned and paid-for futures, liquidated
There in the roaming sea; and pleasantnesses,
Quiet attachments like dogs, pictures and books and tables,
The tobacconist's at the corner, the paperboy:
Serene suburban forevers uprooted and tossed
Out into barking distances, whose waves,
Running like wolves, lope to the leaping kill.

This one, perhaps, accustomed all his life
To order and precision (the tidy desk,
Coy petted lawns at home) grieved most at the disorder
Of his departure, snatched by a mindless wind.
While that one, maybe, educated in kindness, cried
Out against the indifference of his ending.
But this unmarried girl, pale dreaming shell,
How could she cope with disaster or fight extinction
With perfume and dances, or snap
Her handbag against the advances of lumbering death?
Much less could this curled child pit life still teething
Against the heretical storm, soft-eyed in greeting,
For whom life had flowed like a window's ribbon of sky,
Whose rooms and gardens were choirs of blossoming faces.

Government of what is, of living and dying,
Of trial and terror, conformist and nonconformist,
Consider in wish's parliament wider than world,

Where in this loose disaster an architecture appears;
Where the chaos of storm is reduced and refined to the sheer
Line of the confident gull cleaving the clouds' confusion.
For what can we say in lieu of a wavering prayer
Blown back from drowning handshakes, recalling Cuchulain's
     rage,
Except to require some greater, some gentler and more coherent
Pattern of meaning than thumb-flicked pennies spinning
From chancer's call to call; and to number them always,
Those scattered names from our hearths, with all that commits us:
To make them our own as much as keys on a ring;
And to carry them always, through every journey and sojourn,
Their weight in the heart's pocket prompting remembrance.

THE HEART'S TOWNLAND
(1947)

WHITE DEATH, GREEN SPRING

CALENDAR
for John Hewitt

I

The echoing boots advance across the world
While, elbow-propped, I ply an intricate trade,
Or walk in sun-slashed lanes where the wind-twirled
Leaf burns into ash beneath the tree.
Asking myself why my days should be spent
In an unbroken scene, I turn to hills,
Serene and slender, each an argument,
And find my shape in them that face the sea
And that flame-tortured continent although
Rooted within these browsing fields of peace.
Now I can feel the birth-pang and the throe
Of dying Europe strike in harmony.

Now as autumn brushes the loose coat
I grow more reconciled to quietness,
And time becomes more truly a remote
Point on a circle whose whole face is truth.
I can accept these hedge-strung sheets of fields
And meet these people whose closed narrow ways
Pricked me to anger, and, behind lowered shields,
Cajole speech from them and a confidence:
For they are part of that great circle's face,
The arrogant blind, tied fast to history,
Beads tight on a string they cannot trace,
Their contours softened in this month of leaves.

As the year lingers, we pause, lingering
By faltering leaf and sun-scorned blackberry,
Striving to recollect one vigorous spring
Heavy with singing and a craze of wings
That broke the whole mind to a single blaze
From centre to the ring's periphery,
But only find stray shafts that crossed our ways,
Thin breaking beams that faltered and were gone
Into the darkness where the sick tirade
Of time straddled by time clashed in the void.

(O Europe in the heart, those voices made
Our songs their mouths, our words their elegies.)

Now for a time this sea-cold land has tied
The dislocated part into the whole,
And I can walk the reddening countryside,
Rejecting symbols for the tottering leaf,
The hardening blaze of autumn in the lane,
The white smoke curling and the labouring man
Planting his spade. For only parts have pain.
The whole swirls with this smoking countryside,
A balanced circle; and our guilt for death
Ebbs with the evening's birds to quieter grief,
Thinning and widening like a lifted breath
Blown by a breeze that hardly shakes a leaf.

II

Yet winter breaks the branches from the tree,
Turning to rend the year that mothered it,
And, through the part, destroys the entity.
The broken branch denies the rooted tree.
Walking that Sunday morning by the harsh
Masked river and the tilted dying trees,
The water blade-sharp in the bearded marsh,
I heard sick Lawrence: Man is a mistake;
The wisest natural order omits man.
Rejecting all that blighted countryside,
I found myself rejecting all that can
And must fall under winter: all that dies
Should never have been born. Then, suddenly,
I saw you pause beside the dying trees
To rip the throttling ivy, soberly
Reprieving venerable chroniclers,
If only for a time. You faced a choice
And sanctioned life within a sodden field,
While I, obsessed by a sick preacher's voice,
Ignored or saw no choice, and let trees die.
But though my heart saluted you I knew
Those who can kill must also learn to die;
The penalty for death is death anew.
—Yet I am guilty of the fallen tree.

Once you were symbol of the arrogant mind,
Cold hand that blighted miracle at birth,

Philosopher of all the noisy blind
Who flouted those who swore they saw the sun.
It might have been so once; but though you still
Assume opinions with your hat and coat
You have an eye to greet the miracle
In all well-rooted things, in child and tree:
In paintings by that honest man, John Luke,
Who wears no corduroy or politics,
But grows potatoes and, no doubt, can cook:
Or in the shining prose of that quiet man
Who flowers into speech because he must,
But forms each petal with an artist's hand,
Who finds the raindrop glittering in the dust
And kingly speech alive in County Down:
In all that's honest, native, relevant.
You have an eye to greet the miracle.
—But here's the brick wrapped in the compliment
I've thrown at you; so listen to me now:
Adopted children remain orphans still;
Life's no poor poet to be patronised:
Thoreau, who taught you to be regional,
Laboured the land you cultivate in verse.
But kinship is enough. Why should I rail
That only I am I; twin-seeking minds
Roam barren ground outside the broken jail,
And Lawrence murdered England for a twin.
I am content now with my family,
An island in an archipelago,
A branch aware of the deep-rooted tree,
Glad that my children all shall bear a name.

III

My thought owes much to that god-crazy man,
The craftsman, William Blake, whose famous rant
Of faith storms stallion-strong across the span
Of decades rotten with heart's decadence:
Who wrung doubt by the neck and upturned safe
Religion's tepid vessels in a rage:
Who testified where others sought for proof,
And turned mirage into reality:
Who taught an arrogant integrity,
Branding his opinions as the truth:
Because of all men he found certainty

In solitude, and made each thought a myth.
O to the end he played a likely part,
Saint or playboy, singing hymns at death.
—Because, too, his intense and reckless heart
Reminds me of that small and arrogant man,
Preacher, painter, poet, spendthrift, wise
And strangely wayward man, my grandfather,
Who taught me to employ a pair of eyes
But failed to teach my rebel hand to draw.
I did not know my grief the day he died.
But when I read how William Blake faced death,
I felt a curious flush of family pride:
For then I recognised my grandfather.
This was the nature of my ancestry:
Square pegs that strove to wrench the round hole square;
These are the myths in my mythology,
Tall candles in my hand that never fail.
Yet, there were others: those shrewd business men
Who settled in a grey-stoned county town,
Attended the cathedral, said amen
In confident response, and owned a vault
That they might carry property past death.
I pay them tribute too; for their kind bred
Responsibility and rooted faith
In all time-sanctioned and traditional things.

These are the varying threads my flesh will knit,
For I contain the rock and rootless fire,
The spendthrift singer and his opposite
Who hums the song but concentrates on trade.
The wildfire must be harnessed to the grate
And prophets trek back from the wilderness
If only to partake in presaged fate.
—The harvest's worthless till it enters bread.

IV

The snowdrops tilt white heads, acknowledging
The fierce spring tapping at the folded roots,
Children of winter and the need for spring.
O tree that breeds upon the lurking skull,
Green spring sings through unresurrected bone.
Fierce tapping spring that crushes out the dead,
I shall remember all who made my own

A dangerous thought, a darting purpose when
Others postured for the gallery cheer
Or shunted tamely to a terminus:
I shall remember that one, grown more dear
And near with death, who made flesh of belief
And squandered all in one contemptuous cast:
For that one I shall carry endless grief
Uncharred by the fierce prairie-fires of spring
Breaking from unresurrected bone,
The lyric rhyming with the elegy.
I shall remember all who died alone
In winter fastness undisguised by spring,
Believing that the death-knot in the mind
Is lifeline to the ultimate bringing-forth,
The birth of that, awaiting life behind
The finger-tips of thought, behind the death-
In-life; alert for answers that are not
Merely complaisant echoes of one's thought.

Cold snowdrops, sad white dancers, poised between
Two seasons' tyranny, I recognise
In this clear beauty's discipline of green
And stark December white the distilled self,
And pause in greeting as the winter dies,
That I may stiffen into discipline
And feel that pruned and certain self arise
To carry frost into the heart of spring.

AUTUMN RISES

Autumn rises with the morning, cold
With tooth of frost and eye of running rain.
The apples fall directly to the ground,
Green inturned eyes, or tilt themselves in bold
Breasts at the window-pane.

The skull moves in the leaves. The chill sun spills
Thinly on road and field and window-pane,
On slated roofs glinting metallic blue,
On flowing streets and the sky's drifting hills,
Their breasts careless in rain.

The skull moves in the leaves, and the bones turn
Sighing in soil at the slow funerals

Of twig and wing, petal and song-braced throat,
For tidefall in the heart, the shadow's stern
Signature on walls.

The dead, uncovered, rise and walk our way,
Leaving a footprint at the water's edge,
A handmark on a gate. Their open eyes
Stare from the coarsening grass; their pale feet stray
Through every boundary hedge.

Autumn uncovers them. The mournful girl
Walks through echoing rooms, her grief unspent,
With tooth of frost and eye of running rain,
Listening for winter with a piper's skirl
Playing a slow lament.

IN THIS THEIR SEASON

Like ambling butterflies the leaves
Swirl and ebb to the ground. Blue smoke
Stands in relief against the sky,
Bedded with moss-like clouds. Cold sheaves
Of sun fold up and die.

This is the season of an evening's grief
When the whole countryside inclines a head
In meditation: when the smoking leaf,
The leaves swirling to soil, disseminate
The mute insidious sadness of the dead.

Withering leaves, the grey hills wilt;
And, sidling near them, the green sea,
Murmuring, craves their company,
Drawing the mists's long quivering quilt
Over each leaf-shaped wave.

Now in this season of the crying heart,
Grief stands to find in the snowfall of leaves
A second dying of the dead, who start
In this their season from their quietude,
Rustling sadly their long, trailing sleeves.

ADVICE IN SPRING

Today the spring walked, scattering sun in pools
Under the windows, stirring the sensual
Heart to reasonless nostalgia.
I, by a window, waited for the call,
The hill-loud shout for me. But nothing came
Above the wheels. Clearly I saw the play
But heard no music. Spring has not the same
Lilt for a mind that winter's disciplined.

There, by a window, dark above the spring,
I thought of winter and its iron heels,
The truest season in the calendar,
And thought, above a churn of market wheels,
Of one dispassionate star poised in the night,
Staring in pools, glinting in window-panes,
God's lidless cruel eye drawn taut and tight
In contradiction of a wayward spring.

I bring no flowers to a bright singing girl,
Brown in the sunlight, laughing in the rain.
I bring the silence of that glittering eye
And shreds of what the mind can entertain
And then reject as wisdom. You who are
Symbol of silence, grave, articulate nun,
O do not watch that cold disastrous star,
And find your silence a mute, broken thing.

A CAROL FOR CHRISTMAS DAY AND EVERY DAY

Holly-fashioned star
Glittering in the tree,
Older than festival,
Cold in eternity,
I watch on Christmas Eve
And wonder that you led
Those men to Bethlehem
Who never comforted

Any christ-cleft heart
Or sorrowing mind that came
Clamped in, cramped with grief,

And felt that cold gaze maim
The wings of life and love,
Ironic Christmas star
That lighted Bethlehem
And war succeeding war.

Cold star of knowledge, star
Older than festival,
Indifferent to a world
Of saint and criminal,
I throw against your cold
Unblinking irony
The poetry of lives
Broken on history.

I cast against all sure
And reasonable thought
Irrational creeds of men
Who spent their days unbought,
And from their ranting lives
Wrought symbols for all time—
Like Christ on Christmas Day,
A clinched and ringing rhyme.

THE SONG CREATES ALL

Hearing the angel's song
Ecstatic in the cloud,
His heart shook off the rust
Of self and blazed out, proud
In answering song that thrust
Out silence with a gong.

William Blake died singing.

All that had blurred the heart,
Dappled clear thought with doubt,
Splintered and broke in song;
Fire that had guttered out
Skirled up, strident, strong.
The whole reclaimed the part.

William Blake died singing.

Beyond brain's right and wrong,
Consumed by song, he burned,
Transformed to song, each part
Trellised with notes that turned
Him to the thing his heart
Praised in a craze of·song.

William Blake died singing.

Scatter the rust and call
The angel from the cloud,
From crazy brains that sing
Hosannas out aloud
On death-beds, fierce as spring,
The song creating all.

William Blake died singing.

PORTRAIT OF A POET

He culled as it were from air
Not their ghosts but smiling presences
Inhabiting gardens and strict avenues:

Reclaimed the freehold from
The limited demise; the parchment's breath
Responded to his greenfingered caress:

And when he died they found
Inside his opened body immigrant
Poems around his hospitable heart.

ELEGY FOR A DOG

This is his day; for now the finger falls
Upon the pencilled calendar. I think
Each date has craters for some grieving mind.
This is his day; and now old sorrows slink
Out from the heart, and I remember him,
And turn again to face catastrophe:
And spit upon the slick and ruthless wheels
That bruise a poem to an elegy.

The laurel in the park that took him in,
Enduring evergreen, a sentinel
Stubbornly standing over an unmarked grave,
Will listen for him; and my sorrow, still
Articulate, reach down to where he lies.
And, recollecting blood upon the street,
I'll walk back through the traffic in the town
And listen to the absence at my feet.

THOR

Big laughing dog, now silent in the sod,
Again death casts the harsh ash in the mouth,
And, stopped in sunlight, one feels in the blood
The signalled question-mark, the finger-flung
Avowal which outcalls the bid of spring.
Stopped suddenly in sunlight, one recalls
The death in every bright familiar thing,
That moment when the challenge outbids spring.

Big laughing dog, stopped suddenly in sun,
Checked at the edge of this clear rippling spring,
I say that life and death emerge from one
Stem in the mind that sees beyond the spring
Rubble of winter where the autumn fell:
I have a message saying each harsh death
Proclaims as brazenly as that church bell
That death is tribute to the arrogant dead.

Never a preacher of an easy God,
Prophet of heaven-release, I greet each death
As mine; the wheels that murder dogs are shod
With my destruction; therefore I say all
Fragments belong to one great unison,
And, dying each strange death, articulate
The ultimate knowledge chiselled in the bone
That death is tribute to the arrogant dead.

THE DEATH OF A CYCLIST

Perhaps a girl was waiting when he was hurled
Headlong at death; wearing new gloves, a favourite scarf,
Anxious to please: anyway, part of his world
That rang its inadequate bell at the tearaway wheels.

Who, patient in rooms or crying out in the fields,
Can indicate the point where their revolution became
Charged with his demise? Round-eyed like a child's
Abandoned hoop they goggled at public blood.

And, petulant, still miles away from fear,
She tapped her foot, till rumour touched her, whispering,
Widening her suburb to a hemisphere,
Blind to the pretty pictures on her scarf.

MANIFESTO

I

Remember all the people you have loved,
To whom you ran with outstretched arms, who turned
And left you, laughter broken on your lips.
With every step we take we are betrayed.

To love is to betray or be betrayed.
With every step we walk upon a grave.
The voices stilled before their time are speaking:
Remember us, they say, betrayed by time.

With every step, they say, we are betrayed.

Remembering all the people you have loved,
The only certain aristocracy,
Accept that one day you will speak for them,
And, speaking, falter, fall and be betrayed.

The dead, those faces lantern-strung through time,
Become your children and your counsellors,
Small footprints leading to the water's edge:
Those gentle people, all betrayed by time.

With every step, they say, we are betrayed.

Daring to speak for them, betrayed by time,
You too will falter, fall and be betrayed.

II

When honourable spokesmen talk of killing
Remember the girl who died because the world
Blasted her love apart. Remember her dying.

When glib mouths talk of nations, think of one
Maddened mind crying there is no God.
Remember the betrayal. Remember the cause.

Remember. The voiceless know the last betrayal,
The blood and crying under the polished words,
The kiss on the cheek, the hearty handshake. Remember

Your dead, betrayed. None but the dead can counsel.
The intellectual man will kill his friends
For subtler reasons than the spokesman's doll;

But he will kill. Trust none but the dead
And heed their counsel. Listen; the dead are speaking:
Remember us, they say, betrayed; remember.

WHITE DEATH, GREEN SPRING

I

Now, glittering river, quiver all your darts,
Hearts-wounders; do not prick the past to blood,
For present past sends time to servitude,
And should be masked, not known. So let the heart's
Wrung elegies ring distantly, for parts
That warp the whole deny a nationhood.
And, sky-grey river, with your tangled wood
Of clouds and trees, where only a stray wing starts
In trespass, yield that early image, me,
Into the custody of the grown man,
Here at the thin swell's edge, and soberly
Record new silence where grief's loose rains ran:
And then create a perfect counterpart
Among the treacherous waters of the heart.

II

So quiet an evening; now, so quiet a field
Of sky, with gentle lambs of loitering cloud:
Mind is fleeced of thought and memory reeled
Down to a spindle. Listen; such a crowd
Of silence at the door. But o no loud
Querulous quietness; now, past's all repealed,
Grief's grasses and thought's thickets pulled and ploughed,
And a new skyscape suddenly revealed.
So quiet a field of silence. You must turn
And follow printed words' appearances
Across a page, afraid that you may learn
Some frigid truth from those cool silences,
And, trespassing upon eternity,
Dissolve like rain into anonymous sea.

III

The new year turns. Jilted by poetry,
I ply my trade and pass an evening,
No longer knit to that reality
That forms a heart in every rooted thing.

The homeless dread the hooves of history,
And all those roads that lead the wandering
Child beyond the hill show widening
Eyes a raging emptiness of sea:

For wisdom has a house. As the year turns,
Computing knowledge, I assess the loss
Of something greater in the certainty
That braced my living then, now as heart learns
How rolling stones, discarding mesh of moss,
Crack in the frost that spares the rooted tree.

IV

Cold clear flower of winter, ring your bell
For the white death and the green echoing spring;
Life between death and birth, o now impel
Minds between life and death to lift and sing

A midway song of being. You who spell
In white, white death, in green, green echoing birth,

And hold them both, a whole: cold flower, tell
The cleft heart that all's rooted in the earth;

That death's only the veering of a wing,
And life a sun-caught wing; that grief and mirth
Traverse the features of an unchanged face.

Teach those who are, now, clear and intricate thing,
Midway between the harvest and the dearth,
To marry both in one familiar place.

THE HEART'S TOWNLAND

HEARTHOLDER

Heartholder of the horizon's sweep,
Deep and steep of it, creek and cove and cave,
Wave and weave of it, lunge and leap
Of salmon-shimmering things, the grave
Plunge of the slender gull, light as sleep:

Only poetry can cast
Shape and sense upon the wilderness
Bewildering us, combing the last
Land- and sea- and sky-line; yes,
Heartholding-folding all things, furled wings, fast.

DIRECTIONS FOR A JOURNEY

Pay small attention to that talkative man.
(God save us from the Irish realist.)
Assume the proper tartan of your clan
And you'll lack few things; mouths you have not kissed,
Anonymous lovers in anonymous towns,
Those books unread, the lives you did not live:
These will not fret, heartscald you once the noun's
Coupled with its appropriate adjective.

Beware of liberated Irishmen
Emerging from potatoes into prose,
Harrowing pages with a squeaking pen,
Giving us Life in vegetable rows.

Mistrust emancipation; liberty's
A word from the caged parrot's party piece.
Turning your back upon the seven seas
Of exile and those famous centuries,

Go out and find the tartan of your clan.
Then all your rhymes will ring, your metres scan.

THE WHITE BIRD

I made a loaf of bread
And scattered it in crumbs
Under the yellowing tree,
For the white bird with the red
Beak and glittering eyes,
Who sits indifferently
Turning a confident head.

I culled old recipes
And made a loaf of bread
And laid out crust and crumb
As bait or sacrifice.
But he humps stony wings:
Pickpocket starlings come;
The quiet rat pillages.

If I could lay a hand
Upon that confident head
And hold those glittering eyes
And come to understand
That unrelenting beak,
I'd silence all those cries
That desolate the land.

MY FATHER HAD A CLOCK

My father had a clock above the stairs.
Punctilious but benevolent, its hands
Had fingers on our pulses, in our pies;
Was like an uncle, or a grandfather
In the spare room, condoning incidents.
And then—I don't know; unaccountably—
A stranger bought it; took it in his car

To foreign parts, like Ormeau or Malone,
And I was left to climb the stairs alone.

I take the measure of my silence, but
Relapse back to a nursery of sound,
Of knitting needles ticking, or a clock
Stitching the ragged corners of the mind.
So, you who know my footstep on the stairs,
And recognise my voice across a room,
Endure the routine of my sentiment,
A sprinter coasting through pentameters,
An anarchist who packages the law;

For, out of bounds, the high-and-mighty hawk
Stands, sun in hand, biding its alien time
To swoop and sweep away our clockwork toys.

TREEFALL

Escaping from the cuckoo-echoing crowd,
I cycled through the park, from grey to green,
Letting my mind run free with grass and tree.
But they had killed the trees, those that had been
My comforters, sure of the travelling sun,
Alive in that black winter, hope of spring.
Now, in the spring, the severed roots clawed air.
O comfortless, leaf-cheated trees, I string
Death upon death, assessing all that fell:
For we inhale the air they might have drawn;
And, owing all the life they might have lived,
Must tear the night apart to reveal dawn.

MEMORY OF A GIRL WITH A RED SCARF

I remember her,
The red scarf at her throat,
Smiling or sad, that time
Between the wars. I stir
Like pages in a book
At thought of her. For now
Time has made a sea
Too wide for those who look
From island's peak to peak,

Sundered by circumstance.
Remembering a red scarf,
I think and cannot speak
As I would speak, or move
Freely through time like those
Who run without a glance
To see, broken, their love.

THE DEAD PRINCE

The flags fly low today because he's dead,
The gentle prince who lived above our town;
Small girls foregather, starry-eyed with tears.
Deflecting windows shepherd sunshine down
Along the straw-hushed breathless thoroughfares.

Old belfries vie with cracked condolences.
Ecstatically, in resonant churches now,
Choirs glorify his name. But, as we pray,
Thoughts scamper off like children, minding how
Gladly he lived and how he is today.

VIRGIN COUNTRY

She has that quality of innocence,
The gravity above the laughing mouth,
The mind unburgled by experience,
Whose north is unpartitioned from its south.
Curbing that orangeman, the intellect,
Who kills the body to preserve the part,
She never fails to watch for and suspect
The mad republic shouting in the heart:
And will not die between the heart and head,
Each hunger-striking for its daily bread.

THE HEART'S TOWNLAND

I

Between cracks in the flagstones flowers grow.
So bright hours flower oddly through the hard
Pavement of my days. I greet you now,

Townland stooked beneath the hill, stored, starred
With fragments of me, fixed to hedge and tree;
I greet you, cottage, corner, brick and bone,
Door and floor of you, gable and brow,
Townland flowing round adopted stone.

To live's to cultivate a wilderness;
To make a garden from anonymous sand.
The solitary man works to impress
His shape upon the timeless, nameless land
That drifts in oceans from his window-pane.
So I have named the heart's townland that owes
Beneath the colours, the conventional dress,
Allegiance to the desert where it grows.

So once again I praise those lonely men
Who stamped their shape upon chaotic things,
And those, less fortunate, who failed to pen
The stampede that destroyed them. My blood sings
Salute to all who signed before they left.
And, most of all, I praise the ones who knew
The sea behind the shells, who sensed again
The presence of the desert out of view.

In Ballyorney I remembered them
In the quiet cottage, under Yeats's lamp.
(Old poet, you and I have tried to stem
The drunken tide, the sly insidious damp
Killing the house.) Out in the starlight paced
Silence the landlord. I remembered then
The idle acres and the thatch aflame
With moss, and those dead necessary men.

II

Ballyorney

May the blue hill that masks your window-panes
Colour the minds of all within your house
And cast a gentle shade of innocence,
Where thought transcends all violence, and ploughs
An intimate acre with wise indolence,
Stranger to plunging horse and lashing reins.

Now read a lesson from indifferent stone:
Aloofness fosters comprehension;
And from a hill one views a whole townland.
The watcher who's a hill's companion
Stiffens to stone the heart's loose shifting sand
And turns the wail of flesh to calm of bone.

I recollect Glencree, that voiceless place
Where nothing moves but the slow tide of air
Swinging a noiseless curtain against time.
Nothing it seems could alter or impair
That quietness—not even the clock's chime
At the hand's fatal move on the blind face.

But one implacable memory plucks at thought,
Bringing the challenge of that honest mind,
Of one who took the sick world for a cross,
Forsaking all that's intimate and kind,
And died, in the conviction that the loss
Was small beside the chaos that she fought.

I move between two worlds: between Glencree
And the self's courted, murderous Kinsale
Coiled in the burning centre of the ring,
The ultimate betrayal of the Gael
To the fierce fires of Europe whose flames fling
Fingers that scorn the crust's identity.

So I can write a blessing for that place—
Smooth apple of silence, ignorant of the worm,
The coil of fire that sears the passionate heart:
Weather means calm as well as violent storm.
I move between two worlds; for now all's part
Of the white death on that remembered face.

III

But in this northern county, nearer time,
The clock ticks louder and the landlord comes
Hourly, in silence, measuring stick and stem.
Sir, I have paid. Remember the gross sums
Of sorrow, grief's black currency, despair's
Extravagance on unrepentant men.
Sir, I have paid; and though the coppers chime
Gently now, I still rent breath and brain.

IV

Cushendall

Staying with the poet and his wife
In their small fat house beside the glens,
I learned the virtue of those milder moods,
Shaped by knowledgeable innocence,
Where thought and aspiration dwell in peace:
The strange necessity of being kind,
Punctilious even, among violence:
Of keeping house within a well-built mind.

Tenuous, like a spider's web, the fields
Tinted the rain; at loaneñ heads an eye
And ear attended as we passed; drear fowl
Scattered like thrown grain; and one small sly-
Shy child received our greeting cautiously
And wondered after us till the road turned.
Glen-grooved and hillocked, those calm townlands lie
In confidence where history broke and burned.

So the white smiling nun, the carpenter
Who'll take no orders as to how he'll ply,
The painter painting pictures that he'll sell
Without a dealer to a passer-by,
Carry that knowledgeable innocence,
The balanced blade that sheaths itself with style—
O supple grace—embracing the wild cry
Of stricken things and the proud hunter's smile.

V

So the townland emerges from the thought
Of all I loved, the grooved heart's ancestry
Of proud and foolish people whose lives fought
The masks and gloves of glib society,
Those I have praised before, my counsellors.

I learn my pattern in the wilderness,
The hills and valleys balanced in my mind,
Fields stooked with purpose. Now I can assess
The harvest, recollecting those who signed
Before they left to map the barren sand.

FORREST REID

I

He would burn his books and gladly die
If, levelling those walls that hem his mind,
He, mountain-shouldered, sky-proud, could with eye
Moon-raised unmask time's metaphors and find
The naked features of eternity.

To break or blend with time? The question ran
Grooving his years till, grieving, he discerned
No answer waited for the dying man.
Now, spurning thought, the icy mind has turned
For alms from heaven, bread conjured from stone.

II

I would tell you if I knew.
The gull signs the air, but you
Stand at windows wondering
What mystery conceived the wing.

I would break the clouds and show
The circle's face, the ebb and flow
Of time and that eternity
Which gnaws and nags at you and me.

I would make your death a song
Of meaning, old man, with a throng
Of explanations round your bed.
O I would ease your haunted head.

Since revelation at the end
Is all you ask death to extend,
Time itching for eternity
Shrugs off your mild apostasy.

A SONG FOR VICTORY NIGHT

The bonfire lights the foolish faces; sky-
Rockets reel and plunge with dripping fins;
Patriotic music floats and falls:
The small bomb loses and the big bomb wins.

Listen, trees, stern in the star-lost light,
As rich wood crackles in the victory fire.
The catherine-wheel goes crazy with delight.

There was a victory. How much was lost
Under the rubble of the rabble's slum.
(O past, avenge through me the blasted heart.)
The drunken citizen bangs on his drum,
The draught-board mind square-patched with black and white.
Burning wood, o past: churchillianly
The catherine-wheel turns circles in the night.

I watch the scarlet fire consume the sky,
The branches writhing in the murderous flame.
(Hamburg, Rotterdam and Coventry,
People and cities, named, without a name,
Replenish pity in us that will fight
With white, white waters continents of fire.)
The catherine-wheel drops suddenly in flight.

INTERLUDE IN MAY

*

May, green month, unbroken field of sun,
Proud head of blossom, sky-remote and chill
With certainty of line, the pattern won
From winter: now complete the miracle
In thought as well as thing. Summer delays
A year, a lifetime, in the frosted mind
Whose knowledge outgrows wisdom, picks and frays
The pattern into rootless strands of wind.
May, present features of eternity,
Tear from thought's calendar December's dates
And write up *Summer, May and unity*
Among all opposites, bringing all states
Within the boundaries of a fulfilled heart.
That leaf the fingers touched fell to the ground;
The girl turned at the gate and said Depart:
O ring the going and the coming round
With boundaries of an undying heart.

The blossoms whiten on the fulfilled bough,
Treble choirboys singing for a bride.

Heart: where is the word, the answer now?
(The peach tree blossomed when the brown dog died.)
Wait until autumn when the landscape's reaped
Of sight and sound and stored behind the brain,
Till all has given, and the harvest's heaped
Sun-heavy in the heart; then, with the rain
That writes off summer, comes the utterance.
The leaves that widen on the upright tree
Fall into song with summer's decadence.
(The song's the time-birth of eternity.)
May, green month, white head of sun, green-eyed,
Within this leaf, this petal on the hand,
Lies all the history of a countryside,
And, in the mind, eternity's townland.
The peach tree blossomed when the brown dog died.

I

Waiting for the note to chime,
Lacing her with harmony,
In drawing-rooms she passes time
Until the tune shall set her free.

But if the tune should fail, the note
Be late in sounding, her light ways
Will darken, and through shapeless days
Wilt like a forgotten coat

That is not worn but hangs always
Behind a door where no one goes
Except perhaps a child who strays

Upstairs to play: who stops to pose,
Coat-draped, before a glass, and grows
Aware of the dark mirror's gaze.

II

Ask what relevance she has
Within a starving continent
To minds bewildered by the grass
And weary weeds of argument

(The intellectual wilderness
Where thought has killed the root's belief).

She is irrelevant unless,
Remaining like the year's last leaf,

Asserting shape, she learns to pass
Beyond mere linear content
Into the leaves' anonymous mass

Trusting the summer to redress
The pure line made exact by grief
For the wide world's shapelessness.

III

All this sunshine falls
On an indifferent mind
Bereft of miracles
Daylighting the blind.

Miracles emerge
Shell-like from history,
Thrown up with the surge
That builds immaculately

From drifting particles;
Those particles submerge
To attain unity.

But, mind, when will the verge
Of shore rise from the sea
Glittering with shells?

IV

The sun of greatness stands
Immensely in the air.
If I could pluck these hands
And direct that stare

Beyond the wicked gaze
And roundabouts of sense,
From the dividing ways
That murder innocence

In all flagged frontiered lands,
I'd put an end to days
That ring as thin as pence

When the stern sunlight preys
Upon my indolence,
My dry unpeopled sands.

V

Casual words spoken
Dying in echoless air
Too often betoken
Landslides of despair

Entombing the trapped heart.
So much remains unsaid
When feet turn to depart
As to impel the dead

To rise, bereft, unspoken.
The whole shrinks to a part
And heart's sold out by head

Within a penny mart
Of soiled words, when, half said,
We die, with death unbroken.

VI

End it now. Let this green day—
May's last days are dear to me—
Fold and carry it away
Into anonymity:

Who but the blind will lead the blind?
Give the falling petals to
The latent justice of the wind.
End it now, and write adieu

To the face behind the mask;
End it now as the months end,
Invisibly, in sleep, and ask

Soberly for grace to move
Intently selfwards and defend
The nameless centre of your love.

*

June comes in with thunder and white rain.
The gutters swarm; and girls with shining hair
Keek from drooling trees; the cellophane
Glitter of rain sheathes the heavy air
But cracks upon the road in mercury veins
That sketch strange maps upon the blackened stone
And jigsaw wildly into seething drains.
On such a day one can learn much alone
Under a tree, watching the waters boil,
The sailing twigs, a shoulder-shrugging hedge.
There, in the kicking rain-hooves, in the coil
And whirl of watery things, at the frayed edge
Of housed society, the mind takes stock
Of rows of gestures and loose straying words
Crowding within the years; of stress and shock,
And happiness as transient as birds,
Unhandled, failing, running out of stock.

All that has been said, enacted, thought,
Remains unlived in me; that flustering twig,
Jerked by the water from the gutter's drought,
Is each purposeless day: the foolish jig
And jog of it the drifting to an end.
Rain, white rain: o lean, impersonal rain,
Drowning the broken twig, what shall defend
The ignorant part against a world's disdain?
The gutter gathers up the arid days
And I go sailing with the rootless thing,
Forgetful of all free and natural ways,
Forgetting what first caused the throat to sing.
But now a ragged bird headlines the sun
And I move home, italicised upon
The glittering pavement where, reflected, run
The broken images of tree and stone,
Till all is claimed by the cloud-cleaving sun.

THE UPLAND FIELD
for John Boyd

I

Walking with the schoolmaster
About the Antrim countryside
—Lilac hills, remember me—
I bid my sentries stand aside
And let the green air fraternise
With the resistance in my mind,
The sombre look-outs in my eyes;
And tell the hedge, the tree, the field,
The ditch-flowers in the stony lane,
To conjure from the dayligone
Not just a symbol but a sign.
Though his unspeculating mind
Is credulously sceptical,
His lumpish dicta passwords for
The village intellectual,
He's sensitive to the stylish hills,
The Mournes' perpetual marathon
From peak to corrugated shore,
Among the baronies of Down.
And I, who share his countryside,
—Leafshot roads, remember me—
Endorse his speech and silence at my side.

II

The play has changed since that first night
I argued with his obstinate gate,
And faced him in a bookish room.
The atlases are obsolete;
And city pulled tooth after tooth
Spew their bad blood, and citizens
Expelled from sheltering parables
Follow the tracks of violence.
The boots have hammered out new moulds
From forms we counted permanent;
And now that reason holds its head
Images outface argument.
William Blake meant what he said
When he denied the world was round,
With hallelujahs in the stars

And amens on agnostic ground.
Create a world, or suffer theirs,
Quiescent in the hinterland.
The portly figure ruminates
Over autumnal rust, a hand
Chopping each punctured phrase,
As on that summer night when death
Was still a book-word, and the wind
From Europe carried flowers in its breath.

III

I know these people, and disdain
Much that I know: the snarl of drums
Fouling an April evening;
Tight fist and tighter mouth; the slums
Of bigotry, suburban cant;
The stagnant ruts in the the townland:
These were my childhood. But in time,
Though hostile, I may understand,
And retrospectively regret
A moon-meshed bridge, a crying tram,
These roads above the market town,
And call them home; for these I am.
Yet, hostile, I'll identify
With form and substance far away
From ghetto-thinking, tribal lore,
Still young enough to find a way
To the high hill that grips the sun
And holds its harvest in the hail.
So, walking with the schoolmaster
Past sights that grow more vulnerable
In the advancing night, I draw
The scene around me, naming friends
Who've fought the clockwork soldiery
And all that earns death's dividends;
—Grave-locked ones, remember me—
For the wind about the hill
Grows hoarse with voices that deny
The upland field we hope one day to till.

IV

Walking with the schoolmaster
About the poignant countryside

—Violet hills, remember me—
I put my wary guard aside
And tell heart to memorialise
Pianoforte of the rain,
The cut-out shadows on the grass,
Smoke hankering from the Lisburn train;
And furbish old alliances
Between the living and the dead
—Grave-locked ones, remember me—
Against the victories ahead,
Heart's isolation and despair,
Corruption seeping into lives
Entrenched in attitudes of war,
The bandaged flags strung up again.
So, walking with the schoolmaster,
Learning by rote a countryside,
I watch and measure. Look; the stir
Of branches in the hillside field
Beckons; and silhouetted clear
Against a watercolour sun
The truthful tree stands calm and sheer
Beyond complexities of time.
I watch and measure while the sky
Accepts the night—*remember me*,
White upland field—and the last bird slips by.

FLOWERS FOR A LADY
(1945)

MEMORY OF A TOWN

ELEGY FOR A SIXTH-FORMER

Collating memories of you, with your hair
Amazed like candles staggering in the air,
Big hands cut out perhaps for taming fields
Yet handy too with words, I look with a child's
Concern at the dismantling of our world,
Hearing the hiss of tiny butts you hurled
Into the simmering burn, o then, before
This surfacing delinquency of war,
Where I'm the bounder, a remove away
From your correct if tepid loyalty:
And fasten souvenirs of glance and phrase,
A jotter's sketches, while your mocking face
Obliquely glimmers from a hand-cupped flame,
Snatching a breather from a dirty game.

EARLY CASUALTY

He'll watch the moon, unplaiting distances,
Ride out to take a roll-call of the stars.
Hills stand alert; the mild subservient fields
Wait in the mist, tholing the needling rain.
Now he is one with them, being underground.
His eyes smoulder in hedges; inquiring hands,
Unlatching branches, buttonhole the flowers,
Death cast off now that recollection's gone
To earth among the absentminded hills;
And, primitive as grass, he has become
Close with the soil and its accomplices
That use the moonlight's silhouettes and shades,
Moving at night, to draw his body home.

ELEGY FOR A NONCOMBATANT

I

June's like a girl out skipping in the street,
Indifferent to the bric-a-brac of war.
Disaster's still a headline, not as yet
Tanks slit-eyed in the town, boots at the door.
But o my friend
Is wheeled into a polished room to die.

Now that he has become
A leaf turned over on a calendar,
The educated conscience will require
An explanation, and a balance sheet
That tots the good days and subtracts the bad;
But what name do you give the auditor?
The young disdain us who attend their graves.

II

Death is no stranger but it brings new tears
That ridicule the clerics' promises.
Affection is an open city for
Maverick mayhem called an Act of God.
And just, as when
On the night of the first siren we glibly walked
Out from the cinema to the ambushed streets
And ran like rats under the caterwaul,
So now,
I run defenceless through an abandoned dark
Subway under a no-man's-land, alone,
Seeking and fearing the ambivalent light:
Till, probating his life, unearthing cards
Postmarked with blue sea-towns, now sad ghost towns
With promenades abandoned to the sea,
I turn from picking out those journeys'-ends
Congealed in snapshots, to a close-up of
Obedient citizens wound-up for war.
Put plaster on the cut. The wound is mine;
But their infection is not my disease.
His absence clings like an amulet on my breast.

III

Hence, since remembrance probably will last
Longer than the short sum of his years,
Let me essay
To polish and keep sharp
The knives of anger, pity, vigilance.
The dead accuse us who walk on their graves.

ENNISKERRY

Township of spires, incardinated trees,
What greeting have you for a traveller
Walking down from a war? Under your walls,
Built to define and safeguard privilege,
I think of earlier wars, and tap the stones
Hoarding their stories, and tread cobbles hoarse
From crying out against the armies. Late
Primroses at the roadside touch my feet.

Walking from war through unconscripted streets,
I turn from unapocalyptic door.
Who would reply if I demanded bread?
Or if, indeed, I asked for sanctuary?
Town of unthreatened spires, beneficent trees,
What comfort have you for a traveller
Walking from history to mythology,
And back again to darkness, where the streets,
Blacked-out at night, dream of the lamplighter?

ST. STEPHEN'S GREEN, DUBLIN

The north lies backward in a fold of time.
I send you greeting from the singing south
Where there is sun and unselfconscious laughter.
I send a twisted sentiment of love,
A foreign flower in your bleak winter garden.
I send you greeting from a strange city
Where talk stands in for and usurps the deed,
And brash moons seek out lovers in the trees,
Bringing no fear, where there is time to love.

But I who walk these places carry death
Curled like a worm in the brain, twisting the eye,

Sharpening the casual word with bitterness.
No country owns a mind that's dispossessed.
Say sick Cuchulain fought his wars alone.

Old city, with a young girl's face,
Your mask is foreign to my broken streets.
Your easy laughter mocks the living dead.
Take heed of history, for I have seen
Such as you broken and swept away
As the sea smooths the footprints from the sand.
With all your wisdom, still remember this.

City of light and laughter, squares and trees,
Proud with the arrogance of history,
Serene as rainfall on dry summer leaves,
Recall how cultures, loves and histories
Drop with gulls into the quiet rivers
To float, face down, into anonymous seas.

I, watching your roof tops and emphatic spires
By greying windows, or, seated, looking
Into tree-green waters holding birds
And hair-gold weeds, mirroring leaves and children,
Have looked for self-engagement, but have found
Little or nothing more, no, nothing more
Than the acceptance of an easy lie,
That some must live and laugh and others die.

You who remember history, recollect
That history moves like rivers into seas,
Accepting no horizons: that its strands
Of generous sun and dancing limbs are drowned
Or spattered with white shipwreck, whiter bones.
This is an island out of step with time.
Listen to other city sounds at night:
Bombs in the north, the stampede to the hills.

The north lies backward in a fold of time,
Behind unhurried hills and running fields,
Uncertain in their humour as a girl.
I send you greeting in a strange country,
Where only those who love can hope to live,
Where this grey city raises lighted eyes
Out to the river and the anchored sea,
Where only those who love can learn to hope,

Where you crouch black and listening by the hill
Marked at day by quick white wings of gulls;
Where I walk neutral streets alive to war,
And counter war-stressed streets with calls to peace.
I send you greeting in a time of war,
When only those who love can dare to live,
When only those who love will never die.

LETTER TO A BOY IN PRISON

I who walk in the sun,
Seize hope by eager hands,
Talk with friends, hold
Quick stolen dregs of laughter
To the quivering mouth, fold
Unhappy hands in prayer,
Nervous as moths, for you
And victims everywhere.

I send the green of the trees,
The various looks of the flowers,
The rippling run of the hills
And the fields at peace with the world.
Across relentless walls
I send the love you have missed,
The smiles you failed to find,
The mouths you might have kissed.

I send my faith and yours,
Quiet as September skies,
Sure that the day will see
In the flesh our dream of the night:
Sure that the day will free
The lives immured from the sun,
And open the door of your cell,
And the prison that holds us all
Dumb like a muffled bell.

EPITHALAMIUM

So you are married, girl. It makes me sad
At heart to think that you, last summer held
Between hot hands on slow white afternoons,

Whose eyes I knew down to their blackest depths
(Stirred by the indolent smile and the quick laugh)
Are married now. Some man whom I have not seen
Calls up the smile and the laugh, holds in his hands
The welcoming body, sees in the darkening eyes
Sufficient future in a shaded room.
I wish you well. Now, with twin-set and pearls,
Your girlhood gone, that summer on your skin,
You'll settle down, keep up appearances.
I, wed to history, pray for your peace;
That the smile be never twisted in your mouth,
And the pond of your mind never be rippled with sorrow:
That you may sleep your sleep as the world quakes,
And never see the chasms at your feet.

LETTER FROM THE MOURNES

From the cupped peace of these aloof
Uncertain hills, a quiet hint
Of a corner-lurking past, the leaf
Murmuring on the wary tree,
I pen with glib erratic point
Irrelevant lines to the squat city
Dour in its suit of dust, the blunt
Thunder of traffic lulling your room,
Booming a grotesque lullaby.
(Here the wheels are out of time,
Like a drift of smoke loose on the sea.)
Here, in the mountains, where a crazy folk
Coax the sullen soil to yield,
Whose prayers are that the weather walk
Softly, sitting on a stone
In the middle of a lean, mean field
Where a rabbit goggles and is gone,
The silver sheep silent and cold:
Watching the soft sweet swoop of the hills,
I nurse a vague nostalgic prayer,
Slow as the stammer of lame stone walls,
For a golden harvesting this year:
Pray that a miracle may flower,
Though the seeds are wrong, and the soil is sour.

LINES WRITTEN NEAR DOWNPATRICK AFTER AN AIR-RAID

Riparian fields, tidal with spring,
Daffodil-debonair clouds in a slow
Swan-processional river. Look:
Alternatively, there's moored
The island's matching miniature.

But I interpolate
A personal point of view,
Of rubble in the street
Last Easter Tuesday.

On an abandoned quay
Where barges unhumped merchandise,
The bargees loose in the town with tales
For unbelieving girls, new pennies for children,
The only pennants now
Are condescending gulls:

Where I, at my summer's edge,
Caught up by history,
Eyes on the river's clouds, recall
How the souls of the Irish soldiery
Passed in a slow salute of geese.

THE MONK

Back in the twists of time
    A monk frowned in his cell,
Chasing a truant rhyme,
    Cupping the bubble-laughter
Of a white-throated summer.
    Now, a history after,
It is his tale we tell
    Of the looped language of birds,
The athletic stride of the hill,
    Quick wings uncaged by words.
Spirals of laughter spill
    From summer's shaking throat,
Mocking our elegies,
    And the pleas we put
Up to our fathers' God.
    O taste the irony

Of this stout summer, shod
    With quiet shoes of peace.

PAUL ROBESON

The summer faltering, and the town
Mending its shutters for the storms,
With glimpses through the skiffing rain
Of Donegal across the bay,
And Scotland when the early mist is blown,

I've shaped my thoughts to discipline
Nostalgic areas of the mind,
And watch a wave's imperious fin
Import white anger to the shore,
Retreat, submerge, and shoulder back again:

And, dwelling on my hankering days
When wish-world was a rockcut sea,
And poems were rushed messages
Like notes in bottles children send
Out solemnly on summer holidays,

Confident that the sea will bear
Them buoyantly to promised lands,
For some lost cause, some rightful heir—
Say that your proud dark songs have crossed
Far more than the Atlantic getting here.

THE DOG

Hardened to war's enormities
I watched a dog snap at a fly,
Leaving it dead and cold; and this
I judged against brutality
And subtler forms of violence
Planned and designed painstakingly
At armslength from the massacre.
Unthinkingly, instinctively,
He killed for sport, whereas we claim,
And stand for anthems to insist,
That God has also placed his hands
On weapons that the bishops blessed.

THE HOUNDS

But he had seen her naked on a hill
High over Ireland, uninhibited limbs
Firm in the windblown grass, free from the nets,
The hunters and the sleek contemptible
Hounds trained to hunt what masters nominate.
Or he had seen her so once in a dream,
Immaculate as Christmas-morning snow;
And held that private image of her. But
They've trained her too to carry out their part,
And she goes hunting with the masters now,
And she will lead them to his quietude
And watch them put a bullet in his heart.

NORTH-ANTRIM PROSPECT

Treading the shallowy offshore,
The sea's set for America;
Or chafes in turquoise harbours for
The tidal tug to avid distances.

Round the sky's elbow Donegal
Colours the rain, its swimmer's arm
Bent towards the intellectual
Brow of the White Rocks and the sinking sands.

Here mind is rationed to the bare
Essentials, and your eyes will graze,
With local gulls from the cold air,
On rocks awash with unforgiving sea.

THE ISLAND OF SAINTS AND SCHOLARS

Loud and tedious argument,
Words borrowing similar words have bent
This country crooked, until what
Once was firm is wormed with rot.

Now we have only elegies
To mark those seven centuries;

Now we have merely mouths of wind
And senseless echoes in the mind.

And now the orange and the green,
Whatever they may once have been,
Are prostituted to the cant
Of candidates for parliament.

We have betrayed them one and all.
The Dublin intellectual,
The Belfast bigot, have become
The character of Irishdom.

SIXES AND SEVENS

'Art is unconcerned with politics.'
(Concurring hands lift smartly in applause.)
'Sonnet and senate cannot intermix.'
(Poetic justice has no valid laws.)

So we have built up separating walls
Between each room, and, labelling every door,
Have answered only the familiar calls,
Oblivious to the rats beneath the floor.

THE ORATOR

'Remember Pearse,' he said; 'if we
Lose Irish we lose Ireland.' They
Looked and listened stupidly
Like country folk on holiday.

If Yeats were still alive maybe
He could breathe vigour into clay,
Conjure an aristocracy,
And add grandeur to decay.

But he too is accountable
For this dull audience, for he
Was often irresponsible
In bartering all for poetry.

I've read, and heard some people tell
Of petty spite and tyranny,
For psychic sight and psychic smell
Both failed to teach him charity.

If Yeats were still alive maybe
Ireland would cut a dash again
In politics and poetry,
And noncomforming Irishmen.

We need another death. Who knows—
Before the resurrection—
Instead of arrogance and pose
We'll need a Sheehy-Skeffington.

DUBLIN TO BELFAST: WARTIME

Dublin left, with its uncensored lights
Careless of retribution from the skies,
Unreprimanded and insouciant streets,
A goodnight's sleep and morning unimpaired:

You tunnel back to war, where licit light's
A swinging arm redeeming the night sky,
Grabbing for midges dancing in the dark
Over the braced and vulnerable town:

Sobered from extravagance of lights,
Adjusting to the place's temperament,
The brazen gantries and the querulous gulls
Harsh from the islands occupied by storm.

MEMORY OF SAND

In August, on familiar strands, the sea
Sweeps up the summer's leavings; and the wind
Monopolises shelters on the hill
Where he so lately stood to watch,
Behind the islands, shipshape for the night,
The shrinking boats depart;
While, secretly, his disengaging blood
Prepared its own goodbyes.

Romantic word that lacks a synonym,
O heart, recalcitrant heart: the sun's regard's
A ricochet from a dark hinterland,
And light a look-out on the hill;
And you must hoard your unconscripted days
For peacetime pilgrimage
Back to a battleground whose sandy graves
Are bandaged by the sea.

PORTRUSH

I came to you first as a solitary child,
And built a castle with a seaweed lawn,
And then created continents and seas.
Across where Donegal extends an arm
I thought of shipwrecked Spanish mariners
And galleon-treasure glowing in the depths.

Yes; I have given and received in marriage.
My past is laid quiet on a lap of sand.
You who survive the Atlantic storms and smuggle
Sun yearly from Europe, crowned with gulls,
You hold my sighing tides chained to your shores,
Where seas lay down and stretched out paws to play.

Now at the season's end, when clouds become
Barrage balloons alerted by the wind,
And sun deserts the sea, and the slow march
Of death quickens in Europe and beyond,
I put away my bucket and my spade,
And store my shells and pebbles in a jar.

FLOWERS FOR A LADY

FIRST ELEGY

I

Now autumn pauses in these Antrim lanes,
Pulling the red leaves idly, one by one,
The first frosts visible in morning fields

When hills seem bowed in prayer and mists wheel
Under the branches, scattering from the sun.

The beautiful is the most sorrowful,
Lacking eternity. The tree that falls,
Broken and splendid on a wind-torn hill,
Cradled in grass, falls in the murmuring heart,
Leaving the black wound there, while the lost leaves
Lift children's frightened faces, dispossessed.

Now as the last leaves fall her eyes are closed.
She, who was beautiful, is in the trees,
And her beauty falls with the leaves, her sudden smile
Brightens the clouds that stare from hill to hill,
Over the damp fields and the white, patched farms,
Hands acquiescent, those quick eager hands
That nurtured me, and worked for others too.

But somewhere, on a pale twist of a road,
She could be walking towards an unknown town,
Past unnamed fields and unfamiliar hills,
Nervous maybe, and maybe quite alone
When evening thickens and the night draws on;
Carrying memories of this other town,
Its knotted roads and wayward countryside,
And mornings flowering in the passive trees
That outlive all the storms that humble them.

II

I pray for her who does not need my prayers,
Having been better than I, blown by a faith
To incandescent flame. But I can pray
Against an onliness, with anxious prayers
Widespread before her on the empty road,
Bearing an accent of the place behind:
Of grey-faced people wondering at death
Behind drawn curtains in bewildered rooms.

As autumn closes round her funeral,
Tell every stone she walked to say her name,
Tell every blade of grass to turn to flame
And light green candles for her journeying.

III

No one can hurt her now. For it is they,
The rogues and hypocrites who've passed away,
And she alone remains, inviolate.
Her epitaph, if any, will be found
Outside conventional stone and formal words:
Her elegy is all these fading fields
And all these leaves waiting for burial.

They cannot hurt her now her hands are still.
They cannot hurt me when the heart is cold
As the last leaf impatient for the soil.
Her being lies within me like a shell,
Chill and complete, having no need of me.

IV

While I could go and stand upon a hill,
Or lay my head upon a stone and weep,
I hear her say one must not think of death
As more than the turning of a hill-caught road,
Or with less promise for the traveller.

Yes, we can live and wipe away our tears,
Each in his cell behind the flesh and bone,
Convention raising eyes at public grief.
I could not share her suffering though I tried,
And all my prayers were tainted with myself.
But she, being good, transcended flesh and bone,
And, dying every death, had nothing left
To save herself when darkness turned to her.

V

Keep a place for her at the victory
Procession of the prematurely dead
Bringing the exiles home, when all her kind
Walk back to summer from their sufferings,
The angry and compassionate, who weep,
The unhailed aristocracy of pain.
Now the last leaf may fall outside my heart
That holds her beauty singing like a shell,
The quiet voice of her that cannot die:

The gentleness of the shy English girl
Who married into this crazed, sterile land
And bore a son in hope, though rifles spoke
Against his future in the ambushed streets:
The quick lilt of her laugh, and images
Of tilted head and hair; and, towards the end,
The dark fixed look of pain, the tired hands,
And the child's eyes menaced by closing walls.

Now the autumn mourns her burial,
And each slow leaf sighs to her formal grave,
Seeking its springtime in the warmer soil
And all the martyred wisdom of the flowers,
And the grave music of migrated birds.
Now as the year attends her burial,
Let some hushed history await her birth.

SECOND ELEGY

It is strange that I have died while you live on
Although I walked behind your funeral
On that late afternoon when silhouettes
Reached out for apronstrings of sunlight; strange
That I have died while you still follow life,
Spinning new thought, building new histories;
For I sit stiffly with an empty mind
And cannot help myself. O it is strange
That I your child have died, and a new man
Waits to be born in pain in a raw world,
Utterly alone and pitiless:
Having confronted history in the raw
With bitter men and fools; having suppressed
Continuing sorrow and the wounds of love.

The pity is not in death, but in the dying:
For the dead, we're told, unfold in their own time,
Resume continuance of the journey home.
So I shall lift no voice against your going,
But send godspeed on your strange travelling
Into the infinite you recognised,
A patient pilgrimage into the light,
And shall not weep that you have grown so strange.

THIRD ELEGY

Winter deepens, and the first snows come,
Hurrying on the hills, carrying shrouds
To cover the dying land. Stripped branches loll
Like scarecrows on horizons of cold hills
Frozen in flight down to the temperate sea.
Death is indeed living reality,
Wiping identity from flesh and mind,
All evidence of an autonomous soul.
How shall I know her then without her voice,
Her eyes and hair and quick impatient hands,
And all that made her rare, or recognise
The strangeness of her? Maybe it is true
That time brings like to like, and love can draw
Each similar heart into one dwelling place.

Having no proof of immortality,
I can believe in the unravelling
Of each slow coil of time, trusting the truth
That grew within me from the earliest days,
Spreading an actual warmth behind the mind.
For even the tin soldiers at their wars
And mumbling multitudes that acquiesce,
Follow their history; even the stones
Harbour a latent immortality,
Holding the seeds of god in unspent flower.

Christ happens more than once in history.
For he is the high lip of the swollen wave,
And we are troubled particles of foam,
Broken at tide-fall, seeking the surge again,
Sundered by islands and dry continents;
Praying for flood-time and a brimming sea
Unsucked by ebb or marred by grey tide-fall,
God walking the shining acres, being home.

She who was warm is gone beyond me now.
But the great part of her can never die,
For life's too busy tending running wounds
To squander what's been wrested from the dark.
Now she is gone beyond my present reach,
And I surrender her to history.

FOURTH ELEGY

Now the last leaf has melted to the ground,
And death has taken over. Acquiesce,
Resistance over, and the last flag down.
Let there be death then; for these hardening eyes
Find in the stiffening days symbolic grief,
A pageant of the mind. Let no bird rise
Sheer from the fields, or beads of blossom clasp
The branches' vibrant throats, or drips of sun
Conjure to movement stone and the limp grass,
Easing the buds' tight fists, or children move,
Crackling the moment like green crusts of ice,
Breaking the image of a funeral.
Let there be silence while with folded hands
We harden, expiating tragedy.
Let there be death, and let us bow to death,
And see no strangeness in the face that swam
Into her failing eyes, or be afraid
Of lesser things than the mind's widening loss.

FIFTH ELEGY

Children's carols tinge the air
And ebb on the wind back to the hills'
Stern querulous lips; and here and there
A star stares, and the swinging moon's
A toy light on a Christmas tree.
I wait for the voices coming. Soon
They'll unfold on the road, each pale throat taut,
Fraught with nostalgia. By the fire,
I shall remember how they brought
Her a carol a year ago,
Grouped in the garden under her room,
In salutation; and I know,
When they come nearer, that my brain
Will stiffen, and nervous thought turn cold,
Darkened with swelling clouds of pain
And smoking anger. I shall go
Into another room and stand
Cold in its emptiness, and grow
Helplessly sad like a sick child.

SIXTH ELEGY

The sky is terrible with stars,
Souls, they say, that stare towards home,
Still tugged by memory; and some
Nervously flicker, so that tears
Pulse in the wind-cold trees and light
Shadows of hedges, and the dog
Scampers ahead, while I still tug
Unanswering bells, asking the night
For word of her who died too young
One day when leaves marched to their graves
Slowly, making no sound, dark waves
Breaking into the soil. My tongue
Rears with a bitterness of grief,
The words cold in my brain, like stars
That stare and cannot speak, small scars
Of pity, each a shattered leaf.
Somewhere in this dim night she moves
Seeking her place, and her star talks,
While this limp body blindly walks
Cold in its accustomed grooves,
Bounded with silence. O has she
Grown merciless in death, or are
These ears afraid to hear her star
Singing its way in history?

SEVENTH ELEGY

The evening softens. The sky smiles, and birds
Sing after rain; and the heart replies.
Always the resurrection. Eyes
Are burgled by light, and the cry behind the words
Curls and withers away. I come and stand
Outside my grief, a winter's sun
Gloving an aggressive hand,
Clenched against fact. Watching the stumbling run
Of hill and cloud, I feel death lurch away
Like clouds rollicking from hill,
Cloud after similar cloud until
Only the long blue spine remains. I pray
Pardon that I can live, although her death
Is drilled into my bone. The way
Ahead, and all experience,
Shall have the dark depth of an elegy.

EIGHTH ELEGY

Spring sighs in the soil. Perplexity
Of growth nudges the trees. Dark, rush-crowned fields
Shudder with sun, the pale grass flustering
Tremulous arms, flexing muscles free.
Spring breaks in the mind, spattering blood,
Prising the closed grief wide. Now comes a time
When surge of bud and blossom, sun and song,
Practise invasion. Today I stood
Watching two lambs blink at infinity,
And failed to recollect or recognise
The once-abrupt significance; for now
Death has drained familiarity
From place and time; and, unresigned,
I cried against the sun's clumsy caress,
Asking for darkness, sculptured quietness,
Another door to close and hide behind.

Spring ventures, uninformed, making its rounds;
Knocks at the door in passing, leaves
Flowers for a lady, waves, and hurries on.
But now the house is changed; behind
Plaster and brick death's set up residence;
And when the chatter fails,
You'll overhear from brown and yellow lanes
The leafing-over of an elegy.

November 1943-March 1944

AND LIKE CUCHULAIN

A time comes when the stiff resisting self,
Circled and tongued by tides of circumstance,
Breaks through the seething ring to merciless seas
And, like Cuchulain, claws down crumbling waves,
Crazed by the absence of a guilty hand.

ALL THE FUGITIVES

The lonely man dallies on evening sands,
The sea-indented shore. Gull-cold
His mind's suspended; and from finger-tips
Forgotten sand mingles and falls apart.

Walking ahead, towards the horizon's line,
He leaves a track for all the fugitives
Seeking a stronger prison than the heart.

TWO SONGS

One

Time transforms grief's turbulent wings
To sadness, a pale bird idling in cloud,
Frail as the seeping dusk. But polished stones
Of silence weigh down struggling words. O cold
Closed marble mouths, closed granite mouths, relent
And speak to me. O drifting wings of sorrow,
Dip from your sky into my ruined clouds.

Two

Cornfields like brown-legged children straddle hills
Rising from shadows. Green o green are the trees,
Finding the wound in me. In them I drown
Deep from the arid mind, sliding through seas
Into your lovelier world whose shape appears
Only in quietness curled free from words,
From bitten tongue whose lumbering pities flap
Ungainly wings, like shadows of huge birds.
I carry you in all my tragedy,
Green behind my eyes, your leaves in song.
I hold you gently when catastrophe
Turning to snatch at me still finds me strong.

THE FLOWER IN THE SAND

SAINT FRANCIS AND THE BIRDS

Hearing him, the birds came in a crowd,
Wing upon wing, from stone and blade and twig,
From tilted leaf and thorn and lumbering cloud,
Falling from hill, soaring from meadowland,
Wing upon widening wing, until the air
Wrinkled with sound and ran like watery sand

Round the sky's gleaming bowl. Then, like a flower
They swung, hill-blue and tremulous, each wing
A palpitating petal tugged by shower
Of words, till he beneath felt the stale crust
Of self crinkle and crumble and his words
Assume an independence, pure and cold,
Cageless, immaculate, one with the birds
Fattening their throats in song. Identity
Lost, he stood in swollen ecstasy.

A WREATH FOR SHOON

He lies under a laurel bush, the angular head
Twisted awry, the cold mouth fallen wide,
Suddenly dead. An hour or so ago
He was the warmest thing I had, the only trusted thing,
Having much good and little power for evil. O he held
The centre of my heart; and now his blood
Dark on my clothes indicts.

A rough man buried him, cruel with spade
And word, digging an awkward grave,
Seeing no tragedy, but only a black dog dead.
Holding a hard green leaf, I watched my past
Sink into soil, and tried again to learn
To love is to be hurt, and only those
Who do not care are strong. Now this stern house
Cold in the damp trees is wholly dead.

JONATHAN SWIFT

Strolling in public gardens, he saw Death
Sidling behind the flowers, backing off
To leave life to its brief commitment, as
The branches sprang back shut on the private path.

The hollowness roared up at him from chasms.
His dreams massed in the night like refugees
Crowding the dawn's release. His daylight mind
Confronted and unmasked Death's euphemisms.

No ministering angel bent to skim
The scum of self or loosen ligatures

Of clamped horizons clotted on his mind.
The bleeding girl. The fierce erupting drum.

His huge coherence leapt from the monstrous drum,
And broke the axle of the drummer's wrists.
Below, the garden was a butterfly
Assured within the context of its dream.

ELEGY FOR A MAD GIRL

As a child she was solitary,
Always a quiet one,
Turning from voice and hand,
Nervous of intimacy,
Closed from the sun, resigned
To find companionship
In dreams or wandering thought.
Taken by the hand
She'd strain back out of reach
Of threatening circumstance,
Twitching her dress from life,
From all who stretched to touch
The wonder of her face.

She was alerted to
Betrayal everywhere,
Lurking, coy, pitiless;
And walked round to avoid
The snares covered with grass
Set to take prisoners;
Despairingly she'd hide
From what was beautiful,
Cruelly perfect, high
Above compassion, fear,
Serene, inimical:
Perfect beyond belief,
Beyond relief. O here
The brain must stop or break,
Eyes close in disbelief,
Unfit to suffer God.
So she was quick to choose
The safety of the veil,
The dark side of the road.

But those who cannot bend
Are broken off like twigs,
And life flows over them,
Acres without end.
The ordinary world
Moved past her when she fell,
Her fences broken down,
Her privacy uncurled,
Doors, windows blown apart,
Disaster loose on the stairs.
She met death like a child
Playing a grown-up part.

So pity her, and hold
Anger and grief like thorns
Tight in your hands, and touch
The unkissed mouth grown cold.

LETTER TO AN IRISH NOVELIST
for Michael McLaverty

Establishment has taken to the hills.
The capitals are bombed. But you pursue
Survival in minute particulars,
Your landscapes, intimate with sea and sky,
Perpetual, unblemished idiom
Common as dolmens and the Easter whin.

Even this city reveals dignity,
Turning a startled face from history.
If you ignore the adolescent dream,
The club-fists of the mob, the tumbled bed,
It is because, the final pattern known,
You choose the threads. And local hatreds fail
To herd your vistas to a ghetto's close
Or drown you in a puddle's politics.

Chance friendships are not always fortunate.
I think of someone, mutually known,
Complacent as a thrush big with its song
Above the matchstick silhouetted town
Caught in the headlights of advancing war;
And of another portly pedant who

Talks of the revolution from a chair,
Stroking his stomach; and of that old man
Walking in mountains, gnarled with stern regret
At missing greatness (the erratic bus).

And then I think of Ireland. Of blue roads
That rivulet into Aeonic seas;
The fields bogged down with failure; the downfall
Of honest men perverted by a cause
Of dangerous verses irresponsibly
Let loose by poets and adopted by
The semi-literate candidates for power,
Or turned to dogma in schoolchildren's mouths.

Those who have lost a country, with a wound
In place of patria, can sail like winds
Among the islands and the continents,
Flying, if any, only personal flags,
Educated to brave devious seas,
Sceptical of harbours, fortunate
In being themselves, each with his personal war.

And they have charts and compasses, for some
Have made the voyage out before their time,
Confronting tempests, fangs of submarines,
Alerted to the coasts' hostility,
The accents foreign and the flags suspect.
A few received an ocean burial,
Having lost sight of continents too long,
Crazed by a magnitude of space and time,
Agnostic salt in the nostalgic wound.

We shall be wary then, and weatherwise,
Testing our strength of sail, learning the ways
Of sinuous currents singing in the rocks,
And the exotic dreams that come from thirst
And too much loneliness on the world's edge,
The midnight mutiny and the dark hold,
The shark's snarl in the wave, the loitering mines.

In time the navigator holds a course,
And heads for landfall. Yes; but, you'll observe,
The missions follow, organised with flags
And bibles for the natives. Be assured

The paths and footholds left by us will fill
With vendors of a new conformity.
Turn to take counsel from the running sea
That carries shells like mouths to the hushed sand.

WILLIAM BLAKE SEES GOD

He sees the lowering sky distend,
Widen into a wound,
A mouth of song. Coldly they stand,
The precise angels, pruned
To leaf-light singing. William Blake
Lifts his face to God.
But the light leaves of singing break
And he turns thickly, shod
With unbelief, uneasily
Feeling the question-mark
Rear and snarl on him inwardly,
The strangler in the dark.

THE DRUMS
12th July 1944

I

The drums stutter under sunless trees.
The train of sound shuffles through hills and fields,
Braggart of market square and country lane.
Invisible, the muttering hand that wields
The live stick talks; speaks of history.
The latent passion wakened by the hand
Finds an explosive rhetoric to call
Squadrons of hate over the ear-cocked land.
Across rooftops and gardens chaos comes,
Pulsing like swollen bombers on the drums.

II

The drums continue through the sultry night
Under the quiet rain's diagonals,
Loud in the coolness of the hollow trees,
The rhythm unrelieved. Their anger falls

Autumnal in the dusk, unsatisfied,
A sullen masturbation, smouldering.
Then silence towers like a moon-caught tree,
Until the rain resumes its murmuring,
Fingers inciting an unsated drum
To tell of triumphs past and still to come.

CUCHULAIN

I

Cold at the frills of the sea, in the wet sand,
Foam-flecked, he watched an aimless drift of wings
Scooped and swirled by the wind. He studied them
Curiously, with one part of his mind
Swinging out like a scarf after their course,
The other part arrested, like a stone.

He felt the air move like a blade on his tongue,
Probing his crannies with nostalgia,
Ache for the crisp, firm days of the white child
Who walked straight forward, never looking back.
Drained to his heart, he felt his throat form words
That fell defeated back into the sand
Of the dry heart, the desert of the self.

Out on the wind he heard the water call.
'Cuchulain, o Cuchulain killed his son.
The blood like shadows dimpled on the sand
When it was done; and he, depleted now,
Stiffened in recognition, his eyes stones.'

The sea drew nearer, flirting at his feet.
'Remember the warmth of her who nurtured him,
Your son, Cuchulain, quivering with your blood.
Remember the flower-tense hour that placed his seed
In her firm centre, the long braid of her hair
Looping her throat, the challenge in her eyes.
O then you could move mountains with a sigh
And squeeze the world like clay in your hard palm
To your own liking. Then in your swinging strength
You spilled your drinks, knowing your throat could swill
Only a hundredth part at your command:
You showered meat to the dogs, knowing your fist

Could fell a field of cattle ripe for kill:
With scores of credulous boys aping your ways
You had no reason to remember him,
Your son, who took her from you; who would add
Each year subtracted from your calendar.
You were Cuchulain, who could fight and whore
From sun to star-point. Now you calculate
Each sword-thrust, substituting craft for strength,
Avoiding quarrels, words replacing wounds,
Afraid of the inevitable day
When news storms through the streets and crackling fields,
Freezing labour, petrifying talk:
"Cuchulain has fallen like a blasted tree
And lies, his branches crippled, oiled with blood."

'That day strides high on stilts. Its shadow falls
Hard on your eyes. This is a time when men
Go home to the soft chair beside the fire
And pimple turf to flame, and stretch their legs
And turn historian of their roaring deeds.
This is a time for supple sons, Cuchulain,
When the old man hands life on to a lad.
You gave your death to him, but failed to win
His springtime in return. Now you are old,
A greying man alone on a cold strand,
Stripped of all purpose, watching aimless wings.
O out of time, Cuchulain, you must walk
On the world's rim, alone, having no friend,
Avoiding the stretched hand and the glad eye,
A thread ripped from the pattern. Only death
Or the glowering skull of madness can hold back
Inexorable time. The fighting man,
Scatterer of death, shrinks like a child
From his own ending, grown aware of fear.'

At last he turned, and the sea's fathoms stirred
From grief to anger. Raising the red hands,
Garish with blood, he cursed them, lingering
Over each finger's fault. 'O now Cuchulain,
Who severed veins like mowers slaughtering grass,
The angry Hound of Ulster, terrible
In battle-rage; a sombre warrior
Who broke the hearts and bones of happier men:
Your harvest flows from tears and desolation,
Defeat and famine crawling in its wake.

Purveying sorrow to the keening girls.
Your name is terror in the nurses' tales
Told to naughty children in the dark.
Look now, Cuchulain, you have met yourself
Here by the sea, a stranger, foreigner
Than all the alien meadows of the south.

'Cynical waves, death-deep deceptive sea,
Now I meet myself in your green lanes,
A warrior, facing an equal fighting man,
Challenging combat. Look, he smiles at me
And I smile back, thinking the same broad thought
That only one will reach the sand again
And walk the level road into the town,
Back to the houses with the open doors,
Breasted by talking women, back to life
In time. Cuchulain greets a champion,
His counterpart, unbeaten enemy.'

II

'Look, neighbour, look: look at the fighting man
In combat with the waves. Look at his arms
Gleaming with spray, the muscles big like stones;
And hear him singing too. Listen, the words
Come between wind and wave, are spat from the spray.'

    "I have delivered death
    Like grain to flustering hens,
    And in my battle-rage
    Have challenged provinces:
    Professional in death,
    Knowing the choicest place
    In groin and neck and breast
    To send a man to hell.
    Now I Cuchulain face
    An equal warrior,
    As cunning in his ways
    Of feint and countermove;
    For he and I are dyed
    Deep in the blood of boys,
    Pity and mercy words
    For wives' embroidery.
    So death take one of us,
    For life like a crossed girl makes fun of us."

'O look, it is Cuchulain, the strong man,
Fighting the waves, gone mad maybe with grief
At killing his own son, as well he should.
Never in all born time was such a man,
Ditching with girls when all respectable
Men of his age twirled fingers in a corner,
Making the young men just as bad or worse,
Till not a virgin or an owlish lad
Could walk the roads in safety. God is just
And lays his sins like children at his door.
Look, neighbour, look: look at Cuchulain now
Crazed like an old vexed horse snorting at flies.'

Now he was in eternity, and time
The corrugated churning of the sea,
A creaking bird. But like a frozen hand
Thawing in heat the world ached back to him,
Vein after vein, until he shook his head
Free of the water and went back to land
Beside the stiffening boy. But even then,
Delaying the first look, his eyes swept round
The smoky hills and the grey sunless sea,
The blue peninsula drawn like a head
In meditation. Then he saw his son.

III

His words tumbled like pebbles to the sand.

'Each man has a desert in his heart
For the hollow cry in the night's silence,
The wandering whisper and the following feet
That find no rest so long as the heart beats.
The flower in the sand opens answering eyes
To the rare sun. But mostly only sand
Sheets to the mercy of a finite sky.

And I was sand, a figure draped in sand,
The white flower underground, a pebble's fist.

Each in his time must meet himself and kill
Accomplice, counterpart and enemy,
And walk straight from that place and be alone
To find his way through dunes and treacherous grass

Into the town.
                    O broken boy, in you
I killed ambitious immortality,
The bladder-swollen self. Your blood was mine
Seeping into the sand, probing the flower.
Then my final self stood above time
At the sea's subtle fusion with the shore,
Beckoning. But I remembered things:
Hands and hair and laughter and blue fields;
And every road in Ulster veined my heart:
And ran like a scared girl back into time,
And, trembling, found myself on the dry land,
An old man dry as sand, gull-querulous,
Who knows that all the roads lead to the sand
And the accusation of the sea.

Pity an old man with his heap of sand.'

IV

The sea covered the sand, reaching the road,
Up to the walls packed with stones like bread,
Speaking like shells. 'Cuchulain, wandering man,
Come home into the waters, into the sand
Transformed by sea; into the sunken town
That hangs like wavering weeds, green and serene,
Deep in the waters: to the timeless town
Where no clock whirs, no chimney smokes, no wheels
Grumble in streets; for here grass swarms and swirls
Over the cobbles' breasts—for here dry time
Has, grain by grain, entered eternity,
The sand, the town, the permanent poised flower.'

But he was walking on deserted roads,
Confused and aimless, laughing loud at trees,
Crying at nothing more than a turned wing.

And they built legends round him. They still say
He can be seen on roads at the new moon
Looking at the sea, as though he might
Break through the stones and enter the black waves.
But he turns back, with eyes so terrible
That none who saw him walks that same road twice.

July 1944

THE JOURNEY HOME

I

Walking at sunrise I came into a town,
A market town in Ireland where I was born,
Looking for landmarks and remembered spires.
But all was unfamiliar to my eyes.
The monument was gone: the warrior
Bringing emancipation with a gun,
His place usurped by public lavatories.
I missed the workhouse, pawnshop, dole queue, and
The wind-fat flags above the market square,
The pavement beggar and the hungry dogs.

The homecome traveller discovers ghosts
Where he had left the living: tentative
Explorer turning corners, while threadbare
Memories touch his shoulder. Sombrely
He looks for absentees, notes innovations,
His bridges blown, boats burned, the river crossed;
Having only a name, his accent wrong.

Walking among the ruins of my time,
Touching and testing, sad in retrospect,
I met an old man who remembered me,
Anachronistic, long grown out of time,
Too old for readjustment, left in peace
To catalogue and annotate, and sleep.
He showed me the museum, tempting me
Back into history, to renew, he said,
Some old and interesting acquaintances.

There, feathers still in place, was Privilege,
Imperious on a chair, carved like a skull,
Decanting blood. Behind him lay the bones
Of his last meal. Yet, from his inturned eyes,
It was apparent he was drinking wine
And seated on an ordinary chair.
Inscribed above his head I read the words:
Only the blind and ignorant are strong;
Pity acknowledges the source of things.

And there beside him sat the monster Greed,
Salivating, the great belly shaking;

With Famine at his elbow, iron-eyed
And silent, an ancient child, stonily waiting.

Then I saw Bigotry, squat, straddle-legged,
Stones in his hands, the fallen simian brow
Stone-like itself, the small eyes riveted
On a projected image of himself,
Girt like a crusader, a pioneer.

I saw them all. I saw life magnified,
Deftly arranged in cases. I saw God
Struggling in narrow places, breaking chains,
Changing his fetters, until nakedness
Appeared as an ideal, the stripped truth.

They showed man lose his manness in the mob,
Changed to a thing of throats and bloody hands,
Of separate species. I watched the sombre core
Throb in existence, the permanent sorrowing heart,
The itch of godhead, the grave's fingers stretching.
I saw my hundred selves and wept for me.

II

The town was smaller than it used to be,
Closer to the soil. I saw machines
Disciplined as heart, tended by men
Who stood above, outside them, knowing the fields
As well as the geared wheels. Society,
They said, was like a flower poised in the sun,
Seeking its perfect shape, then withering
Into readjustment with the soil.
They had broken through the circle of the mind
And raised a house out of the shards of time,
A house with many windows, permanent
On its own crust of time, but, like the flower,
Living in death, death-rooted, echoing
The dark maternal soil. I listened to them,
Stumbling on new language, pruning words,
Learning the accent of community,
Seeing a synthesis of heart and head.

A man said:
          'Having travelled past the lie
Of nationhood, we honour this small town,

A place we know and live in. We embrace
The fields around us, then the neighbouring towns
With whom we trade our surplus, with whom we vie
In sport and architecture. By degrees
We can conceive the whole vibrating island,
But only as the sum of these field-towns,
Having no corporate being. Fields and towns
And people. So we define and know the island.'

A woman said:
        'After the wars were over,
After the heads were hidden underground;
After the national anthems and the talk,
The promises, the damp-eyed promises;
After the boomerangs came home again,
And the stone entered even the simplest heart,
I found these people who acknowledged death
Here in the sunlight in the rivering grass.
With death in them they brought life to this town.
No hymns or speeches. And some others too
In other places brought their candles' light
Into the darkness, with the night in them,
Small pools of flame, live tongues in the stone's silence.

'The crowd is faceless. Only the intimate few
Have hope of the hand of God cool on the brow,
And sink their godness in the pool of God
That stands deep as the heart. O I came here
Benighted, darkness toiling in the loins,
Death unacknowledged, stiff, unsatisfied,
Until I found the pattern.'

        A child said:
'I was born in chaos, in a national war,
Conceived in fear, suckled at sour breasts,
My father's head lowering in the rocks.
Here, I study flowers and the ways
Of birds, and how the seeds are blown by winds
Into various fields over trained hedge
And boundary, each bearing a harvest.
I too have looked at death, acknowledging.
Arm-in-arm we walk with the field's dead.
But still the core is spotted with the past;
The manumitted slave still hears his chains.

I, half in sun half shadow, see two worlds:
One like a crusted pond, standing and stale,
The other, washed with sun, articulate.'

They said:
              'First comes the vision, a rare seed,
Blown by uncompassed winds, swelling to flower
In unconfinable anguish. The voice must speak
Of it, hands render it homage, eyes
Look for its translation into flesh.
Then like a depth of water dedication
Cools and refines the brain; the hands learn craft,
Patience, the voice biding its time. But hot
Was its conception; hot is the consummation.
In time revolt barks like a pistol shot.
The self stands naked, the vision manifest.

'Then come the stones, the fingers and the laughter,
Shame creeping like insects on the skin,
Fear big as awareness. But the anger
Of loneliness sharpens the mind, for love
Unedged billows in sentiment. And last,
The plan unfolds as surely as the spring,
Sober with roads and houses, turretless,
But warm with the first flowering of the mind.

'The nearest thing to happiness is purpose.
Consult a crowd and watch the pamphleteer,
The lone distributor spreading the news,
Intent on God or merely revolution.
Look at his eyes, his face, his head, his hands,
And see completeness, the dedicated mind,
A standing stook among the scattered sheaves.

'For loneliness is immortality.
The cold stone lies upon the rain-washed hill.

'At night the wind unscrews in the long lanes.
Timeless, it cries in time. We hear our voice,
And gird against the bonds our lineaments,
Angry to pass from shape to unison.

'Loneliness is the mark of a known time:
The wind's sad rage spirals across the world.

'We who have found our shape in brick and furrow
Have built a tomb, and wait for the third day.

'Our voice is long and thin as the night wind,
Voice of the heart seeking the depthless sea.'

III

At dusk I climbed the small familiar hill,
Above the lights' white necklaces. Alone,
A silhouette, I watched the stiffening fields
Submerged in shivering mist. Someone was crying
Obscurely in my mind, greyly in pity
For the weak straws scattered and smashed in time,
Carried by patient wings and built anew
Innocently in face of history
And the frail sorrow stammering in the heart.
I called, cold in the stars, black in the sky—
In spite of ignorance and weakening hands,
Of cloudrift, rains grown gentle, generous suns,
An end of travelling through an echoing world—
For time to fill the arid heart with song.

July 1944

SWORDS AND PLOUGHSHARES
(1943)

LINES BY SLIEVE DONARD

The men who made these walls,
Rimming the higher ground with younger stone,
Aproned with mist or shoulder-high in sun,
Intent, absorbed and yet contemplative,
Pausing, did they lift their heads to hear
The hunted echo scurrying through the whin,
Peer for the shadow driving the stuttering sheep
Askew in flight, and the cattle lumbering
In the swollen valleys glittering with fear?

And speculate,
Above the parishes and baronies,
Picking out spires like pins and the roads' threads,
On some disaster climbing the rockface
To where this obstinate regiment of stone,
Boulder to boulder, guards the empty peak?

RAIN TOWARDS EVENING

Sadder than pale Deirdre, the white rains falling
Scatter like spiders spinning to the ground.
    Cold as the silver mists twisted round Donard,
    With graven eye assessing from his stand
Under the drooling tree, he calculates
In the moment's balance the bulging world squeezed small
    As a porous sponge clenched in the knuckled fist:
    Noting the insects flustering under tall
Swaggering hedges, as the water lopes
Lipping the pavement edges, floating leaves
    Their tiny arks of hope. Sadder than
    Pale Deirdre chained to his tree he grieves
Seeing no hint of sun, as insects run
Foolishly under the hedges; knowing though birds
    Salute the rift in the clouds, there will be none
    To pity the flood-wrecked things, stark by their stones.
Sadder than pale Deirdre the white rains fall,
Than pale Deirdre, the saddest of all queens,
    While he, cold as the silver mists round Donard,
    Looks from his tree, through the bars of the white rains.

EASTER 1942

The long lines of the dead,
As the grey moons move the sea,
Conscribe my heart and head
Back into history.
'He is a fool,' they said,
'Adrift on the tide.'

I turn them in my mind,
Names uttered with hate or love,
Whose kind was not my kind,
Who scorned O'Connell's glove,
The blind who led the blind,
Sowing the wind.

In streets and rooms I see
The long lines of the dead
Breaking from history.
'He is a fool,' they said,
'Turning his face away
To yesterday.'

I hold them by the hands,
Sad on this Easter day
For the running sands
Under the houses of clay,
And a voice somewhere responds,
As the dream demands.

They still bring Easter flowers
Placating the restless dream.
Despite the severing years
When life flew loose from the scheme,
A half-remembered verse
Or a song endures.

POEM FOR TODAY

What can we say who have exhausted words of meaning,
Who have wept our hearts empty of a generation's tears?
What can we say that is new in the face of sorrow,
Lacking in language and in silences;
What can we say when they come for our reply?

Lock books away, turn pictures to the wall;
Cast yesterday's roses from sight that the pain may be lost;
Turn key on memories, and bolt the mind
Fast against grief too threatening to be housed.

What can we say who have said it all already?
Who have seen the years fall
Into an ever-open grave,
Too vast for a posy of flowers, a rectangle of stone.
What can we say, here, by the hardening fire,
As the clock ticks history, and the flowers drip blood?

IN IRELAND NOW

In Ireland now, at autumn, by frugal fires,
We hurry to lock the present out with the closed door
And night-slammed windows; huddling into a past
Where life at times could turn a nonchalant head,
We watch the heads of flame swirl in the draught,
The demon dancers on reflecting walls,
Backed by an angry wind strumming the wires.

And think, on the edge of a crumbling continent,
Of local hills goodnaturedly at play
With wind and sunlight pampering girlish fields,
Trying to comprehend, while we condemn,
The passionless slaughter of millions, all faceless, unknown,
Though the mass resolves into a singular
Soul pulsing in your wrist, the killer's pulse.

In autumn now, when leaf and hope are failing,
And days draw curtains earlier than before;
In autumn now, when leaves and men are falling,
Thoughts shuffle back into the dying year,
Looking for rampant sunshine in the town,
Where curtains hang like crape in mourning now.

In autumn now, when leaves and blood are falling,
And field and thought bend under seasonal shadow,
In season of harvest by sickle and bayonet,
We turn back pages on the calendar
For innocence, perhaps, and nonchalance,
While winter's onslaught gathers overhead.

IN THE MEANTIME

In the meantime, be aware of too much laughter,
Lest it should mock the prematurely dead;
Cautious of sorrow crowding on the stairs,
Lest ghosts should claim the living for the dead.

Let the grey skies be symbols of our hearts,
And the skeleton branches the bones of our summer desires;
Let the autumn air settle like leaves upon us
And the furrows in the fields lie on our foreheads.

Let shadows nudge at our heels in windy lanes,
And the smell of the year's decay cling in our nostrils;
Let us scatter the dust of our sins, and bow our heads
That were too arrogant by far in the proud summer.

In the meantime, let us be quiet in empty rooms,
Conversant with the crowding silences;
Let us be quiet, and have done with shouting
Now, at the ebb of the year that has stolen our love.

TRAIN AT MIDNIGHT

Train, hurrying over hungry lean
Insurgent fields flaunting their green
Tatters of flags, pause to aver
Your anger and compassion for
This unreal country, always out of time.

Announce your heresy to them,
Hearing in sleep approaching doom
Of wheels and prophecy of steam,
Clenched in the cold fist of a dream,
Tense in another space, another time.

Send out from your arcade of smoke
A salutation that will wake
Dreamers across the countryside
To pledge allegiance as you stride
On towards the final termini of time.

YOU, SITTING IN SILENT ROOMS

You, sitting in silent rooms,
Afraid of thought, with anger
Arrogant in heart:
Look at your handiwork;
Look at the four square walls
Boxing you in,
Look on your own grey self in the mirror.

Over the decades you sweated, crushing
The wild thing under your boots.
Through summers and winters you laboured to iearn
How to erect a hoarding against the world
And the thing you fought with. You have forgotten the day
You finally killed it and hid the remains in the bush:
How you wondered to laugh or weep at the liberation:
How you stole away in the night to your iron bed
And rose in the morning free, a king in yourself.

But I remember the day, the place, the minute:
How the cry in your throat wrenched to a snarl,
How your wife wept in her chair when you were not looking,
How your sons watched the change come in your eyes.

In my grave I have seen and heard these sad things happen,
The evil dream is my face at the open window.
Listen at doors and windows. I am risen.

You, sitting in silent rooms, alone,
God to a handful of men and one pale woman:
Look at the stones you have built that have calloused your hands
And knock at the peace of your heart. For I am risen.

A CRY

If it was Samson I
Would drag this mad house down
Loud about their ears—
But I being only I
With hands like melting snow
Must thole the fools, and crown
Joy with a cap of tears.

If it was Samson I
Would raise great shouting hands
Out to the crying dawn—
But I being only I
With slave hands quiet as dew
Bind them with white prayer bands,
And put my soul in pawn.

If it was Samson I
Could move mountains with faith,
That God-inspired ally—
But I being only I
Loose as wind-clutched straw
Must raise pale hands at death,
Seeing no white christ die.

THE POOR MAD GIRL'S LOVE SONG

The wreaths have perished where he is lying
Foreign and white under the ground.
His voice is the throb of the night wind sighing
In the shivering wires. The furtive sound
Of rain dropping like tears drips
The passing of disconsolate days.

They say it is madness for me to think
His soul is a tree or a blackbird flying.
(Deep in the flood of love I sink,
Hearing his voice in the night wind crying
To the fretful stars among the trees.)
This is the poor mad girl's love song.

Red from the mouth of the merciless ground
His blood breaks through and lies on the grass.
Listen, and you will hear the sound
Of someone singing behind the trees.
This is the song of the poor mad girl
With the hopeless hands. Therefore have pity.

But maybe I'll die tonight in bed
And wake to my place in the promised land
And maybe, upstanding among the dead,
He'll be waiting me, a kiss in his hand.
This is the wish of the poor mad girl
With the empty hands. Therefore have pity.

SOLILOQUY OF AN OLD NATIONALIST WOMAN

Down in the black city
Under the grey hill,
Ghosts crowd close in ambush,
Quick to do you ill.
Faces at the windows
Are scarred with history still.

Down among the places
Where the bones were laid
Stark beneath the starlight,
Living with the dead,
Shadows move to name you
For the graves you made.

See up on the mountain
Figures watching still;
Dead men leave their stories
For their sons to tell.
God alone can save you
With a miracle.

God alone can save you
From the bitter street
Where ghosts are quick to hurt you
And corners watch and wait:
No one else can save you
From legendary hate.

Down in the black city
Under the bird's wheel,
Hunger and her children
Genuflect and kneel
Before the scarlet altar
Whose candle-points are steel.

Under the grey mountain
Voices bleed in prayer;
Ghosts rise up to hurt you,
And out of the thin air
Voices and footsteps gather
To stalk you everywhere.

THE VISITOR

He walked the black roads, under trees
Whose brittle leaves cracked underfoot,
Versing his tongue in recent news,
Selecting apposite words to prune
And shape the story-telling. Peace
Kept step beside him for a while,
Walking the black miles by the fields
That sprawl out to the Antrim hills,
Under the chill wires' keen,
And in the west the sun's dead smile.

The empty house, unanswering door,
Forced him to put his words away
And walk the angry road in fire,
Seeing the town's spires lurch and sway,
Drab hills abandoned on the shore.

PRAYER FOR A YOUNG MAN

Clothe him with profound silence,
For prayer to illuminate
His destination. Spirit of place,
Glimpsed, if ever more than a trick of the light,
Offer, confer your shawl to comfort him
Whose emblem is a turf-cart on the road,
Plodding with evening and the hills behind,
Evoke the strangeness that men may know
And tell that he is of you. Lay
A peasant woman's hands in blessing on him,
With your history alive in his veins.
This is his prayer, who casts
Stones at the gods in other temples;
For your temple is a seat by the fire,
And your weapons belong to a different soil.
This is his prayer at stairhead and window,
Still that of a stranger coming in,
With different dialect and foreign ways,
But claiming you, by right of one who sees
Still on the hills the beacon, and hears
In city streets the lilts of history.

PLAINT OF THE WORKING MEN

Why do you revile us, the unfortunate ones?
Who have lived our lives greyly, without harm,
Without wish or any wanton desire to harm,
Content with our crooked huddle of squinting houses
Where the soot came in, and the roar
Of traffic and gnash of machines was our lullaby;
Content to let live; condemned to let die?

Why should the bomb stalk us who are all unworthy
Of time and money needed to kill a man?
Whose only vice was a pint and the twopenny pools,
Who tightened our belts in the slumps and went to the shore
When summer came and we had the railway fare.
What are we to the unknown men who rule us?

Only desirous of sleep and sun in the window,
Food and tobacco, a shilling for drink and the pools;
And for us who are young, a girl whose ways are rare
Before they fall foul of ugly bargains with want.
This, lord and master and factory boss, is our petition,
And though it is worldly and selfish it is all we desire.

THE GUEST

I saw Death striding through the land;
His mouth was cruel, and his eyes
Hard like stones thrown up by northern seas;
The blood of generations drooled from his hand.

I saw him enter quietly, cautiously:
Welcomed by mine host as a friend,
Dusting his shoulders, taking up his hand,
Assuring him of hospitality;

Running to air the best four-poster bed,
Arrange a late cold supper. But
Now he has laid aside his cloak and hat,
Showing the staring sockets and the head

Stripped down to ultimate bone. Nobody there
Stands up or speaks out to oppose

The glaring challenge of his vacant eyes,
Skeletal fingers barring the street door.

He indicates *be merry*; their forced mirth
Under the clock, rings boast, like graveyard earth.

EVENING IN DONEGAL

Cuchulain, '*a dirty fighter*', killed his son
And gave a hard name to a neutral strand.
Evicted once again by war, I come
To say '*adjust, adapt, acclimatise*';
But see a fighting man climb from the waves.
The blood of Conla is on all our hands.

THERE WAS SUN TODAY

There was sun today, and a girl who smiled
Crooked welcome; there were birds
And dimples in the sky. A child
Laughed in his pram, greater than words.

War paused for breath today; the guns
Stood down, at ease; rhetorical
Accomplices of violence
Faltered into a dying fall.

There was sun today. Expectant eyes
Kindled alight; a young girl smiled
In crooked welcome. All-clear skies
Returned the raptures of a child.

SONG TOWARDS SPRING

Soil crumbles in the hand, and spring
At last seems likely under kindlier skies.
Old stones conceive, insinuate a song
Under the tread of flat gregarious feet.
Love will ignite from patches of sunlight,
Hope scamper through fields to the entrances
Where summer treks back from the underground.

PRELUDE TO AN EPITAPH

I will speak softly of one who has gone
Down to a sea untrammelled by sky,
As a sigh of sun drowned in the green
Echo of leaves. Softly I
Will speak of one who has gone to sea.

I will construct a pillar of words
Tall to his memory on the shore,
That he may hear the wings of birds
Turn in the sky to make my prayer
To the unknown sea for his safe oar:

That men may stand and murmur his name
Down by a sea untrammelled by sky,
Wondering why one passed by fame
Should be remembered. Softly I
Will speak of one gone down to sea.

THE PATTERN

Out of these hills and fierce, historic fields,
Out of this froth of trees and silent stretches
Of solitary soil where hurrying winds
Gossip and separate: out of this sky
Holding the island cupped to the ear of God:
Out of each clenched bush and sauntering river
Swaggering to sea: out of the frail
Flotsam of the shipwrecked centuries,
I speak, builded with their bone and anger.

Every stone in every crazy wall
Stumbling across the sky-line, every road
Streaming like ribbon from ballooning hills,
Every flare of whin and sudden slash
Of water knifing trenches in the fields:
A panic of birds loud on the heels of the day,
Push eager, arrogant fists through every word.

The gambolling, coltish fields of County Down,
And the quiet menace of the Antrim plains
Dappled by drifting clouds and the slow rains

Lurking behind the wind on reticent hills:
And the strange city, patient in its hates,
Smeared always with commemorative blood,
Its angry martyrs urgent and alive,
Where dogma has its store of stones to fling

And sinuous smoke insinuates and spreads
Down through the lilting arteries of streets
To the black heart pulsing its own false time:
All these are in the pattern, and the sea,
The latent sea of history always flowing,
Casting its shipwreck and its mariners
Stark on the fleeing beaches of the mind.

THE GIRL

Walking with water from the well, the firm hips swaying,
The nervous tread of feet lost in the leaves,
The unpinned hair dark, loose, her head held proud and high,
She walked this way a thousand years ago,
The loose blue veil of hair dark in the lane's shadows,
The water chuckling with each quiet footfall,
The Gaelic liquid-smooth in throat, a sweet burn flowing,
Before the foreigner, when sea and sky
Were safe, and down-to-earth brutality strode naked,
With lust and living short of love and life.

RUSSIAN SUMMER
(1941)

RUSSIAN SUMMER

Sun sprawls through tributary streets
Silverly blinding naked glass
Of shops; clatter of white plates
In restaurants, and clash
Of clipped convulsive talk denote
The fever of blood, for tomorrow we die.

Tinting yellow crisps of sun-drugged hay
Stooked like penny coconut cakes in a pastry shop,
Day is kind to lovers in the grass,
Waking the hasty kiss,
The careless cigarette,
The trivial things that tomorrow will forget,
Into the conscious ache of history.

Night has postponed fear,
And there is nothing but sleep and stars and silent love,
Though the hypnotic rays move like scars on the sky-surface
Touching the heart for a moment to remembrance;
But when the blind is down it is nothing,
Nothing at all but the assuring coolness of slim sheets
And the stealthy creak of a chair, and the moan of the cistern.

The blood of a generation subtracted from life
Is the cost of the holiday from fear and fear of acknowledging
     fear;
And the lovers in the grass or in the cinema seats
Feel it on their hands and between their lips
And know that it is only a lull and an interval.
And knowing it they laugh, or press hot lips
On lips in an agony to forget.

NOTES AND INDEX

Publishing History

Verse

A Poem: Russian Summer (Dublin: Gayfield Press, 1941).
Three New Poets. With Alex Comfort and Ian Serraillier (Billericay, Essex: Grey Walls Press, 1942).
Swords and Ploughshares (London: Routledge, 1943).
Flowers for a Lady (London: Routledge, 1945).
The Heart's Townland (London: Routledge, 1947).
Elegy for the Dead of The Princess Victoria (Lisburn, County Antrim: Lisnagarvey Press, 1952).
The Garryowen (London: Chatto and Windus, 1971).
Verifications (Belfast: Blackstaff Press, 1977).
A Watching Brief (Belfast: Blackstaff Press, 1979).
The Selected Roy McFadden. Edited by John Boyd (Belfast: Blackstaff Press, 1983).
Letters to the Hinterland (Dublin: Dedalus Press, 1986).
After Seymour's Funeral (Belfast: Blackstaff Press, 1990).

Co-editor, *Ulster Voices, Irish Voices* 1941-42, *Lagan*, 1945-46, *Rann: An Ulster Quarterly of Poetry*, 1948-53, and *Threshold*, 1961, all in Belfast.

Prose Writings

'A Trend in Poetry', *The Dublin Magazine*, October-December 1944, Dublin.
'A Note on Contemporary Ulster Writing' (from a lecture at the New Ireland Society, December 1945), *The Northman*, Winter 1946.
'Conversation in a Shaving-Mirror', *Poetry Ireland*, No. 13, October 1951, Dublin.
'The Pard of Armagh, A Note on Æ, George Russell', *Rann* 15, Spring 1952.
'Reflections on Megarrity', *Threshold* No. 5, Spring-Summer 1961, Belfast.
'The War Years in Ulster 1939-45', *The Honest Ulsterman*, No. 64, 1980, Belfast.
'The Dogged Hare: a study of W.R. Rodgers', *The Ulster Tatler*, 1983.
'No Dusty Pioneer: a personal recollection of John Hewitt', *The Poet's Place* (Gerald Dawe and John Wilson Foster eds.), Institute of Irish Studies, Belfast, 1991.
'The Belfast Forties', *Force 10*, Sligo 1994.

Recordings

'Roy McFadden and Laurence Lerner select from their own poetry'. BBC, 1959.
'Two Poets: Roy McFadden and Seamus Heaney'. BBC, 1966.
'Roy McFadden Reads'. BBC, 1992.

Critical Studies: in *Rann 20* (Belfast); Michael Longley, in *Causeway: The Arts in Ulster*, Belfast, Arts Council of Northern Ireland, 1971; *Northern Voices* by Terence Brown, Dublin, Gill and Macmillan, 1975; D.E.S. Maxwell in *The Macmillan Dictionary of Irish Literature* (ed. Robert Hogan), Macmillan,

London, 1979; John Boyd in Introduction to *The Selected Roy McFadden*, Belfast, Blackstaff Press, 1983; Philip Hobsbaum in *The Honest Ulsterman*, Belfast, 1993.

THE HUNGER-MARCHERS

Magee's Nursery (p. 3)
See also 'Nursery Land' (p. 119); 'The Astoria' (p. 91).

Miss Purdy in Old Age (p. 5)
See also 'Ballyhackamore' (p. 164).

Tiveragh (p. 5)
See also 'Cushendall' (p.256); *The Poet's Place*, Gerald Dawe and John Wilson Foster (eds.), Belfast 1991.

A Dog, An Afternoon (p. 7)
Like 'An Attic in Holborn' (p. 78), this is a poem derived from a picture: in this instance, from a photograph of a fox terrier belonging to my childhood. That moment of time reaches out from the photograph to grasp the present. At the bottom of the photograph, there is a shadow of the head of the photographer.

The Hunger-Marchers (p. 8)
Memories of the Jarrow Marchers continue to remind me of a Northern English, nonconformist, dimension in my inheritance.
See 'For the Record' (p. 48).

5 Anglesea Road, Dublin (p. 10)
An afternoon visit to Brendan Behan's last formal residence.
"... We have bought a house after much searching, on Anglesea Road, rather a snob area, opposite the RDS. It costs £1,470, and we have paid £400 already. So if you could send the £750 it would mean we could complete the purchase."
   —Letter from Beatrice Behan to Iain Hamilton dated 26th November
       1958. *The Letters of Brendan Behan*, edited by E.H. Mikhail. Macmillan;
                                                    London, 1992.

Confirmation Class (p. 10)
Preparatory to confirmation in the Church of Ireland, classes were held in the vestry for the candidates, when one argued with the curate, and approached a cross-roads of belief or unbelief. A journal entry reminded me of my own experience. At confirmation, I knelt before Louis MacNeice's father, the Bishop of Down, Connor and Dromore.

Miss Walters (p. 11)
See also 'Mr McAlonen' (p. 54).

Irish Street, Downpatrick (p.12)
See also 'Lines Written near Downpatrick after an Air-Raid' (p. 275); 'Quail Holdings' (p. 165); 'The Other Grandfather' (p. 51).

Burns Night (p. 14)
"Now that poor Robin was dead, all the birds of the air fell a-sighing and a-sobbing to some purpose ... Both the Angus-shire Fencible Infantry and the Cinque Ports Cavalry were stationed in the town. Such an occasion was a

godsend to these and to the Gentlemen Volunteers—good drinkers every man ...

The dead volunteer's sword and unpaid-for hat were laid on the coffin lid ... Fencibles, infantry, and cavalry lined the streets for the half mile that lay between the Town Hall and the grave. The drums were muffled, and the bells tolled. So Robin went to his last lair.

The Dead March in *Saul* (a piece of the sort which the poet had always found repugnant to his musical taste) was played.

Three volleys by the 'awkward squad' were fired over the grave ... At home Jean, who all the morning had endured the pains of labour, gave birth to a ninth child, a boy."

— *The Life of Robert Burns* by Catherine Carswell; London, 1951.

Autograph Album (p.16)
During my childhood I was taken to Celebrity Concerts at the Wellington and Ulster Halls in Belfast. Renowned singers and performers appeared regularly; and seats were available at modest (unsubsidised) prices.
See also 'Jean Armstrong' (p. 175).

Prior Title (p. 17)
In conveyancing, previous ownership of property; derivations, successions, and bequests.

Belgravia in Winter (p. 18)
As with many other parts of London, Belgravia is impressive for the survival and upkeep through the generations of buildings, not as museum-pieces but as living, functioning addresses; and at the same time, suggesting histories of previous residents, known and unknown.
See also '34 Tite Street' (p. 65).

AFTER SEYMOUR'S FUNERAL

Hyde Park (p. 24)
'Take heed of that fabulous boy'. Statue of Peter Pan in Kensington Gardens, by George Frampton, erected in 1912; commissioned by J.M. Barrie.

The Dancers, Sloane Street (p. 24)
Bronze figures in the north garden between Cadogan Place and Sloane Street, London, by David Wynne; erected 1971.

The Hill (p. 25)
'The redhaired maid they'd brought from Manchester'. See 'Sancto's Dog' (p. 100).

A Dead Chief (p. 26)
A chief engineer, from County Armagh, with a long memory for poems learned by rote at the local school.

Jack Yeats at Fitzwilliam Square (p. 27)
In 1945 items of food were still scarce or rationed, and in Dublin tea was avidly sought after. 'Discreetly deprecating hands/Conferring some mundane necessity' belonged to friends and admirers concerned to supply the old man with scarce commodities: Life sustaining Art. Visits to Fitzwilliam Square are also described by Louis MacNeice in *The Strings Are False,* and by Hilary Pyle in his biography *Jack B. Yeats* (London, 1970; 1989).

Carrie Coates (p. 28)
Caroline Clements Coates (*née* Rea), 1865-1954. In childhood a neighbour and close friend of AE's (some anticipated marriage); a lifetime correspondent and fellow Theosophist. See *Letters from AE* edited by Alan Denson (London, 1961). My mother befriended her at the Theosophical Society in Belfast.

The Upanishads (p. 29)
See *The Ten Principal Upanishads: Put into English by Shree Purohit Swami and W.B. Yeats.* London, 1937.

June Blossom (p. 31)
Before the war, pierrots were common to most seaside resorts, and now in retrospect are an intimate part of childhood in the Thirties.

Pim (p. 33)
'He said his father had known Oscar Wilde'. Herbert Moore Pim, 1883-1950. Poet, novelist and essayist. *Unconquerable Ulster* (1919) has a foreword by Sir Edward Carson, QC, MP. (The friend was in fact Lord Alfred Douglas.)

The Little Black Rose (p. 36)
Refers to a poem with that title by Aubry de Vere (1814-1902).

> The Little Black Rose shall be red at last;
> What made it black but the March wind dry,
> And the tear of the widow that fell on it fast?
> It shall redden the hills when June is nigh.

See also *Dark Rosaleen* by James Clarence Mangan (1803-1849).
Roisin Dubh, one of the romantic names for Ireland.

End of Season (p. 37)
See 'Memory of Sand' (p. 279).

After Seymour's Funeral (p. 38)
Thoreau: 'We do not live by justice, but by grace'.
'Wait a little longer ...' See Alex Comfort, *The Song of Lazarus* (London, 1945).
'Who answers the call
Of Reverence for Life'
—Albert Schweitzer's credo. See *My Life and Thought, an Autobiography* by Albert Schweitzer, translated by C.T. Campion, London 1946; and *Albert Schweitzer, His Work and His Philosophy,* by Oskar Kraus, London, 1944.

Joseph Campbell: Born Belfast 15th July 1879, Joseph Campbell (Seosamh Mac Cathmhaoil) poet, patriot, scholar died in Co. Wicklow in June 1944. "Campbell died, June 5th, alone. Neighbours raised the alarm on June 7th. Body found stretched across the hearth, the kettle overturned and the lid under his head ... A quiet funeral ... Not a single one of his books in print until the publication in 1963 of Austin Clarke's edition of his collected poems, *The Poems of Joseph Campbell* (Dublin, 1963)."

—'Notes Towards a Biography' in *The Journal of Irish Literature: A Joseph Campbell Number,* September 1979.

Hans Crescent (p. 42)
'The day's first-footed by the calvary'. In the early morning the Household Cavalry proceeded unceremoniously along Sloane Street, past the window displaying Aston Martin cars, and the shop with superior little dogs for sale.

Old Style (p. 43)
Mary Anna Foster. Gentlewoman; Greek scholar; Irish nationalist. For a time she was Aunt Anna on Children's Hour, BBC, Belfast. She was a cousin of the educationalist and philanthropist, Vere Foster (1819-1900). My mother knew her at the Adult School in Belfast.

My Mother's Young Sister (p. 45)
See also 'Immigrants' (p. 122).

The Statute of Limitations (p. 46)
The Statute of Limitations (1874) imposed a limit on the time within which proceedings could properly be instituted after a cause of action occurred. But the statute did not begin to run where the party concerned was outside the jurisdiction.

Old Tennis Courts (p. 47)
During the 1920s and 30s private tennis courts were a feature of some of the larger residences around Belfast; and here and there in the suburbs small tennis clubs consisting of two or three courts, mainly grass, were maintained by local enthusiasts. After their day passed, they lingered for a long time in decay, weedgrown, sometimes with the rotting net still attached to lolling posts. Neglected, they prompted not only regret but response to a challenge from the past.

For the Record (p. 48)
When my children were young, I persuaded them that I had been born in County Durham, and that as 'a barefoot lad' during the years of depression I had sold bundles of sticks around the doors to eke out a living.

Grand Old Man (p. 48)
'Erinmore'. A brand of pipe tobacco.

Three Cousins (p. 50)
'The Other Grandfather' (p. 51); 'Quail Holdings' (p. 165).

The Rockery (p. 52)
While assembling poems for this collection, I discovered an early, forgotten

poem in manuscript, dated 1st September 1944, which anticipated the later poem by almost fifty years.

> Among the broken images to-night
> One swung back, recollected, unimpaired,
> Smooth through the traffic-roar of time: a white
> Child beside a rockery of flowers.
>
> And I recalled his thought; how he had planned,
> Beneath the stones and flowers, a hidden garden
> With water playing and the sun's thin hand
> Arranging the cold leaves. And in his faith
>
> He was content to stand by the closed stone,
> The dream unrealised, content to stare
> Dream into stones until the tree had grown
> Black to the window and the house lights flowered.
>
> O mind grown cold outside a sterner stone:
> Constantly prune your thought, and, body, stand
> Safe among people and, untouched, alone
> In roaring streets and see the garden there.

The Bar Library (p. 53)
Barristers' workplace in Royal Courts of Justice, Belfast, consisting of an anteroom for consultations and an inner sanctum for Counsel. See my short story 'Quinn', published in *New Irish Writing* edited by David Marcus on 11th November 1982.

Mr McAlonen (p. 54)
A protagonist in the Peace Pledge Union 1939-45, who, in spite of being 62, with high blood pressure, displayed *Peace News* for sale in a hostile environment.

Evictions (p. 58)
In the Troubles of the 1920s, before I was one, my family was evicted by militants. The poem fancies my being old enough to ride a tricycle, greeting a child refugee from another area, as we switch ghettos.

The Little B.A. (p. 58)
'Do you remember a
Letter to William Allingham?'
—Letter (undated) from Madame Bodichon. See *Letters to William Allingham,* edited by H. Allingham and E. Baumer Williams. London, 1911.

Captain Thompson (p. 59)
My brother was in fact named James Thompson after my father's benefactor.
See *Helston* (p. 103)

Gone Away (p. 61)
See 'Sancto's Dog' (p. 100).

LETTERS TO THE HINTERLAND

2 September 1939 (p. 65)
The day before Britain declared war on Germany; the last day of peace. See 'My Mother's Young Sister'.

34 Tite Street (p. 65)
Formerly number 16, where Oscar Wilde lived from his marriage in 1884 until his arrest in 1895. Wilde was attracted to the street when he saw Ellen Terry on her way to sit for her portrait in Whistler's studio in the White House. At the date of the poem, the house was, apparently serenely, still in domestic use.

Style (p. 66)
'The lady nobly dying' was May Morton, poetess, and secretary of Belfast PEN Centre. The 'Bedside companion' for many years a distinguished journalist, had, from a distance, been admired by a youthful fellow-poet.

Victories (p. 66)
See 'Heroes' (p. 137).

The Disappeared Ones (p. 67)
Los Desaparecidos of Argentina, a description here applied to missing buildings and citizens, removed by the Troubles.

Old Mr Kershaw (p. 67)
One of the assimilated English connection that had come to Belfast in the early years of the century, equipped with trade or profession.

The House (p. 69)
Produced as a poster-poem by the Arts Council of Northern Ireland, illustrated by Arthur Armstrong.
    The house was originally the residence of my young muse when I was 18 or so. It was subsequently owned by an elderly lady for whom I acted as solicitor. One morning she was discovered lying dead in the hallway in mysterious circumstances. After an interval of thirty years, I revisited the house, with conflicting emotions.

The Den (p. 70)
See 'Style' (p. 66).

Doctor Serafico (p. 73)
Rainer Maria Rilke (1875-1926): dubbed 'Doktor Serafico' ('Serafico' after Saint Francis) by his friend Princess Marie von Thurn und Taxis Hohenlohe, because 'Rainer Maria Rilke' was 'far too long'.
    Rilke began what he considered to be his life's work, the *Duino Elegies*, in 1912. For ten years he despaired of being able to complete them. Then, in February 1922, at the small Chateau de Muzot, in the Valais, Switzerland, he was caught up in a hurricane of creativity during which he completed the cycle of elegies, and also produced 'Sonnets to Orpheus'.
    Of Marthe, Rilke wrote: "My heart is wrung in a strange way: Marthe,

whom I discovered aged seventeen in the utmost misery, was my *protégée*, a
working-class girl, but with that downright genius of heart and mind
probably only found in French girls. What amazement, what indescribably
full, indeed overflowing, happiness she gave me during a certain period by
her alert understanding of all that is greatest and best, in which she even
outdistanced me. I doubt if any other human being has ever made it so clear
to me to what extent a spirit can unfold itself if one provides it with a little
space to live in, a little quiet, a scrap of blue sky."
                            —*Rainer Maria Rilke* by E. M. Butler, Cambridge 1946.
Of his impending death, Rilke wrote to his friend Rudolf Kassner on 15th
December 1926: "So it was this that my nature has been forewarning me of
so insistently for the last three years: I have fallen sick in a miserable and
infinitely painful manner, a little-known cellular change in the blood
becomes the starting-point of mercilessly cruel processes dispersed over
the entire body. And, I who never wanted to look it in the face, am now
learning to settle down with incommensurable, anonymous pain. I am
learning it with difficulty, with a hundred revolts, and such dim dismay."
                            —*Rilke, Man and Poet*, by Nora Wydenbruck, London, 1949.

"I have found a book of essays on Rilke waiting me; one of Rilke's ideas
about death annoyed me. I wrote on the margin:
    Draw rein; draw breath.
    Cast a cold eye
    On life, on death.
    Horseman pass by."
                            —W.B. Yeats to Edith Shackleton Heald, 1938.

Telling (p. 76)
"Where there is the *will* to say something there is always a *way*; imagination
and technique act as one ... For what is style but matter in motion!"
        —W.R. Rodgers introducing *Awake! and Other Poems*. London 1941.

Oil Painting: The Manse at Raloo (p. 78)
See 'Calendar' (p. 237); 'The Lay Preacher' (p. 168); 'The Raloo Sermon'
(p. 131).

An Attic in Holborn (p. 78)
Refers to 'Death of Chatterton', the painting by Henry Wallis, in the Tate
Gallery, London.

Gig (p. 79)
'The Methodist church hall'. The hall where my elder brother excelled as
senior-sixer of the Wolf Cubs, 24th Pack, and where, a generation later, my
second son demonstrated his prowess as a drummer in a pop group.

Elocution Lesson: Hot Cross Buns (p. 80)
As with private music lessons, elocution lessons were usually given in the
teacher's house, often on Saturday mornings. (I had thought of calling this
poem 'Saturday Morning at Mrs Kenmuir's'.) They could lead eventually
to a diploma, and they were sometimes related to amateur dramatics. See
'The Grand Central Hotel' (p. 96).

Brothers-in-law (p. 81)
See 'The McKelvey File' (p. 141) (VI. 'A Hearty Meal').

Ballad Singer: Chichester Street (p. 81)
The singer was Margaret Barry. See 'Paddy Reilly and Others' (p. 226).

The Variety Market, next to the Law Courts, was the subject of a clearance order, but carried on regardless, under protest. Opposite, the fire-brigade headquarters had a tower like a watch tower overlooking the area.

'And here and there a petal'. See 'The Tree' by Alex Comfort in *A Wreath for the Living* (London 1942). "Continuing comrades of/Comfort from the war." The same Alex Comfort.

The Round Pond (p. 83)
'A J.M. Barrie of the park'. See *J.M. Barrie and the Lost Boys* by Andrew Birkin; London, 1979. *Moments of Being* by Virginia Woolf; London, 1989.

Walled Garden, Irish Street, Downpatrick (p. 83)
See 'Lines Written Near Downpatrick after an Air-raid' (p. 275).

In Passing (p. 84)
See 'Time's Present' (p. 103).

The Girl (p. 87)
The girl referred to is in a poem of the same title published 43 years previously. See 'The Girl' (p. 318).

The Milkman (p. 87)
An attempt to make a poem from a dream.

High Low (p. 88)
See 'The Upland Field' (p. 263).

A Word in his Ear (p. 90)
See 'Grand Old Man' (p. 48).

Reunion (p. 90)
In 1939 Michael McLaverty published his first—and, some think, his best—novel. With the outbreak of war it did not receive the recognition it deserved. In 1979 it was reissued as a paperback and is now a classic. To celebrate its reissue, Michael McLaverty entertained three friends to a meal, dedicatees of his collection of short stories, *The Road to the Shore*: Robert Greacen, John Boyd and myself.

The Traveller (p. 91)
The Traveller was the man who called for the grocery order. He was a friend, like the milkman and postman known and addressed by name. As was the man making the deliveries on 'the hooded cart'. As, indeed, was the horse.

The Astoria (p. 91)
For a generation Magee's Nursery preserved for Ballyhackamore and the Upper Newtownards Road the remnants of rurality. See 'Nursery Land' (p.

119); 'Magee's Nursery' (p. 3). Then, in 1934, at a time when a new generation of cinemas reached out to the suburbs, the Astoria "supplanted lettuce by a let's pretend", and the green acres disappeared. The Astoria provided family entertainment for four decades, including the war years, when, after the threat of aerial bombing had passed, the Saturday night queue became part of the landscape.

See *Fading Lights, Silver Screens* by Michael Open (Belfast 1985).

NOTES FOR THE HINTERLAND

These poems, originally included in *The Selected Roy McFadden* (Blackstaff Press, 1983), formed what Philip Hobsbaum describes as a 'mini-collection' of previously-uncollected poems.

Ballyshannon (p. 95)
William Allingham (1824–1889), born at Ballyshannon, poet and diarist, Customs officer; husband of the painter Helen Allingham. See 'The Little B.A.' (p. 58).

An opposing stance to the obsession with self-publicity affecting writers and particularly poets. See 'Self-Generation' (p. 118); 'Poetry Reading' (p. 76); 'After Seymour's Funeral' (p. 38); 'The Public Readings' in 'Sketches of Boz' (p. 105)

Post-War (p. 95)
The end of the war and the election to Westminster in 1945 of a Labour government, in spite of continuing austerity, offered hope, if only for a time.

The Grand Central Hotel (p. 96)
Built in 1892, 'The G.C.' was Belfast's principal hotel. Not unlike the Shelbourne in Dublin, it provided a meeting-place for a variety of people and associations, in surroundings more formal than those of the public bars and cafés. During the 1939–45 war, it was patronised by officers in the British army and their associates. Outside, on the kerbstone, anti-war vendors of *Peace News* stood in jeopardy. With the onset of the Troubles, the hotel went out of business and became a British army barracks until 1980, suffering serious bombings.

' ... past where the stony head/Hangs, lidless, lintel-high.' Stylised female head over entrance to Bank of Ireland, Royal Avenue. See *Belfast: An Illustrated Architectural Guide* by Paul Larmour. Belfast, 1987; *Central Belfast: A Historical Gazetteer*, by Marcus Patton. Belfast 1993.

Conveyancer (p. 98)
Chaque notaire s'emporte le débris d'un poète.

Mortgage Redemptions (p. 99)
Redemptions brought together solicitor and client after an interval of perhaps 25 or 30 years.

Sancto's Dog (p. 100)
The poem is an adult's wry exploration of the lingering scenes of childhood and what succeeding generations had done with them. Defying bathos, it ends with a child's uncomprehending fear at his mother's departure to an unknown destination: *O where is Vote?* It was common practice for candidates at local elections to provide transport to the polling stations. *Your mother has gone to vote.*

Time's Present (p. 103)
In my childhood, a box of King George V chocolates was a sumptuous present for a lady. It belonged to a time when you were promised 'a thousand a year or a wife/husband' if you accepted the last sandwich or biscuit on the plate.
Rutherford Mayne: pseudonym of Samuel Waddell, 1878-1967; a prominent protagonist in the Ulster Literary Theatre as actor and dramatist. He was employed by the Irish Land Commission.

Helston (p. 103)
Helston, in Cornwall, renowned for its Floral Dance, is where my brother died suddenly while on holiday. He saw Cornwall as part of a Celtic commonwealth, and would not have objected to being buried there.

A Death in Maryville Street (p. 104)
Short of the murder and maiming that characterised the Troubles, traffic hold-ups and diversions, as a result of bomb warnings, were a continuing frustration. A death in Maryville Street, of natural causes, seemed almost incongruous against a background of a bombed and barricaded town.
See 'Fire Bomb' (p. 145).

Sketches of Boz (p. 105)
'Boz', pseudonym adopted by Dickens for the sketches contributed to various journals that began his writing career. The origin of the pseudonym is explained by Foster: it was "the nickname of a pet child, his youngest brother Augustus, whom, in honour of Goldsmith's *Vicar of Wakefield* he had dubbed Moses, which being facetiously pronounced through the nose became Boses, and being shortened became Boz. "Boz was a familiar household name, Dickens said, long before he was an author, and so he came to adopt it". *The Dickens Index* by Nicholas Bentley, Michael Slater and Nina Burgis. Oxford, 1990.

The blacking factory
Warren's blacking warehouse at Hungerford Stairs, "a crazy, tumbledown old house, abutting of course on the river, and literally overrun with rats", where the 12-year-old boy worked ten hours a day.

The appraisal
While his father was incarcerated as a debtor in the Marshalsea, it became necessary for the young Dickens to appear before an official appraiser to have his clothing valued. The official apparently turned a blind eye to the old family watch which the boy wore with pride.

Ellis & Blackmore
In May 1827 Dickens became a junior clerk to solicitors in "a poor old set of chambers in Holborn Court" (later in Raymond Buildings nearby) at a weekly wage of half-a-guinea. He turned up for work in a blue jacket, with a soldier's cap worn "rather jauntily on one side of his head". The firm's petty cash book contained the familiar names of Weller, Bardell, Rudge and Knott.

Hungerford Market
A large building erected in 1833 for the sale of food and miscellaneous ware. The site is now occupied by Charing Cross Station.

Mary Hogarth
Sister-in-law and close companion, who died when she was 17.

48 Doughty Street
Leased by Dickens in March 1837 at a rent of £80 per annum. A "frightfully first-class Mansion", it had twelve rooms on four floors, and involved the employment of four servants. Mary Hogarth resided there as one of the family, and died there, in Dickens's arms, in May 1837.

Mary Beadnell
The young Dickens proposed to and was rejected by her in 1833. In 1855, as Mrs Winter, she wrote to the then-famous author. Dickens eagerly replied and arranged a private meeting. When he discovered that she "had become very fat and commonplace", he recoiled. Later he drew a cruel picture of her as Flora Finch in *Little Dorrit.*

Miss Ellen
Ellen Lawless Ternan, youngest of three sisters with a theatrical background, at eighteen was taken up by the forty-five-year-old Dickens, and became his mistress, continuing in a clandestine relationship until after his death in 1870. She later married a schoolteacher.

The Public Readings
See 'Self-Generation' (p. 118); 'After Seymour's Funeral' (p. 38).

A WATCHING BRIEF

A Watching Brief was first published by Blackstaff Press in December 1978. Following objections by the author, the book was withdrawn from circulation. It was reprinted and, with a different cover and typographical amendments, published in September 1979.

Reprieve (p. 116)
Many chemists used to provide an ancillary service in the destruction of unwanted family pets: cats and dogs mainly; occasionally birds. The victim was incarcerated in a metal box, with a sliding panel to allow chloroform-soaked cotton wool to be inserted. A fee of half-a crown was charged. The corpses were removed and disposed of by the city's cleansing department.

Postscript to Ulster Regionalism (p. 116)
See *Ulster Poets 1800-1850* by John Hewitt. Privately printed, Belfast (1950);
The Rhyming Weavers by John Hewitt, Belfast (1970). See also 'Calendar';
and 'No Dusty Pioneer', my reminiscences of John Hewitt in *The Poet's Place*,
edited by Gerald Dawe and John Wilson Foster. Belfast, 1991.

The Island (p. 118)
One of the Skerries, off Portrush, County Antrim. See 'Portrush' (p. 280).

Managing Clerk (p. 119)
'Adduce in Registery of Deeds/Candle's epiphany'. Recollect:
"How far that little candle throws its beams.
So shines a good deed in a naughty world."

Nursery Land (p. 119)
See 'Magee's Nursery' (p. 3).

Theatre: Lunchtime (p. 120)
When I was a student I used to spend lunchtimes with Joseph Tomelty, who
was then manager of the Group Theatre in Belfast. We sat in the tiny box-
office, where he took, and sometimes tried to evade, telephone bookings
for the evening's performance.

Immigrants (p. 122)
In 1905 my mother's father James Steel, a Scot, brought his young family
from the 'English North' to Belfast, where he became chief draughtsman
of a local shipyard.

White Stockings
Perhaps as a consequence of having mothered nine children, my
grandmother took to her bed in her early fifties and continued as a semi-
invalid throughout my lifetime.

Luna
The youngest of four sisters, she died of tuberculosis when she was 23. See
'My Mother's Young Sister' (p. 45).

Geordie
See 'I Spy' (p. 122).

The Raloo Sermon
An amateur painter, a collector of books and curios, my grandfather was
also a lay or relief preacher for the Unitarian Church. As a young girl, my
mother often accompanied him to churches in the countryside. He ended
his days at Raloo, County Antrim. He presented his painting of the local
church to the minister. Many years after his death I glimpsed it on the wall
in a house occupied by the minister's widow. See 'Calendar' (p. 237); 'The
Lay Preacher' from the sequence 'Quail Holdings' (p.165); and 'Oil
Painting: The Manse at Raloo' (p. 78).

Coffee at Crumble's (p. 132)
Campbell's was the favourite meeting-place for writers and painters during

the 1930s and 40s: Campbell's Patisserie, Café and Snackery, at 8 Donegall
Square West, Belfast, overlooking the City Hall. On the top floor, at a table
by the window, local practitioners met and talked. Joseph Tomelty, Sam
Hanna Bell, Denis Ireland, Richard Rowley, Louis MacNeice, Jack Loudan,
were among the writers; Paul Nietsche, William Conor, J. Langtry Lynas,
Rowel Friers and George MacCann ('Maguire' in *Autumn Sequel*) were
among the artists. 'The Table in the Window', a radio programme produced
by Sam Hanna Bell and broadcast by the BBC on 9th November 1961,
contains the recorded voices of some of the habitués.

In the poem, Derek Walsh, Dan Armour and Maynard Chatterton
remind me of Denis Ireland (autobiographer, Senator, raconteur), Jack
Loudan (journalist and playwright), and Richard Rowley (Richard Valentine
Williams, 1877-1947, poet and playwright.)

'May I presume to sit beside the ghost/Of William Butler Yeats?' See
'Yeats's Ghost' by Denis Ireland, *The Northman*, Winter 1941-42.
Concertinaed. I disagree with Fowler's opinion regarding the addition of -ed
to "words with unEnglish terminations", and with his preference for the
apostrophe. See *Modern English Usage* by H.W. Fowler, 1960 edition, page
126.

Baptism (p. 138)
John Gibson, a protegé of Tyrone Gutherie's, was drama producer at the
BBC in Belfast, before moving on to London. He produced my radio play
The Angry Hound in 1952.

Sound Sense (p. 138)
'Sam Bell it was who raised a somnolent head.' Sam Hanna Bell (1909-
1990): novelist, BBC feature-writer and producer, co-editor and co-founder
of *Lagan.*

D-Day (p. 139)
An elaboration of Michael McLaverty's account of his retirement from the
teaching profession, and the eagerly-awaited day of liberation to unfettered
writing. See *The Silken Twine: A Study of the Works of Michael McLaverty* by
Sophia Hillan King; Dublin, 1992.

The Law Courts Revisited (p. 146)
Something of a scandal in the court offices when it was published, the poem
has since been read at a gathering of legal luminaries, anecdotally acceptable.

VERIFICATIONS

The first of my books to be published in Belfast. The title was intended to
indicate a reassessment and confirmation of earlier convictions and attitudes.
I had tested and found valid the intuition that the innocent eye was of more
value to a poet than the uniformity encouraged by the classroom. I also
confirmed the importance of style: illumination of language controlled by
acquired craftsmanship. And I continued to be aware that poetry, as
distinct from verse, has a music which backs and permeates the words.

Knowing My Place (p. 154)
Originally entitled 'Keeping My Place'. I was advised that the title had already been used.

Smith (p. 157)
Cu-Chulain: Hound of Culain, the Smith.

Daisymount Terrace (p. 158)
After we were evicted in the Troubles of the 1920s (See 'Evictions' p. 58) we found accommodation at Dundonald, on the outskirts of Belfast. Daisymount Terrace was a terrace of small grey houses next to Gape Row. (See Agnes Romilly White's novel of that name; reissued Belfast, 1988; *The Most Unpretending of Places: A History of Dundonald, County Down*, Belfast, 1987).

The Johnson Girls (p. 159)
'Nonetheless there was common/Ground ...' The grounds were always known by the name of a previous owner, Stringer. See 'Stringer's Field' (p. 160).

First Funeral (p. 161)
See 'The Statute of Limitations' (p. 46).

Downpatrick (p. 163)
Comparable with our exodus to Dundonald twenty years previously, as a result of our house having been wrecked in the Belfast air-raid of 1941, we found shelter in Downpatrick. I was aware that my father was born there, and that his mother's people had been prominent in the town for some 200 years, but I was more committed to my mother's people and their emigration from the north of England. Later, Downpatrick and what I was able to discover about my ancestors, became a personal mythology.

Ballyhackamore (p. 164)
See 'The Innocent Eye' (p. 23).

Quail Holdings (p. 165)
My father's mother's family, Quail, lived in Downpatrick, County Down, for precisely two centuries, from 1700 to 1900. Of the various trades which they promoted, that of cabinet-maker persisted throught the generations. Their furniture was described as 'Irish Chippendale'.

My grandmother's marriage was disapproved of by her elders, and she was disinherited. At the age of 39 her husband was thrown from his horse and killed. The business was sold, and the widow with five of her six children left Downpatrick for Belfast. Only my father, aged 12, remained behind. My grandmother's sister (Great-aunt Anna) disowned the family burial vault and is said to have thrown the key into the River Quoile.

In 'The Lay Preacher' I tell of my other Grandfather (*Steel*: the name a half-rhyme with *Quail*) preaching at the Unitarian church in Downpatrick, accompanied by his young daughter, later my mother. Waiting for her father after the service, she encounters the Quail burial vault, containing the forebears of her future husband, while his father lay buried in the

Cathedral graveyard, in his mother's grave, with only her name on the stone.

Gray Quail was my grandmother's eldest surviving uncle, *in loco parentis* towards her and her siblings.

The name of Mary Quail appears in the family tree, a sister to my grandmother and Anna, without dates.

A Sad Day's Rain (p. 169)
See 'Portrush' (p. 280).

Laureate (p. 172)
In 1970 my daughter Grania shared first prize in a national poetry competition for children organised by *The Observer*. Her poem subsequently appeared in an anthology, *Under the Moon: Over the Stars*, Belfast 1971.

Tuesday (p. 174)
During the depression of the Thirties shawls as outdoor apparel were commonplace in the poorer parts of Belfast. Women wearing them were known as 'shawlies'.

The Ards Circuit (p. 174)
The Ards Circuit was the course for the Tourist Trophy Races from 1928 to 1936. The 1928 race was won by Kaye Don in a Lea Francis. See 'Victories' (p. 66).

Uncle Alec (p. 174)
One of my mother's brothers who joined the army in the Great War at the age of 16, and was wounded and shellshocked at the Dardanelles.

Stranmillis Road (p. 176)
'Drummond Allison's war'. I met Drummond Allison when he was a very youthful officer in the British Army: enthusiastic, talkative, innocent. "His tragedy ... is implicit in the bare recital of his dates, 1921-1943."
—*Poets of the 1939-1945 War* by R.N. Currey. The British Council, 1967. See also *The Yellow Night* by Drummond Allison, poems published posthumously by the Fortune Press, London, in 1944.

Tom's Tale (p. 178)
Told to me by an old man in Lisburn in the 1940s.

The Trap (p. 179)
Based on an account given to me by John Hewitt, and given to him by his father, of an old man (grandfather of a prominent citizen) being taken to the asylum.

THE GARRYOWEN

After Long Silence. Not altogether silence, since I continued to publish in periodicals: but the first collection nonetheless since 1947. The poems were chosen by Cecil Day Lewis and Ian Parsons, directors of Chatto & Windus. The title proposed by me was *The Garryowen*, and when I inquired whether a gambit famous in Irish rugby would be known to English readers, Ian Parsons assured me that as a paid-up member of Blackheath Rugby Football Club he heartily approved of both the tactic and the title.

Glenarm (p. 183)
A good part of the interval between collections had been spent in earning a living and rearing a family. Fittingly, the first poem in the new collection is dedicated to my wife. It was inspired by a photograph of her as a young girl on holiday at Glenarm, County Antrim.

Independence (p. 183)
Included in the Oxford Book of Irish Verse, edited by Donagh MacDonagh and Lennox Robinson, London, 1958, it celebrates Ghanaian independence.

Synge in Paris (p. 185)
In 1965 I was one of six poets (the others being Padraic Colum, W.R. Rodger, John Hewitt, Thomas Kinsella and Seamas Heaney) to be asked to dedicate a poem to the Lyric Players Theatre, Belfast, in celebration of the laying of the foundation stone of the new building by Austin Clarke. 'Synge in Paris' seemed an appropriate choice in associating the theatre with a major Irish dramatist.

Poem for John Boyd (p. 185)
See 'The Upland Field' (p. 263).

Memories of Chinatown (p. 186)
Part of the Knock-Belmont area where I grew up was locally known as Chinatown. 'Jackie Dugan' was originally written for my children. He was a real character. He was so well received that I invented his contemporary, Clutey Gibson.

The Arcadia (p. 190)
The Ladies' and Children's Bathing Place at Portrush, County Antrim.

Folkminder (p. 193)
Michael J. Murphy was a member of the Irish Folklore Commission, and subsequently on the staff of Department of Irish Folklore, UCD. He has collected folklore all over Ulster and written several books, including *At Slieve Gullion's Foot*, Dundalk 1941, and *Tyrone Folkquest*, Belfast 1973.

Night-Fishing (p. 194)
This is another Cushendall poem.

Grania at Three
Included in a BBC archival recording with Seamas Heaney on 8 December 1966.

The Garryowen (p. 200)
Term used to describe a tactic in Irish Rugby football, when the ball is kicked high ('up and under'), giving time for a maverick assault.

Brendan Behan (p. 201)
On its appearance in *The Irish Times* after Brendan Behan's death, W.R.

Rodgers considered this poem to be "the best thing written about Brendan".

Second Letter to an Irish Novelist (p. 202)
See 'Letter to an Irish Novelist' (p. 291)

The Golden Boy (p. 203)
A greatly abbreviated version of the poem originally published in 1966, on the third anniversary of John F. Kennedy's death.

In Drumcliffe Churchyard (p. 203)
Written after the return of W.B. Yeats's remains to Ireland in 1948. I owe the last line to Ian Parsons.

SPEECH FOR THE VOICELESS: POEMS 1947-1970

I Won't Dance (p. 207)
Relates to the Troubles of the early 1920s.
cf. "I am of Ireland,/And the Holy Land of Ireland,/And time runs on," cried she./"Come out of charity,/Come dance with me in Ireland."—W.B. Yeats, 'Words for Music Perhaps'. Cuala Press, 1932.

Spring Breaks the Heart (p. 208)
See note to 'Coffee at Crumble's' (p. 339)

Death of a Mahatma (p. 209)
Mohandas Karamchand Gandhi (1869-1948) was assassinated on 30th January 1948. At the cremation, Pandid Nehru declared: "A light has gone out from the world."

Death Dive (p. 210)
'That film you saw in childhood'. Probably *Hell's Angels* (1930) directed by Howard Hughes.

One Who Got Away (p. 214)
Originally published in *Life and Letters*, April 1949, under the title 'Derriaghy'.

New Words for an Old Tune (p. 217)
'The Castle of Dromore'.

Belfast (p. 218)
"It was the Celtic-speaking Irish or Erinn, who had mastered most of Ireland by the beginning of the Christian era, who called this crossing place *Beal Feirsde*. The name literally means the mouth of, or approach to, the sandbank or crossing. The Farset stream, entering the Lagan almost at its mouth, takes its name from this sandbank crossing: *fertas* translated can mean a sandbank, a sandbar, a crossing-place or a ford."
    —*Belfast: An Illustrated History* by Jonathan Bardon. Belfast, 1982.

Star (p. 221)
See 'i.m. Edith McFadden' by Valentin Iremonger, *Horan's Field*, Dublin 1972; and *Sandymount, Dublin*, Dublin 1988. "It is the first poem I have

written since 1946." Letter dated 6th September, 1950 from Valentin Iremonger to Roy McFadden.

Dinah Kohner (p. 222)
Dinah Kohner (1936-64) "seemed to have every gift of nature. Even those who met her casually during her schooldays carried away an unforgettable impression of her vivid dark beauty ... She joined the Peace Ship *Hope* to sail for Equador. What she achieved there, in a few brief months, is now part of the medical history of that country. It was as a result of a last-minute decision, just before the *Hope* left for New York, that she flew with a team of doctors to a distant jungle mission hospital, to help people who desperately needed her. The plane failed to take off from the airstrip on its return flight, and crashed in the jungle.

Mr Oisin Kelly of Dublin has carved a memorial plaque which has been placed in the entrance hall of the New Building. The framed manuscript of Roy McFadden's poem hung there already."
—Elizabeth H. Maxwell in *A History of Richmond Lodge School.*

Paddy Reilly and Others (p. 226)
First published as a foreword to *Threshold* No. 18, of which I was guest editor.
Margaret Barry: 'Queen of the Tinkers'; came to prominence as a ballad-singer and folk-singer in the 1950s, and made several recordings. Earlier she was a street singer. See 'Ballad Singer: Chichester Street' (p. 81).

'You who departed like MacMurrough'. "The story of the Anglo-Irish invasion of Ireland begins as a personal drama, with two warrior kings, Dermot MacMurrough of Leinster and Tiernan O'Rourke of Breifne, pitted one against the other ... of the overthrow and exile of MacMurrough."
—F.X. Martin in *The Course of Irish History,* Cork 1967.

ELEGY FOR THE DEAD OF *THE PRINCESS VICTORIA*

Originally published by The Lisnagarvey Press in 1953.
A popular Larne-Stranraer steamer, *The Princess Victoria* sank in a violent storm on 31st January 1953. 128 passengers were drowned.

THE HEART'S TOWNLAND

"In an article in *Poetry Ireland* in 1950, John Hewitt, then on a high tide of regionalism, could still confuse sentiment with dogma. Of myself, he said: 'Roy McFadden began, as I have indicated, snugly within the fold of a contemporary English school, but, pushed out of this by a strong Yeatsian influence, has become more and more individual as he matures. His last volume is entitled *The Heart's Townland* (1947) and demonstrates that he has gained the primary regionalist position, love of place, safely enough'. I never belonged, let alone snugly, to an English school of poets. Most English reviewers, for whatever reason, saw my work as Irish as early as 1941.

I simply contributed to English magazines and anthologies which included poetry and prose by contemporary English writers. The influence of Yeats, which I readily acknowledge, though it was superficial, did not push me out of anything; together with the influence of John Hewitt which is apparent in the volume he mentions—an influence which I warmly acknowledge— it only pushed me, I hope, towards the writing of better poems. I was unaware that 'love of place' proved that I was an Official Regionalist. So much requires definition. Place: what place? Tiveragh and its environs? And so much is left out. Love of place, however defined, when it becomes dogmatic, becomes dangerous".

— 'The Belfast Forties', *Force 10*. Sligo, 1994.

Calendar (p. 237)
Addressed to John Hewitt, this poem reflects my association with him in a common concern with regional values and appearances. See Hewitt's essay 'The Bitter Gourd' (first published in *Lagan* in 1945, and subsequently included in *Ancestral Voices*, Belfast, 1987). My reservations concerning the reality of an 'Ulster' culture, largely undefined, hardened into friendly scepticism. See 'No Dusty Pioneer' in *The Poet's Place*, Belfast, 1991. See also 'Postscript to Ulster Regionalism' (p. 116).

'Thoreau who taught you to be regional': Henry David Thoreau (1817-62), essayist, poet, naturalist, born at Concord, Massachussetts. See *A Week on the Concord and Merrimac Rivers* (1845), *Walden, or Life in the Woods* (1854), *A Writer's Journal*, edited by Laurence Stapleton, London 1961.

The Song Creates All (p. 244)
"My Dr. Friend
Lest you should not have heard of the Death of Mr. Blake I have written this to inform you—He died on Sunday Night at 6 o'clock in a most glorious manner. He said He was going to that Country he had all His life wished to see & expressed himself Happy hoping for Salvation through Jesus Christ— Just before he died His countenance became fair—His eyes Brighten'd and He burst out in singing of the things he saw in Heaven. In truth he Died like a saint as a person who was standing by Him Observed ...
Yrs. affection[y.]
G. Richmond."
—Quoted in *The Life of William Blake* by Mona Wilson. London, 1948.

Elegy for a Dog (p. 245)
A muddy paw-mark survives on my copy of Topham's *Company Law*. When the poem appeared in *The Irish Times* in February 1945, Oliver Edwards wrote an appreciative letter, which led to an introduction to his wife Barbara and, subsequently, to the emergence of the quarterly, *Rann*.

Thor (p. 246)
See 'After Seymour's Funeral' (p. 38).

White Death, Green Spring (p. 248)
'Quiver all your darts'.

"Quiver," the man in the Land Registry said, *The Irish Times* spread open at the literary page. "You mean: *replace in quiver?*"
"Yes," I said; "as with gun, *holster-up.*"
He nodded, and handed me the Land Certificate. "Quiver that," he said in the direction of my briefcase.

The Heart's Townland (p. 253)
In the summer of 1945 I stayed with Oliver and Barbara Edwards in their house at Ballyorney in County Wicklow. Yeats's biographer, Joseph Hone, lived nearby; and not far away, was the cottage where the poet Joseph Campbell had recently been found dead. (See 'After Seymour's Funeral' (p. 38)). During my stay I met Yeats's widow and his daughter Anne, and I was taken to see the printing machine of the Cuala Press.

Later, I stayed with John Hewitt and his wife in their small house at Tiveragh, outside Cushendall. While the title has a Hevittean ring, the poem nevertheless extends to both townlands, and beyond them to the wastelands of the war years.

'under Yeats's lamp'. In their house at Ballyorney Barbara and Oliver Edwards proudly possessed a ruby lamp which had belonged to W.B. Yeats.

Forrest Reid (p. 257)
Forrest Reid (1876–1947) lived at Ormiston Crescent, off the Upper Newtownards Road, in my part of the town; but I never met him. However, I heard about him secondhand. It was John Boyd who told me of the old man's fervent wish for a revelation at the end.

See *Forrest Reid: A Portrait and Study* by Russell Burlingham: London, 1953; *The Green Avenue: The Life and Writings of Forrest Reid, 1875-1947* by Brian Taylor: Cambridge, 1980.

A Song for Victory Night (p. 257)
A large bonfire was set alight in Wallace Park, Lisburn, to celebrate the victory of the Allied forces over Germany. The poem, appropriately (for me), was published by John Middleton Murry in *The Adelphi.*

Interlude in May (p. 258)
'The peace tree blossomed when the brown dog died'. See 'After Seymour's Funeral' (p. 38)

The Upland Field (p. 263)
See 'Leaving Lisburn' (p. 210).

FLOWERS FOR A LADY

Elegy for a Sixth-former (p. 269)
'Where I'm the bounder, a remove away'. Greyfriars language. See *The Magnet*, 1908-40; *Frank Richards* by Mary Cadogen, London, 1988.

Early Casualty (p. 269)
See 'First Funeral' (p. 161); 'Elegy for a Noncombatant' (p. 270).

Enniskerry (p. 271)
'I turned from unapocalyptic door'. See *The White Horseman: Prose and Verse of the New Apocalypse*, edited by J.F. Hendry and Henry Treece. London, 1941.

St. Stephen's Green, Dublin (p. 271)
See 'Dublin to Belfast: Wartime' (p. 279).

Paul Robeson (p. 276)
See 'Autograph Album' (p. 16).

The Orator (p. 278)
'We'll need a Sheehy-Skeffington'. "Francis Sheehy-Skeffington was an anti-militarist, a fighting pacifist, a man gentle and kindly even to his bitterest opponents, who always ranged himself on the side of the weak against the strong, whether the struggle was one of class, sex or race domination."
—Hanna Sheehy-Skeffington in *Dublin 1916*, edited by Roger McHugh. London 1966.
"The officials appeared to panic, martial law was imposed and more people were arrested than had actually taken part in the rising. The pacifist, Sheehy-Skeffington, although he had taken no part in the rising, was arrested and shot without trial."
—*The Course of Irish History*, edited by T.W. Moody and F.X. Martin. Cork, 1967.

Memory of Sand (p. 279)
See later version, 'End of Season' (p. 37).

Portrush (p. 280)
See other 'Portrush' (p. 162).

Saint Francis and the Birds (p. 288)
Included in the *Oxford Book of Irish Verse* edited by Donagh MacDonagh and Lennox Robinson. Oxford, 1958.

Letter to an Irish Novelist (p. 291)
Stanza 4; 'Aeonic seas'. AE, pen-name of George William Russell, 1867-1935. "A compositor's difficulty in making out the word 'Aeon' with which Russell had signed an article, and which he printed AE—?, had suggested the pen-name now familiar to many who could not tell the poet's real name".
—*A Memoir of AE* by John Eglinton; London, 1937.

William Blake Sees God (p. 293)
"On Peckham Rye (by Dulwich Hill) it was, as he in after years related, that while quite a child, of eight or ten perhaps, he had his first vision. Sauntering along, the boy looked up and saw a tree filled with angels, bright angelic wings bespangling every branch like stars. Returned home he related the incident, and only through his mother's intercession escaped a thrashing from his honest father, for telling a lie".—*The Life of William Blake* by Alexander Gilchrist, edited by Ruthven Todd. London, 1942.

Cuchulain (p. 294)
"When Cuchulain was in the east, learning feats of arms from Scathach so that he might win the hand of Emer, he fought against another woman-warrior, Aife, an enemy of Scathach; and he overcame her and had a son by her. All this is told in a long saga called 'The Wooing of Emer'. The boy is to come to Ireland when he grows to manhood, and he is not to tell his name on the demand of a single warrior. 'The Tragic Death of Aife's Only Son' tells of the boy's coming to Ireland and of his death at the hand of his own father. It is the story of Sohrab and Rustum, the theme also of Hildebrandslied, evidently an ancient Indo-European motif. The Irish text is very short, so short that we must suppose that the manuscript versions of these stories served merely as an outline which the reciter could develop as he went along." —*Early Irish Literature* by Myles Dillon, Chicago, 1948.

The Journey Home (p. 299)
In 1944 a prospect of peace inspired hope of a more enlightened society in the post-war years. This poem envisages a journey back to the sloughed-off iniquities of the past.

SWORDS AND PLOUGHSHARES

Easter 1942 (p. 308)
'Who scorned O'Connell's glove'. It is said that, having killed a man as a result of a duel, Daniel O'Connell thereafter always wore a glove on his right hand in church when he was in contact with the altar-rail.

Evening in Donegal (p. 316)
'A dirty fighter'. Cuchulain's 'ultimate weapon' was the spear called the 'Gae Bulga' or breach-maker. 'This could be used only in the water, by a warrior fighting in river or at ford; once it entered his opponent's body, the spearhead opened and thirty barbs shot forth, burying themselves so deeply in the flesh that they could not be withdrawn but had to be cut out. When Cuchulain left Scatthach to return to Ireland, she gave him the Gae Bulga, for it was the only one of its kind'.
                    — *Golden Legends of the Gael* by Maud Joynt. Dublin. No date.

RUSSIAN SUMMER

Russian Summer (p. 321)
On 22nd June 1941, the German armies invaded the Soviet Union, and the war moved to the east, leaving behind a summer's respite and relief.

Published separately as a pamphlet, with a woodcut illustration by Leslie Owen Baxter, by Gayfield Press, Dublin, in 1941: 'Made and printed by Cecil Salkeld November 1945'. Cecil ffrench Salkeld (1908–69) was a painter, poet, playwright and raconteur, who in 1955 became Brendan Behan's father-in-law. One of the characters in *At Swim-Two-Birds*, Cashel Byrne, was modelled on him. It is said that Cecil Salkeld went to bed in 1957 and got up on only one occasion, for Brendan's funeral. It was indeed from his bed in 1941 that he greeted Robert Greacen and myself as 'the Holy Luthers of the preachin' North'.

Title Index

2 September 1939 *65*
5 Anglesea Road, Dublin *10*
34 Tite Street *65*

A Carol for Christmas Day and
Every Day *243*
A Cry *311*
A Dead Chief *26*
A Death in Maryville Street *104*
A Dog, An Afternoon *7*
A Man Observed
    Standing Beside a Grave *46*
A Sad Day's Rain *169*
A Small Incident in Town *45*
A Song for
    One Who Stayed *223*
A Song for Victory Night *257*
A Word in His Ear *90*
A Wreath for Shoon *289*
Advice in Spring *243*
After Hallowe'en *161*
After Seymour's Funeral *38*
After the Broadcast *104*
All the Fugitives *287*
Allotments *136*
An Attic in Holborn *78*
An Exhibition of Themselves *7*
And Like Cuchulain *287*
Another Autumn *210*
Another Place *4*
Armistice Day *145*
Autograph Album *16*
Autumn Rises *241*
Autumn Voyager *208*

Ballad Singer:
    Chichester Street *81*
Ballyhackamore *164*
Ballyshannon *95*

Baptism *138*
Barnardo Boy *79*
Bed and Breakfast *23*
Belfast *218*
Belgravia in Winter *18*
Birthday Poem *89*
Brendan Behan *201*
Brothers-in-Law *81*
Burns Night 14

Calendar *237*
Captain Thompson *59*
Carrie Coates *28*
Child's Funeral *209*
Christmas Eve *120*
Class of 1926 *15*
Coffee at Crumble's *132*
Confirmation Class *10*
Contemplations of Mary *190*
Conveyancer *98*
Crocus *216*
Cuchulain *294*

D-Day *139*
Daisymount Terrace *158*
Death Dive *210*
Death of a Mahatma *209*
Detail for a Painting *30*
Dinah Kohner *222*
Directions for a Journey *250*
Doctor Serafico *73*
Downpatrick *163*
Dublin to Belfast: Wartime *279*
Dylan Thomas *215*

Early Casualty *269*
Easter 1942 *308*
Elegy for a Dog *245*
Elegy for a Mad Girl *290*

Elegy for a Noncombatant 270
Elegy for a Sixth-Former 269
Elegy for the Dead
    of The Princess Victoria 233
Elevoine Santi 228
Elocution Lesson:
    Hot Cross Buns 80
Emigrants 55
End of Season 37
Enniskerry 271
Epithalamium 273
Eurydice 121
Evening in Donegal 316
Evictions 58

Family Album 194
Family Group 171
Fire Bomb 145
First Blood 70
First Funeral 161
Flower Piece 224
Flowers for a Lady:
    First Elegy 280
    Second Elegy 283
    Third Elegy 284
    Fourth Elegy 285
    Fifth Elegy 285
    Sixth Elegy 286
    Seventh Elegy 286
    Eighth Elegy 287
Folkminder 193
For the Record 48
Forrest Reid 257

Gallagher's Donkey 35
Gig 79
Glenarm 183
Going to Church
    One Morning 88
Gone Away 61
Grand Old Man 48

Hans Crescent 42
Heartholder 250

Helston 103
Herbertson at Forty 8
Heroes 137
High Low 88
Holly Tree 207
Homecoming 218
House Under Construction 51
Hyde Park 24

I Spy 122
I Won't Dance 207
Idyll 33
Immigrants 122
Impostors 146
In Drumcliffe Churchyard 203
In Ireland Now 309
In Passing 84
In the Meantime 310
In this Their Season 242
Independence 183
Interlude in May 258
Interpolation 72
Irish Street,
    Downpatrick 1886 12

Jack Yeats
    at Fitzwilliam Square 27
Jean Armstrong 175
Jimmy Kershaw 213
Jonathan Swift 289
Jump 19
June Blossom 31

Kew Gardens 156
Knowing My Place 154

La Servante
    Au Grand Coeur 229
Latecomer 117
Leaving Lisburn 210
Les Plaintes d'un Icare 229
Letter from the Mournes 274
Letter to a Boy in Prison 273
Letter to an Irish Novelist 291

Lines by Slieve Donard 307
Lines Written near
    Downpatrick after
    an Air-Raid 275
Liverpool Boat 217
Love 80
Lucy Gray 170

Magee's Nursery 3
Managing Clerk 119
Manifesto 247
March 153
McKelvey Revisits Scenes
    of Childhood 16
Memories of Chinatown 186
Memory of a Girl with a Red
Scarf 252
Memory of Sand 279
Miniature 19
Miss Purdy in Old Age 5
Miss Walters 11
Mortgage Redemptions 99
Mr McAlonen 54
Music for an Anniversary 213
My Father Had a Clock 251
My Mother's Young Sister 45

New Words
    for an Old Tune 217
New Year's Eve 3
Night Out 32
Night-Fishing 194
North-Antrim Prospect 277
Nursery Land 119

October
    and the Leaves Again 228
Oil Painting:
    The Manse at Raloo 78
Old Knock Graveyard 44
Old Mr Kershaw 67
Old Style 43
Old Tennis Courts 47
One of the Fallen 215

One Who Got Away 214
Out in the Country 115

Paddy Reilly and Others 226
Parvenus 43
Paul Robeson 276
Philanderer 137
Pim 33
Plaint of the Working Men 315
Poem for John Boyd 185
Poem for Today 308
Poetry Reading 76
Portrait of a Poet 245
Portrush 162
Portrush 280
Post-War 95
Postscript 219
Postscript to
    Ulster Regionalism 116
Prayer for a Young Man 314
Prelude to an Epitaph 317
Premonition 204
Prior Title 17
Proxy 9

Quail Holdings 165

Rain Towards Evening 307
Remainders 84
Remembering Orpheus 11
Reprieve 116
Retribution 140
Return 220
Reunion 90
Roger Casement's Rising 184
Runaway 140
Russian Summer 321

Saint Francis and the Birds 288
Sancto's Dog 100
Second Letter
    to an Irish Novelist 202
Self-Generation 118
Sheepdog Trials 189

Shop Soil 72
Side Ward 71
Soliloquy of an Old
    Nationalist Woman 313
Sixes and Sevens 278
Sketches of Boz 105
Smith 157
Song for a Turning Tide 224
Song Towards Spring 316
Sound Sense 138
Spring Breaks the Heart 208
St. Stephen's Green,
    Dublin 271
Star 221
Stranmillis Road 176
Stringer's Field 160
Style 66
Sunday-School Excursion 32
Survivor 85
Synge in Paris 185

Telling 76
The Arcadia 190
The Ards Circuit 174
The Astoria 91
The Backward Glance 212
The Bar Library 53
The Colonel 68
The Dancers, Sloane Street 24
The Dead Prince 253
The Death of a Cyclist 246
The Den 70
The Disappeared Ones 67
The Dog 276
The Dogged Past 211
The Drums 293
The Eiffel Tower 173
The Foster Twins 34
The Garden
    of Remembrance 86
The Garden Seat 13
The Garryowen 200
The Girl 87
The Girl 318

The Golden Boy 203
The Grand Central Hotel 96
The Guest 315
The Healer 212
The Heart's Townland 253
The Hill 25
The Hole 89
The Hounds 277
The House 69
The Hunger-Marchers 8
The Innocent Eye 23
The Invisible Menders 35
The Island 118
The Island of Saints
    and Scholars 277
The Johnson Girls 159
The Journey Home 299
The Last Length 225
The Law Courts Revisited 146
The Little B.A. 58
The Little Black Rose 36
The Low Glen 4
The McKelvey File 141
The Milkman 87
The Moment of Truth 223
The Monk 275
The Orator 278
The Ordeal
    of Clutey Gibson 176
The Pattern 317
The Poor Mad Girl's
    Love Song 312
The Riderless Horse 179
The Rockery 52
The Round Pond 83
The Silverman Plea 53
The Song Creates All 244
The Statute of Limitations 46
The Stuffed Fox 26
The Summer's Gone 204
The Trap 179
The Traveller 91
The Upanishads 29
The Upland Field 263

The Visitor *314*
The White Bird *251*
The White Rabbit *6*
Theatre: Lunchtime *120*
There and Back *37*
There was Sun Today *316*
Thor *246*
Those Glorious Twelfths *188*
Three Cats *55*
Three Cousins *50*
Time's Present *103*
Tiveragh *5*
Tom's Tale *178*
Train at Midnight *310*
Treefall *252*
Tuesday *174*

Two Songs *288*

Uncle Alec *174*

Victories *66*
Virgin Country *253*

Walled Garden,
   Irish Street, Downpatrick *83*
Welsh Funeral: Carnmoney *85*
White Death, Green Spring *248*
William Blake Sees God *293*
William Cowper *49*
Words *214*

You, Sitting in Silent Rooms *311*